IT'S LEGAL BUT IT AIN'T RIGHT

Evolving Values for a Capitalist World

In most of the world today, the issue is not whether or how to embrace capitalism, but how to make the best of it. The currently dominant capitalist values include competitive individualism, instrumental rationality, and material success. The series explores questions such as: Will these values suffice as a basis for social organizations that can meet human and environmental needs in the twenty-first century? What would it mean for capitalist systems to evolve toward an emphasis on other values, such as cooperation, altruism, responsibility, and concern for the future?

Titles in the series:

Neva R. Goodwin. Editor. *As if the Future Mattered: Translating Social and Economic Theory into Human Behavior*

Severyn T. Bruyn. *A Civil Economy: Transforming the Market in the Twenty-First Century*

Jonathan Harris. *Rethinking Sustainability: Power, Knowledge, and Institutions*

Nikos Passas and Neva Goodwin, Editors. *It's Legal but It Ain't Right: Harmful Social Consequences of Legal Industries*

David Ellerman. *Helping People Help Themselves: From the World Bank to an Alternative Philosophy of Development Assistance*

It's Legal but It Ain't Right

Harmful Social Consequences of Legal Industries

Nikos Passas and Neva Goodwin, Editors

UNIVERSITY OF MICHIGAN PRESS

Ann Arbor

Copyright © by the University of Michigan 2004
All rights reserved
Published in the United States of America by
The University of Michigan Press
Manufactured in the United States of America
⊗ Printed on acid-free paper

2007   2006   2005   2004   4   3   2   1

A CIP catalog record for this book is available from the British Library.

Library of Congress Cataloging-in-Publication Data

It's legal but it ain't right : harmful social consequences of
legal industries / Nikos Passas and Neva Goodwin, editors.
    p.   cm. — (Evolving values for a capitalist world)
       ISBN 0-472-09869-1 (cloth : alk. paper) —
       ISBN 0-472-06869-5 (pbk. : alk. paper)
     1. Business ethics.   2. Business ethics—United States.
3. Corporations—Corrupt practices—Case studies.   4. Corporations—
Corrupt practices—United States—Case studies.   5. Capitalism—
Moral and ethical aspects.   6. Globalization—Moral and ethical
aspects.   7. Lobbying—Moral and ethical aspects.   8. Business and
politics.   9. Political corruption.   10. Social responsibility of
business.   I. Passas, Nikos.   II. Series.
HF5387.I87   2004
174'.4—dc22   2004006182

To my parents, Aphrodite and Emmanuel.
I owe them more than they can imagine.
—Nikos Passas

To the contributors to this book,
and to all others who are
striving for a shift to an
economic system that works for
people, instead of people
working for the system.
—Nikos Passas and Neva Goodwin

Contents

Introduction

A Crime by Any Other Name

Nikos Passas and Neva Goodwin

Billions of U.S. dollars and enormous intellectual and human capital are spent annually fighting the "crime problem," which is essentially constructed as a "street crime problem." Students of white-collar crime and several nonprofit organizations have tried to call attention to "crimes in the suites," but these efforts have had limited impact on actual public policy (Clinard 1990). There is convincing evidence that corporate misdeeds victimize more people—even entire societies—than street offenders; nevertheless, public perceptions and policy priorities continue to support practices whereby "the rich get richer and the poor get prison" (Reiman 2000).

Recently, the threat of transnational organized crime (TOC) has become prominent in media, policy, and intelligence circles. Without any universally accepted definition of TOC, the emphasis is usually on misconduct perpetrated by stereotyped ethnic and marginal groups, while most authors neglect the interfaces between legal and illegal enterprises (Passas 1999b, 2003). For example, Britain's National Criminal Intelligence Service (2000, 6) stated that an organized crime group meets the following criteria: "contains at least three people; criminal activity is prolonged or indefinite; criminals are motivated by profit or power; serious criminal offences are being committed." In principle, there is no reason why this definition would not apply to big corporations with established records of repeated felony convictions (e.g., General Electric). However, the groups that the intelligence service deems to represent threats are mostly Albanian, Turkish, African, Colombian, West Indian, and Asian ethnics, along with some "British Caucasians" and motorcycle gangs. So even when official agencies attempt to define the problem, some of the most serious and powerful offenders are in practice excluded.

Biases in criminal justice and other legal areas do not stop here. By concentrating on what is officially defined as illegal or criminal, an even more grave threat to society is left out. This threat emanates from corporate practices that are within the letter of the law but have serious adverse social consequences. Quite often the main reason why such practices remain legal and accepted by society is that industries mobilize financial and other resources to avoid stricter regulation. The point is most dramatically illustrated in recent revelations regarding the tobacco industry, one of several industries whose products, practices, or side effects are seriously at odds with the public interest. Additional examples may be found in the gambling industry, weapons producers, energy companies, private security firms, petrochemicals, pharmaceuticals, biotechnology firms, offshore financial institutions, law firms, and antiquities traders, most of which will be discussed in this book.

This book is not about crime—not even white-collar and corporate crime. Readers interested more in such issues can turn to the relevant sociological and criminological literature (Braithwaite 1984, 1985; Calavita and Pontell 1993; Coleman 1987; Fisse and Braithwaite 1993; Levi 1995; Pearce and Tombs 1998; Ruggiero 1996; Shapiro 1990; Simpson 2002; Snider 1993; Stone 1975; Yeager 1995). The book is also not intended as a wholesale indictment of corporations in general. Rather, it is about how corporate power can be and does get abused. It is about the unhelpful and damaging influence corporations exert on law- and policymaking processes.

This book argues that we have set our priorities wrongly by overlooking misdeeds whose consequences are even more threatening than what is legally designated as crime. Unfortunately, instead of attempting to remedy this problem, we are moving in the opposite direction. Globalization creates situations that require ever more effective regulatory action and oversight, but part of the neoliberal agenda around the globe is to deregulate businesses and further reduce the role of the state. Not only does this have criminogenic consequences of its own (Passas 2000), but it also furthers certain types of misconduct that undermine democratic processes and sustainable economic growth.

The first section of this introductory chapter will outline some types of corporate practice that are entirely lawful yet are often more harmful than what is defined as crime. It would not be helpful to stretch the concepts of crime and criminality to cover these practices, yet their negative impact is so substantial that even fervent proponents of free market systems can see that these practices generate more harm than good for society overall. The immediate effects often fall on underprivileged people or countries, but in a broader way there is harm to global capitalism itself.

The second section will deal with a different kind of corporate misdeeds, where it is appropriate to apply a revised or newly focused definition of crime, following both the logic and spirit of criminal law. Many companies tread a very fine line, moving actions from one place where they would be criminal to another where they are not so defined yet continuing to make money in the places that would disallow these offshore activities. Globalization has greatly facilitated such "crimes without lawbreaking." This section of this chapter will suggest ways of reconsidering our notion of crime to encompass such situations.

Lawful but Awful

We are going to discuss a certain class of unintended, harmful side effects, things that happen because they produce benefits to some corporation and that are not stopped because the corporation in question is not where the bad effects are felt. We need a name for this class of thing: economists and environmentalists—in a rare instance of unified thinking—have provided the needed term (albeit a rather clumsy one), *negative externalities*.

The underlying idea, on the economic side, is a theory of market functioning that says that markets convey to all economic actors (producers, consumers, and so forth) signals that indicate whether the results of actions are wanted or unwanted. If a producer puts out an Edsel, the market sends back the signal that nobody wants it. If people like the environmentally concerned image of Ben and Jerry's ice cream, they choose that brand. The market conveys these preferences to the producers, and we get more Ben and Jerry's ice cream and fewer Edsels.

The problems—and they are many—happen when some of the people (or animals or ecosystems) who are affected by economic actions cannot express their reactions through the market. For example, the people in the infamous "cancer alley" region did not like having ugly, smelly factories built nearby and did not want to suffer their carcinogenic effects, but this was a poor region whose residents did not show up in the market response to the cancer alley industries. These people were effectively outside of—external to—the market. Similarly, there is a difference between a home-owner who gives the neighbors pleasure from her front garden and one whose barking dogs create a nuisance, but this difference is also largely external to the relevant (real estate) market. The house with the pretty garden may have a higher resale value, but not because of the neighbors' pleasure; the impact on neighbors in this case is a "positive externality": a case where an economic act has a desirable result that is not fed back through the market to alter the behavior of the economic actor. Fortu-nately, the market is not the only conveyer of information: positive exter-nalities—where the good effect is not reinforced by a market signal—can be reinforced by neighbors' smiles and other noneconomic rewards. There are some important areas where the lack of market reinforcement for pos-itive externalities is a real problem: for example, corporations that provide good educational opportunities for their workers may not reap the full eco-nomic benefits if workers gain skills that they can transfer to other jobs. However, an exclusive focus on negative externalities will give us quite enough to discuss.

Economists care about externalities because the justification of markets is that the information they convey—especially through prices—will motivate economic actors to do what is best for the whole of society, "as though led by an invisible hand," in Adam Smith's famous metaphor. When this does not happen, the market is simply not doing what it should: economic theory no longer applies, and if society cannot rely on markets to guard its interests, the question of market regulation becomes urgent.

Environmentalists care about externalities because the best-known examples are negative environmental externalities, where producers gen-erate (as by-products) pollutants that harm people who are not in the mar-ket loop. Their concerns, their health, their grief or anger do not get trans-lated into market signals that would say, "Stop polluting."

Everyone else cares about negative externalities, too, it turns out (once they get past the awkward and unfamiliar phrase), because concern for fairness is a human universal. And it is clearly unfair for an economic actor to profit from an action that harms someone else.

That is the central topic of this book: the ability of a number of indus-tries to generate huge negative externalities, forcing society to bear significant portions of the real cost of these products. Ironically, at the same time that arguments in favor of economic liberalization have gained support after the end of the Cold War, hidden industrial subsidies have grown in the form of costs externalized—passed on to an ever wider circle of stakeholders affected by corporate actions. At this time these unacknowledged costs of legal businesses are mainly borne by groups without voice: the weakest and least privileged groups. However, negative externalities are potentially destructive to economic growth, democratic institutions, and processes of democratization in many parts of the world. In the extreme, negative externalities may also fuel discontent and militancy, the effects of which could spill over to neighboring or even distant places. Therefore, even those who are not concerned about the people who lack voice have other reasons to care about negative externalities.

A common feature of all of the industries examined in this book is their ability to define their conduct as legal while blocking attempts at regulation designed to reduce harmful effects and externalities. The ability to attract substantial pools of capital is often part of this equation. At the same time, the case of the National Rifle Association (see Diaz, this volume) shows that the ability to mobilize nonmonetary resources can be just as effective. In some cases, grassroots organizations are energized in efforts to ensure the availability and low price of desired goods. In other cases, such organizations are in fact funded or activated by big industries, such as tobacco (thus earning them the title "Astroturf organizations"; see Daynard, this volume). All organizations seek to influence their task environment (clients, suppliers, competitors, and regulators). What distinguishes the industries we will highlight is that they are not only highly successful and resourceful but also ultimately detrimental to society. This reality contradicts standard assumptions about the overall advantages society is supposed to derive from the success of legal enterprises. In a sense, the more these industries flourish, the more societies fail. Indeed, the success of some legal businesses, such as weapons traders or private correctional corporations, can be taken as an indication of societal failure.

The industries with very substantial negative externalities can be divided into three general categories. First, some may be classified as antisocial because their product per se is harmful. Tobacco, weapons, pesticides, and gambling are four obvious cases (see chapters 2, 3, 4, 6, and 9). Demand certainly exists for those products and services. A strong argument can be made, however, that society would be better off if those industries did not operate at all or radically altered the way their products are made and marketed.

Second, other businesses furnish legal and desired goods or services, but their production or marketing processes generate hazardous wastes or socially undesirable consequences. This category is illustrated by the factory farming of chickens and hogs as well as by the energy, petrochemical, and pharmaceutical industries, private security firms, offshore financial institutions, and the antiquities business as they now tend to operate (see chapters 5, 7, 8, 10, and 11). One variation within this category—not the sole subject of any chapter in this book—is that of "facilitators," industries that assist others in externalizing the costs documented in this book by keeping practices legal and holding critics or controllers at bay. Such services are provided by accounting, law, and lobbying firms. (On lobbying, see Silverstein and Taylor, this volume.) Some of these firms specialize in assisting antisocial, marginally legal activities, while others do it only occasionally.

Finally, there are industries that deliver privatized public functions or that support public functions but do so in ways that produce predictably adverse consequences (mostly, but not always, unintended). Perhaps the process of privatization has gone too far. Or perhaps some privatized functions require special supervision that the system does not provide. Examples of this category include private security firms (which supply mercenaries and private armies; see Howe, this volume), or private corrections corporations, established to make profits while managing prisons. Here we find an inherent conflict between public interest and private profit. The more such industries grow, prosper, and increase their market share, the worse off societies become in terms of both financial and human capital—that is, more people find themselves behind bars, stigmatized, disenfranchised, wounded, dead or captured in private wars, homeless, unemployed, forced to emigrate, and so on.

There is a common assumption that if an industry is legal, it is basically benign and beneficial to society. This obscures the fact that, on balance, society is negatively affected by allowing certain operations and practices to continue. Not everything that is good for business is good for America or the rest of the world. Negative externalities that remain hidden from public view are sometimes more dangerous than recognized social problems, such as crime. Unfortunately, the generators of these externalities often have retained their viability by shaping public opinion and the legal environment. They manipulate the media and persuade policy- and lawmakers or purchase their support through extensive lobbying and political campaign contributions. As a last resort, these industries can effectively blackmail legislators and policymakers by raising "national economy" types of arguments: "overregulation" and "government interference" in these businesses will render them uncompetitive or unprofitable, forcing them to cut down production or services, lay people off, and thereby negatively affect local communities or the whole country.

Whether or not the beneficiary of an externalized cost has contributed to public ignorance or confusion, the enduring possibility of externalizing costs usually depends on keeping the externalities unclear, poorly understood, or regarded as inevitable. Alternatives are thus not considered or are assumed to be too costly. Critics of the industries in question are few and tend to be associated with partisan or radical groups, which are unable to reach a wide audience or which alienate those who do not subscribe to their political views. Thus, the major negative externalities arising from legal practices and legitimate industries have not been successfully constructed as a social problem. As a result, little or no public debate occurs regarding what can or should be done about them.

Our first task, then, is to address the issue of perceptions by defining the problem. Previous attempts to construct a social problem out of routine activities of powerful actors have had limited impact as a result of misplaced moralizing, the use of loosely defined criteria of wrongdoing, and the introduction of subjective standards regarding what is desirable, what is harmful, and what should be criminalized. To avoid these pitfalls, we need to identify observable negative externalities, including physical, financial, and environmental costs as well as the undermining of democratic systems, economic growth, and international trade and the creation of an environment in which crime can flourish while some other valuable potential withers away. These categories will be outlined in the remainder of this section.

Physical Costs

Few industries can rival the amount of pain and suffering caused by the tobacco industry. About 4 million people are killed by tobacco products every year. The estimated loss of life in the past century is 100 million people. Unless something changes our direction, tobacco will kill 1 billion people in the twenty-first century. Lifetime smokers contract diseases that cause them to die, on average, seven years earlier than nonsmokers. About fifty thousand Americans each year who do not smoke die as a result of inhaling toxins from other people's cigarettes, and another one thousand die from fires caused by cigarettes. All this is in addition to the misery of addiction and its consequences for quality of life (see Daynard, this volume).

Another industry with obvious physical costs is the production of firearms. In 1997, 32,436 Americans were killed with these products. Firearms are the second-leading cause of traumatic death related to a consumer product in the United States and are the second-most frequent cause of death, in any category, for Americans aged between fifteen and twenty-four. The overall rate of firearms death in the United States is eight times higher than that of twenty-five other high-income countries together (see Diaz, this volume).

The so-called defense industry causes untold deaths and injuries through the international sale of weapons, which fuel conflicts and make them deadlier. The world indicates sympathy for the plight of the Kurds under Saddam Hussein's regime in Iraq but ignores the atrocities they suffer at the hands of the Turkish army, which is supported by the United States. The Onyx Program, for example, has allowed Turkey to build, under a coproduction agreement with the U.S. Lockheed Corporation, one of the largest assembly lines for F-16 fighter planes (see Bondi, this volume). These planes "have been used to attack villages and kill civilians in violation of international humanitarian law. In other instances, the planes have been used deliberately to destroy civilian structures, contributing to the general process of forced dislocation" (Human Rights Watch Arms Project 1995, 31).

A Human Rights Watch researcher has produced an overview of human rights violations that have taken place when oil and electricity corporations support strong-arm governments in Third World countries in order to extract natural resources. The findings of this study are shocking, including campaigns of rape, torture, and slavery that benefited Unocal in Burma; mass graves dug in Indonesia with Mobil's bulldozers; citizens massacred in Chad and Cameroon by forces associated with Exxon; and unarmed villagers in Nigeria shot down by soldiers in Chevron helicopters (Ganesan 1999).

A report on the effects of Enron's practices has noted the following:

- In the Dominican Republic, eight people were killed when police were brought in to quell riots after blackouts lasting up to 20 hours followed a power price hike that Enron and other private firms initiated. The local population was further enraged by allegations that a local affiliate of Arthur Andersen had undervalued the newly privatized utility by almost $1 billion, reaping enormous profits for Enron.
- In India, police hired by the power consortium of which Enron was

a part beat non-violent protesters who challenged the $30 billion agreement—the largest deal in Indian history—struck between local politicians and Enron.

- The president of Guatemala tried to dissolve the Congress and declare martial law after rioting ensued, following a price hike that the government deemed necessary after selling the power sector to Enron. (Vallette and Wysham 2002, 3)

Multinational corporations often use private security companies to further corporate aims in developing nations while employing brutal methods (Cilliers and Mason 1999; Silverstein 1997; Zarate 1998). In addition, private security companies have provided mercenaries to warring parties in civil strife, prolonging conflict and increasing violence and cruelty (Ballesteros 1994).

Ken Silverstein and Jess Taylor's chapter notes how the pharmaceutical industry expends massive resources to develop drugs for obesity, foot fungus, baldness, and the improvement of sexual life. At the same time, the industry spends virtually nothing for the (very easy and cheap) development of drugs against curable tropical diseases that kill four times as many people as AIDS every year (see also Silverstein 1999). The same industry has been found to hide side effects of its products in Third World countries (Clinard 1990), to produce and market drugs known to cause harm even after they have been banned in the companies' home countries (Cashman 1989), and to experiment on human subjects without their consent (Braithwaite 1993). The search for maximization of profit by all means thus leads to hundreds of thousands of unnecessary deaths and injuries every year in developing countries.

Financial Costs

In the United States alone, the annual health care costs of cigarette smoking amount to more than $50 billion, while another $50 billion is wasted in productivity losses. These financial externalities easily outweigh the entire industry's profits. Even employment would rise if everyone stopped smoking (see Daynard, this volume). One is hard pressed to find a more counterproductive and parasitic industry, and it has also been directly involved in formally defined transnational criminality, such as subsidy frauds and the smuggling of cigarettes to avoid the high taxes some countries have imposed (Associated Press 2000; Jamieson 1999; USDA 1990).

The financial losses emanating from the gambling industry are staggering (see Kindt, this volume). In 1996, for example, Americans lost $47.6 billion in legal gambling. As O'Brien (1998) pointed out, this amount is more than double the total sales of Coca-Cola in that year. Additional costs are generated by bankruptcies, rates of which have skyrocketed in areas with legal gambling facilities. For example, Nevada's rate is 50 percent higher than the U.S. national average, and Atlantic City's rate is 71 percent higher than the state of New Jersey's average (SMR 1997). Despite the industry's promises regarding job creation and economic growth, empirical studies show that at best, people leave other jobs to seek employment in casinos. The overall economic impact of legal gambling has been negative for people who live or do business unrelated to gambling in the areas concerned (O'Brien 1998; Pavalko 2000; Vogel 1997).

The cost of inaccurate financial reports and other statements from public companies is gigantic. Beyond the big scandals involving WorldCom, Global Crossing, and Enron (see Klinger and Sklar, this volume), a number of companies took advantage of the boom years in the stock market and the economy to misrepresent their growth and operations, in the process misleading millions of investors whose assets (including stock holdings, mutual funds, and pension funds) suffered serious declines both directly and as a result of the undermined public confidence in the wider market.

Environmental Damage

Our environment is often treated with disregard or as a virtually limitless resource that can be exploited without grave consequences. Yet the abuse the environment takes is sometimes irreversible (e.g., extinction of species) and always harmful to humans. Big and "efficient" industrial farms, for example, are both damaging the environment and destroying a large number of lives every year in the United States. Mark Ritchie's chapter points out that just one hog operation can produce as much fecal waste as a city of 360,000 people. This waste is most often stored in open pits, where it decomposes into nearly four hundred volatile chemicals. More than 500,000 people work on these corporate farms and are exposed to the chemicals every day. There are myriad cases of farm workers dying from asphyxiation from these pits. Many hog farms have inadequate waste water treatment facilities, which means that the enterprises pollute lakes, rivers, and underground water basins. Ritchie shows that this is not just hypothetical: the runoff of manure and artificial fertilizer from farms throughout the Mississippi River basin has caused a five-thousand-square-mile dead zone off the coast of New Orleans.

Peter Riggs and Megan Waples's chapter covers the pesticide industry, the products of which needlessly pollute the environment and cause harm to humans and the ecosystem.

The practices of biotechnology companies also require closer scrutiny. They not only engage in highly debatable experiments, creating and then patenting life forms (and calling them "milk factories" or other reifying terms), but also cause a drastic reduction in biodiversity through the disappearance of plant species. Year after year, Third World farmers are obliged to purchase the genetically engineered, pesticide-resistant seeds marketed by big transnationals, who sue the farmers for patent infringement if they save seeds for the next year's crop. Corrupt governments collude with transnational seed and chemical companies in encouraging farmers to abandon varieties that have been cultivated and developed for centuries, leaving farmers dependent on purchased varieties (King and Stabinsky 1998–99; Shiva 1997; on the case of corporate farming and rice crops in Pakistan, see Rizvi 2000). When a bad season leaves farmers lacking in cash, they find themselves in a highly vulnerable position.

Death, disease, and children's cancer rates have drastically diminished in areas where nuclear power plants were shut down (Mokhiber 2000).

The forest industry has been found to ruthlessly exploit and damage the environment, often with the tacit support of local (corrupt) political elites (e.g., on Papua New Guinea, see the Barnett Report 1989). Even the World Bank has come to acknowledge that deforestation can no longer be blamed exclusively on poor farmers, slash-and-burn agriculture, or demographic pressures but results to a large extent from corruption and out-of-control logging companies (Horta 2000).

There are countless other examples of depletion of natural resources as a result of lawful activities by petrochemical, oil, and waste management companies or mining companies assisted by private security firms (among the compilers of these data, see Center for Investigative Reporting and Moyers 1990; Cilliers and Mason 1999; Eaton 1997; *Economist* 2000b; Katsh 2000; Pearce and Tombs 1998).

Undermining the Democratic System

Contrary to arguments that globalization and neoliberal reforms foster and support democratization processes, there are plenty of instances where the opposite has taken place. Investigative reporters revealed that a group of North American investors led by Chase Bank unequivocally urged the Mexican government to "eliminate the Zapatistas to demonstrate their effective control of the national territory and security policy" (Silverstein and Cockburn 1995). This blatant interference in Mexican internal affairs was intended to warn the government that investor confidence could suffer (that is, massive flight of capital would occur) if the Chiapas issue was not quickly resolved. A senior fellow at a Washington, DC, think tank has been quoted as saying that "financial markets might not respond positively to increased democracy because it leads to increased uncertainty" (Silverstein and Cockburn 1995). This sort of meddling in other countries' internal affairs is not atypical. As U.S. Marine Corps General Smedley Butler confessed eighty years ago,

> I spent 33 years . . . being a high-class muscleman for big business, for Wall Street and the bankers. . . . I helped purify Nicaragua for the international house of Brown Brothers in 1909–1912. I helped make Mexico and especially Tampico safe for American oil interests in 1916. I brought light to the Dominican Republic for American sugar interests in 1916. I helped make Haiti and Cuba a decent place for the National City Bank boys to collect revenue in. I helped in the rape of half a dozen Central American republics for the benefit of Wall Street. (quoted in Clinard 1990, 158)

A new instrument in the hands of multinational corporations is the growing industry of private security firms. Given the lack of accountability and regulatory oversight in that industry, it is hardly surprising that they face charges that they are tools of neocolonial exploitation in Third World countries and that they use barbaric methods to maintain order (Cilliers and Mason 1999; Howe, this volume). Powerful states also use private security firms to promote foreign policies through covert channels that offer plausible deniability, especially when these strategies involve embargo busting, violations of international accords (e.g., in Croatia and Bosnia), siding with opposition groups (e.g., in Chechnya, Tajikistan, Azerbaijan, Georgia, Kashmir, Sierra Leone, Zaire, East Timor, and Papua New Guinea), the fueling of civil wars, tacit protectionism of domestic companies, and hidden rewards to "alumni" of security forces no longer needed after the end of the Cold War (Sapone 1999; Silverstein 1997; Zarate 1998).

In this light, even positive aspects of the continuing operation of such firms, such as the provision of foreign employment for retired and unemployed practitioners of violence (Howe, this volume) can be seen as an externality: the exportation of domestic problems to poor and developing countries. This is why Herbert Howe advocates "leashing the dogs of war" by means of national and international regulation. Current practices involving the licensing of such private security firms by home governments leave much to be desired. Given that these enterprises constitute hidden tools of foreign policy, it is possible that licenses will be granted despite a record or likelihood of law violations. Moreover, the discretionary power of powerful countries (e.g., the United States or United Kingdom) to block the services of private security companies in given countries means that only certain regimes under certain conditions have access to private sector assistance. When help is unavailable from the United Nations or other organizations, this power would place additional burdens on some governments, increase their dependence on unaccountable and secretive decision makers, and thereby unduly influence national policies. At both the domestic and international level, many industries can and do generate similar externalities as they shape state policies against the public interest through campaign contributions, lobbying, or revolving-door traditions. The same occurs when democratic governments are forced to submit to unaccountable bureaucracies, such as the World Trade Organization and the International Monetary Fund (Mander and Goldsmith 1996).

Crime Externalities

Many industries generate crime externalities without necessarily committing crimes. A case in point is the gambling industry, which has been shown to correlate with high crime rates (Kindt, this volume; O'Brien 1998). Some firms or industries interface willingly with criminals, while others turn a blind eye or passively benefit from the operation of criminal organizations. Criminogenic effects can be direct or indirect—either facilitating crime or engaging in it. Just a few examples include

cigarette smuggling across national borders to avoid taxes and levies (although in some cases, it appears that some companies also participated in or directed such practices; see *European Union v. R. J. R.*

Nabisco et al., October 2002, Eastern District of New York; Case no.
CV 02 5771)

the illegal dumping of toxic wastes generated by chemical firms (Szasz
1986)

the use of financial institutions in secrecy jurisdictions for the commission and cover-up of financial frauds (Blum 1984) and for money
laundering (Blum and Block 1993; Minority Staff 2001; Passas
1995)

the connivance of private galleries and museums in rewarding the looting of art-rich countries, the smuggling of stolen antiquities, and the
destruction of cultural property (Conklin 1994; Gerstenblith, this
volume)

insurance companies and financial institutions benefiting from and
refusing to acknowledge organized arson (Brady 1983)

oil companies fueling genocide and ecocide for the sake of exploration
and profit growth (Eaton 1997; Katsh 2000)

a variety of companies exploiting child labor and ignoring violations of
human rights (Baez et al. 2000; Wells 1998)

mercenaries provided by private security firms participating in looting,
massacres, mass rapes, and war-related crimes (Sapone 1999; Silverstein 1997; Zarate 1998)

Undermining Economic Growth

Some lawful business practices create extraordinary financial costs that
engender systemic risks both domestically and internationally, as in the
case of collapses or near-collapses of financial institutions. The savings-
and-loan institutions disaster in the United States, which cost taxpayers
between $500 billion and $1 trillion, was not caused entirely by fraud. The
main culprits were deregulation and relaxation of accounting methods of
reporting, effectively allowing insolvent institutions to continue operations and compound their losses (Calavita and Pontell 1990). The Long-
Term Capital Management hedge fund almost brought down the world
financial markets when it legally placed gigantic bets the wrong way with
other (very wealthy) people's money. As long as it produced double-digit
returns on the basis of some Nobel laureate–inspired formulas for investing, no one paid attention to its activities. When it was about to fail, top
federal regulators and Wall Street leaders sat together to bail it out. At
least this time taxpayer money was not involved (Warde 1998).

Most of the externalities outlined earlier have additional negative effects on economic growth. Exploitation and abuse, whether performed legally or criminally, inevitably contribute to the impoverishment of parts of the population and increase the already wide gaps between the rich and the poor in unsustainable fashion. The widening of these gaps has indeed accelerated during the past decade, characterized by economic globalization and neoliberal policies (Passas 2000). However, these processes can only go so far before they bring about a painful and universally experienced economic downturn.

Undermining International Trade

Neoliberalism preaches free markets and minimal state intervention in trade. It argues that state protectionism hampers international trade and economic growth and introduces inefficiencies and waste. Yet one can easily find a plethora of protectionist policies in the countries and groups of states leading the neoliberal bandwagon, such as the United States and the European Union. U.S. law allows the establishment of foreign sales corporations, which are offshore shelters that U.S. exporting companies can use to exempt about 15 percent of their profits from taxation. In 1997, the European Union took action against this at the World Trade Organization, which ruled in the European Union's favor, but the dispute continued (Desai and Hines 2000; *Economist* 2000a). At the same time, the European Union has been protecting several industries, especially the agricultural sector, through export subsidies and import levies (Passas 1991). In the end, subsidies, export dumping, and a long list of formal and informal barriers to developing-country exports remain intact. The consequences are reduced incomes, lower employment, less access to foreign exchange, and lower confidence in the multilateral trading system. No wonder that most developing countries consider the system to be a rich man's club, in which the industrialized countries promote world trade rules to serve these countries' interests (Watkins 1997).

Opportunity Costs

Some biotechnology firms holding patents on gene sequences and cell lines use their power to prevent other agencies or companies from finding socially responsible and productive applications for these technologies. For example, Myriad Pharmaceutical could use its breast cancer gene technology to identify environmental and other causes of the problem and thereby prevent breast cancer. "Instead, it is using its technology and patent rights to sell a diagnostic test which informs the individual how much damage has already occurred in their genome. Exploiting patents requires selling consumers a product, not keeping them from contracting disease" (King and Stabinsky 1998–99, 85).

Others have argued that the American Cancer Society should redirect its significant resources toward the prevention rather than treatment of cancer. Both the American Cancer Society and the National Cancer Institute, the two largest organizations devoted to fighting cancer, have come under criticism for profiting from the "cancer epidemic" and for their alleged "incestuous conflicts of interest" with the pharmaceutical and medical industries (Epstein 1999).

Other industries, such as the private corrections corporations, marginalize very substantial numbers of people and render them unemployable (Yeoman 2000). More generally, we can identify—but can hardly quantify—opportunity costs resulting from the loss of natural resources, tax avoidance, the need to take care of those injured and ill as a result of corporate actions, or the subsidization of wealthy enterprises. It is tempting to dream about what societies might achieve through a rational, productive, efficient, and fair allocation of the financial and other resources wasted by amoral or morally bankrupt corporations.

Corporate "Crimes" without Lawbreaking

The controversy over what is crime is not new. For example, when Sutherland introduced the concept of white-collar crime during the 1940s, he was so concerned about lawsuits by the companies that he omitted the names of the companies his book cited as white-collar offenders (Sutherland 1949; the uncut version appeared as Sutherland 1983). The problem was that because the law did not define their misconduct as crime, they could not be branded as criminals. Decades later, some criminologists still refuse to adopt any standard other than existing criminal law. It is clear, however, that national laws cannot provide the sole basis on which to define crime, either for domestic or for international and comparative purposes.

What is or is not prohibited by criminal law may be decided by corrupt legislators, dictators, ruthless corporations, resourceful lobbies, or other powerful actors. Such actors should not be allowed to determine the scope of a social scientist's object of study or a public policymaker's actions. In addition, even if all legislative processes were well intentioned, laws change from time to time and from place to place. In U.S. society, insider trading, antitrust violations, misleading advertising, and many other malpractices addressed by Sutherland were not formally treated as crimes, despite their obvious similarity to street crimes and the serious harm they cause to society and the capitalist system.

For all these reasons, we need substantive criteria to guide our definition. Earlier attempts to grapple with this issue showed how tempting it is to adopt completely nonlegal criteria (Schwendinger and Schwendinger 1975). However, this approach can lead to definitions that are criticized as subjective or relativist. It is important to define crime in a comprehensive manner, but without going too far beyond the law. Along these lines, a working definition of crime is *misconduct that entails avoidable and unnecessary harm to society, is serious enough to warrant state intervention, and resembles other kinds of acts criminalized in the countries concerned or by international law* (Passas 1999a). This way of conceptualizing crime is little more than a consistent application of legal standards to classes of misbehavior that the law has omitted.

Cross-border malpractices often present the clearest cases of "crimes without lawbreaking" (Passas 1999a). Asymmetries in legal definitions and law enforcement enable corporations to do legally in other jurisdictions what is prohibited at home. Processes of globalization have multiplied such opportunities. Compartmentalized corporate structures effectively raise fire walls to protect the company and its executives from knowledge of wrongdoing and liability. Financial transactions that are disallowed or must be reported in the home country can be booked to offshore subsidiaries and branches. Research, experiments, and manufacturing and distribution of commodities or services that are outlawed or controlled in some countries can take place in countries with friendlier regulations.

Asymmetric environmental regulation illustrates the criminogenic process—that is, the process by which crime is encouraged. Increased awareness of serious health and environmental hazards in Western societies has led to legislation protecting the environment from industrial pollution, even if that might narrow the profit margin of affected corporations—for example, companies that generate toxic waste are constrained by laws regulating its disposal. Unfortunately, this legislation has not had the intended effect of drastically reducing the risk of improper treatment of toxic waste. Instead, it created asymmetrical regimes, which ultimately gave rise to an illegal market for waste disposal. An example of this process occurred when the Resource Conservation and Recovery Act of 1976 came into effect. The rules defining what is "hazardous" and subject to regulation differed from state to state within the United States. Large differences in the cost of disposal created incentives to engage in cross-border export of waste to those states that left particular substances unregulated. At the same time, there was a severe shortage of appropriate facilities to deal with the volume of toxic waste. This shortage, along with the drive for profit maximization, finally brought in organized criminals whose state-licensed companies illegally dumped the waste for the benefit of the chemical industry, saving up to 80 percent of the disposal costs.

In this instance, environmental groups were no match for the power of corporations to influence lawmaking. The chemical industry successfully lobbied against regulation of production methods, which could have been altered to generate less waste. The industry also avoided criminal liability in the event that their waste was discovered to have been illegally dumped by cheap hauling contractors. Control agencies, underfunded and plagued by incompetence or corruption, did little to remedy the situation. Corporations dodged blame while reaping substantial benefits from nominal regulation and organized crime (Szasz 1986).

Similarly, at the international level, regulatory discrepancies along with substantial economic and political asymmetries have given rise to an enormous market for toxic waste. Many Third World countries either do not regulate toxic waste or do so much less rigorously than industrial states. This provides the opportunity for companies to get rid of their dangerous waste in areas where rules are lax or nonexistent (Center for Investigative Reporting and Moyers 1990; Critharis 1990).

Corrupt practices offer another illustration of crime without lawbreaking. Companies operating in countries with slow or inefficient administrations may pay "speed money" to "get the job done." In other cases, companies fear the loss of contracts if they are reluctant to match a competitor's bribes. Again, legal asymmetries produce a shield against the discovery or punishment of corruption. The money handed over as bribes may end up in a secrecy jurisdiction with anonymous accounts. Additional protection is offered by the differential treatment of bribes to foreign officials. In some countries they are a serious offense, while in others they have constituted tax-deductible business expenses until recent efforts to fight corruption more aggressively (Passas 1997).

The pharmaceutical industry also illustrates how transnational corporations manage and exploit opportunities for crimes without lawbreaking. Initial tests of drugs can be conducted in the Third World, where safeguards are lower, civil lawsuits are unlikely, and other forms of protest have slim chances of success. Countries with lax standards are used for first approval and manufacture so that Third World markets can be entered before final approval is made by stricter Western agencies. Components of dangerous and banned drugs can be made in places allowing their manufacture and then marketed in countries that have not banned them (Braithwaite 1993). The global South has been used not only as a laboratory but also as a dumping ground for dangerous products (Bryan 1981; Clinard 1990). When drugs with serious side effects are exported, the published list of side effects gets shorter the farther south the drugs go. Defective and harmful products, such as the Dalkon Shield intrauterine device, can be exported and sold around the world despite being banned in their home countries (Cashman 1989; Mintz 1985).

There are numerous other examples of crimes without lawbreaking. Companies may employ child labor in poor countries that allow it and then export the products to countries where such production is illegal (Burra 1995). Taxes may be evaded legally through the practice of transfer pricing, which allows profits to be booked in countries with no income tax (Piccioto 1992; see also the preceding discussion of foreign sales corporations). Dirty money can be laundered in countries requiring no reporting, even for large cash deposits, and then transferred to Western banks that may not know the money's criminal origin—and do not care to find out (Levi 1991). A recent report has pointed out that U.S. banks have ignored money laundering and other crimes perpetrated through correspondent accounts provided to foreign banks; in this way, the banks "have become conduits for dirty money flowing into the American financial system and have, as a result, facilitated illicit enterprises, including drug trafficking and financial frauds" (Minority Staff 2001). Globalization has enabled financial institutions to do overseas what they are not permitted to do at home. As the Bank of Commerce and Credit International scandal has shown, it has become possible for a financial institution to have no home at all (Passas 1995).

Advice on how to engage in harmful practices without breaking laws can be purchased from lawyers, accountants, private business operators, and former government or military officials who act as consultants. The more a company grows into new geographic areas, the less subject it is to control, accountability, and consolidated supervision. With fragmented regulation in the context of globalized markets and enterprises, transactions can be structured so that no country's laws are broken, even though the final outcome is "criminal." Thus, corporate criminals can slip through the asymmetries of the international regulatory patchwork (Michalowski and Kramer 1987; Passas 1999a).

Conclusion

Why do certain industries engage in egregious, large-scale antisocial activities? Why do they produce so many hidden externalities? What hampers society's efforts to control such enterprises and limit the externalities? While this book will not provide all the needed answers, we can indicate the directions in which answers may be sought. The first places to look are in

- corporate power;
- special ability (e.g., through large pools of capital) to convince policymakers and to shape public opinion;
- weakened guiding power of conduct norms (due to widespread rationalizations, such as "Everyone else does it," "If we don't do it, someone else will," and so forth);
- the ideology of free market capitalism;
- arguments about trickle-down benefits of corporate operations that make those expecting such benefits less likely to inquire into or even bother about externalities;
- culturally reinforced resistance to taxation and government intervention; and
- short-term vision obscuring serious future problems.

We have seen that many industries operate entirely within the legal structure, yet the net balance of their effects is negative. When laws are not violated, controllers and regulators are not expected or allowed to do anything about these problems. This is why the issue is particularly challenging from a policy perspective, especially because in many cases criminalization does not appear to be a viable or desirable option. Experience has shown that prohibition can sometimes produce more problems than it solves. However, there is a clear need to control the worst of the legal but harmful practices.

The economic prescription is simple: industries must internalize the costs they are now avoiding. Their prices, in a sense, must tell the truth. This means that the purchase price of any product should reflect all real costs associated with its production, distribution, use, and even disposal. However, this prescription is often hard to follow because prices imply quantification, and there are many ill effects of crimes without lawbreaking and lawful but awful corporate practices that cannot be expressed in numbers. For example, how could one measure the cost of the dislocation and dismemberment of cultural monuments and the loss of opportunities to understand past civilizations and societies that result from the looting of artwork and the massive illegal antiquity trade to which galleries, museums, and "civilized" art-collecting countries turn a blind eye (Conklin 1994; Gerstenblith, this volume; Margules 1992)? There is no price tag on the recent looting of cultural centers in Iraq after it was attacked by the U.S. and British forces. This loss to humankind was a predictable externality of warfare that was communicated to those planning and executing the invasion. Yet, while the Iraqi Ministry of Oil was well guarded and suffered no looting, many invaluable artifacts from one of the world's earliest civilizations were destroyed or stolen, finding their way out of the country along trade routes that, according to newspaper reports, had been established by traders in anticipation of the war.[1] How can one quantify the demoralization of the general population, which may experience feelings of powerlessness or normlessness when they see that conduct akin to crime is tolerated and even rewarded (Passas 2000) or the disruption of social life in entire communities or countries?

Accepting the difficulty of measuring and internalizing all costs, many critical questions can still be addressed. How can society attempt to reduce negative externalities without destroying industry's ability to produce appropriate goods and services? What industry-specific responses have proven most effective? Are there any common strategies and tactics that can be tried across the board?

The measures to be considered range from the short term to the very long term, from the individual level to collective action, from the informal to the official and institutional, from challenging theoretical assumptions to hands-on actions. Many specific suggestions are tendered in the chapters that follow.

Epigrammatically, some of the most common policy themes that emerge in this volume are the following:

- establishment and consistent enforcement of national and international standards
- introduction and observance of industrywide codes of ethics
- the promotion of grassroots involvement, citizen initiatives, and nongovernmental actions (which presupposes increased awareness of problems, another important goal of this book)
- use of tax policies to encourage or discourage harmful corporate practices
- limiting the influence of industries in law- and policymaking, including the control of lobbying activities and campaign contributions
- transparency and accountability of companies, either informally through the Internet or through the use of the justice system and civil actions/lawsuits

Most generally, the authors in this volume see the need for transparency, accountability, and regulation. But this effort will not really succeed without a reshaping of cultural norms and the acceptance of responsibility by those whose decisions shape corporate behavior.

Corporate executives are not always aware of the ultimate consequences of their actions or failures to act, whether because of compartmentalization, specialization, or neglect. These leaders need to be challenged and asked, When do you become responsible? When should you know that your corporate practice is wrong? Individual responsibility is about saying, "I won't do it because it's wrong." This can be supported by accountability (creating legal and other institutions that allow those affected by externalities to challenge the individual and institutional actors) and transparency (making it easy for others to see the externalities). Responsibility goes beyond but is strongly supported by accountability and transparency, giving conscience a hearing even when there is little likelihood of getting caught.

Changes in the norms that guide behavior in corporations will require wide public support. A key goal, therefore, is to change social attitudes so that people both inside and outside the industries in question no longer think that whatever is not illegal is okay. In some cases it is desirable to change laws; more often, the need is to redefine legitimacy. The two may have to be pursued in parallel. Changing laws sometimes changes legitimacy (gambling unfortunately became legitimate when it became legal). Changing legitimacy sometimes changes laws (as illustrated in issues relating to the environment or with tobacco).

This book is a beginning. Significant challenges remain: to better define the problems, to further document and analyze some of the most significant externalities, to launch a debate toward the redefinition of legitimacy in business practices, and to propose concrete and practical courses of action. Recognizing that our mission requires a change in social attitudes, the first task is to create wide awareness that many practices that are now legal (actually or potentially) can cause us all grave harm.

NOTE

1. The number and type of items lost or looted at the time remains unclear as of January 2004. Dealers from Sardinia to London continue to get arrested for selling Iraqi antiquities, and experts do not know whether a collection of thousands of artifacts gone missing is listed as a single item or not (House of Commons, Culture, Media and Sport Committee 2003).

REFERENCES

Associated Press. 2000. "Tobacco Exec Charged with Smuggling." March 26.

Baez, C., M. Dearing, M. Delatour, and C. Dixon. 2000. "Multinational Enterprises and Human Rights." *Yearbook of International Law* 8:183–338.

Ballesteros, E. B. 1994. *Report on the Question of the Use of Mercenaries as a Means of Violating Human Rights and Impeding the Exercise of the Right of Peoples to Self-Determination*, U.N. ESCOR, 50th sess. at 15, U.N. Doc. E/CN.4/1994/23.

Barnett Report. 1989. *Commission of Inquiry into Aspects of the Forest Industry Final Report*. Unpublished report to the government of Papua, New Guinea.

Blum, J., and A. Block. 1993. "Le Blanchiment de l'Argent dans les Antilles: Bahamas, Saint Maartin et Iles Caïmans." In *La Planète des Drogues*, ed. A. Labrousse and A. Wallon, 73–102. Paris: Seuil.

Blum, R. H. 1984. *Offshore Haven Banks, Trusts, and Companies*. New York: Praeger.

Brady, J. 1983. "Arson, Urban Economy, and Organized Crime." *Social Problems* 31:1–27.

Braithwaite, J. 1984. *Corporate Crime in the Pharmaceutical Industry*. London: Routledge and Kegan Paul.

Braithwaite, J. 1985. "White Collar Crime." *Annual Review of Sociology* 11:1–25.

Braithwaite, J. 1993. "Transnational Regulation of the Pharmaceutical Industry." *Annals, AAPSS* 525:12–30.

Bryan, D. A. 1981. "Consumer Safety Abroad: Dumping of Dangerous American Products Overseas." *Texas Tech Law Review* 12:435–58.

Burra, N. 1995. *Born to Work: Child Labour in India*. Delhi: Oxford University Press.

Calavita, K., and H. N. Pontell. 1990. "'Heads I Win, Tails You Lose': Deregulation, Crime, and Crisis in the Savings and Loan Industry." *Crime and Delinquency* 36:309–41.

Calavita, K., and H. N. Pontell. 1993. "Savings and Loan Fraud as Organized Crime: Toward a Conceptual Typology of Corporate Illegality." *Criminology* 31 (4): 519–48.

Cashman, P. 1989. "The Dalkon Shield." In *Stains on a White Collar*, ed. P. Grabosky and A. Sutton, 92–117. Sydney: Federation Press.

Center for Investigative Reporting, and B. Moyers. 1990. *Global Dumping Ground: The International Traffic in Hazardous Waste*. Washington, D.C.: Seven Locks Press.

Cilliers, J., and P. Mason, eds. 1999. *Peace, Profit, or Plunder? The Privatisation of Security in War-Torn African Societies*. Halfway House, South Africa: Institute for Security Studies.

Clinard, M. B. 1990. *Corporate Corruption: The Abuse of Power*. New York: Praeger.

Coleman, J. W. 1987. "Toward an Integrated Theory of White Collar Crime." *American Journal of Sociology* 93:406–39.

Conklin, J. E. 1994. *Art Crime*. Westport, CT: Praeger [Greenwood].

Critharis, M. 1990. "Third World Nations Are Down in the Dumps: The Exportation of Hazardous Waste." *Brooklyn Journal of International Law* 6:311–39.

Desai, M. A., and J. R. J. Hines. 2000. *The Uneasy Marriage of Export Incentives and the Income Tax*. Working Paper W8009. Cambridge, MA: National Bureau of Economic Research.

Eaton, J. P. 1997. "The Nigerian Tragedy: Environmental Regulation of Transnational Corporations, and the Human Right to a Healthy Environment." *Boston University International Law Journal* 15:261–307.

The Economist. 2000a. "Going Too Far in Support of Trade." December 16, p. 88.

The Economist. 2000b. "Sudan's Oil: Fuelling a Fire." September 2, pp. 62–63.

Epstein, S. S. 1999. "American Cancer Society: The World's Wealthiest 'Non-Profit' Institution." *International Journal of Health Services* 29. Available at http://www.preventcancer.com/losing/acs/wealthiest_links.htm.

Fisse, B., and J. Braithwaite. 1993. *Corporations, Crime, and Accountability*. Cambridge: Cambridge University Press.

Ganesan, A. 1999. "Corporation Crackdowns." *Dollars and Sense Magazine*, May–June. http://www.dollarsandsense.org/archives/1999/0599ganesan.html.

Horta, K. 2000. "Warning: World Bank Policies Destroy Forests; Internal Report Documents Bank Contribution to Deforestation." *Multinational Monitor* 21 (6): 13–14, 28.

House of Commons, Culture, Media and Sport Committee. 2003. *Cultural Objects: Developments Since 2000*. London: House of Commons, The Stationery Office.

Human Rights Watch Arms Project. 1995. *Weapons Transfers and Violations of the Laws of War in Turkey*. New York: Human Rights Watch.

Jamieson, R. 1999. "'Contested Jurisdiction Border Communities' and Cross-Border Crime: The Case of the Akwesasne." In *Global Organized Crime and International Security*, ed. E. C. Viano, 85–97. Aldershot: Ashgate.

Katsh, G. 2000. "Fueling Genocide: Talisman Energy and the Sudanese Slaughter." *Multinational Monitor* 21 (10): 13–16.

King, J., and D. Stabinsky. 1998–99. "Biotechnology under Globalisation: The Corporate Expropriation of Plant, Animal, and Microbial Species." *Race and Class* 40 (2–3): 73–89.

Levi, M. 1991. "Pecunia non Olet: Cleansing the Money-Launderers from the Temple." *Crime, Law and Social Change* 16:217–302.

Levi, M. 1995. "White Collar Crimes and Other Crimes of Deception: Connecting Policy to Theory." In *Crime and Policy: Putting Theory to Work*, ed. H. D. Barlow, 247–68. Boulder, CO: Westview.

Mander, J., and E. Goldsmith, eds. 1996. *The Case against the Global Economy*. San Francisco: Sierra Club Books.

Margules, P. L. 1992. "International Art Theft and the Illegal Import and Export of Cultural Property: A Study of Relevant Values, Legislation, and Solutions." *Suffolk Transnational Law Journal* 15:609–47.

Michalowski, R. J., and R. C. Kramer. 1987. "The Space between Laws: The Problem of Corporate Crime in a Transnational Context." *Social Problems* 34 (1): 34–53.

Minority Staff of the Permanent Subcommittee on Investigations. 2001. *Correspondent Banking: A Gateway for Money Laundering* . Washington, DC: U.S. Senate Committee on Governmental Affairs.

Mintz, M. 1985. *At Any Cost: Corporate Greed, Women, and the Dalkon Shield*. New York: Pantheon Books.

Mokhiber, R. 2000. "Radiation: Children at Risk." *Multinational Monitor* 21 (6): 8–9.

National Criminal Intelligence Service. 2000. *The Threat from Serious and Organised Crime*. London: National Criminal Intelligence Service.

O'Brien, T. L. 1998. *Bad Bet: The Inside Story of Glamour, Glitz, and Danger of America's Gambling Industry*. New York: Random House.

Passas, N. 1991. *Frauds Affecting the Budget of the European Community: Report to the Commission of the European Communities*. Brussels, unpublished.

Passas, N. 1995. "The Mirror of Global Evils: A Review Essay on the BCCI Affair." *Justice Quarterly* 12 (2): 801–29.

Passas, N. 1997. *Regional Initiatives against International Corruption*: Report to the United Nations Crime Prevention and Criminal Justice Program. E/CN .15/1997/3. Vienna, Austria: United Nations.

Passas, N. 1999a. "Globalization, Criminogenic Asymmetries, and Economic Crime." *European Journal of Law Reform* 1(4): 399–423.

Passas, N., ed. 1999b. *Transnational Crime*. Aldershot: Dartmouth.

Passas, N. 2000. "Global Anomie, Dysnomie, and Economic Crime: Hidden Consequences of Globalization and Neo-Liberalism in Russia and around the World." *Social Justice* 27 (2): 16–44.

Passas, N. 2003. "Cross-Border Crime and the Interface between Legal and Illegal Actors." *Security Journal* 16 (1): 19–37.

Pavalko, R. M. 2000. *Risky Business*. Belmont, CA: Wadsworth.

Pearce, F., and S. Tombs. 1998. *Toxic Capitalism: Corporate Crime and the Chemical Industry*. Aldershot: Dartmouth.

Picciotto, S. 1992. *International Business Taxation*. New York: Quorum Books.

Reiman, J. 2000. *The Rich Get Richer and the Poor Get Prison*. 6th ed. Boston: Allyn and Bacon.

Reuters. 2000. "EU to Sue U.S. Tobacco Firms over Alleged Smuggling." July 20.

Rizvi, M. 2000. "Corporate Farming Comes to Pakistan: The Harvest of Globalization and Business Influence." *Multinational Monitor* 21 (10):17–20.

Ruggiero, V. 1996. *Organised and Corporate Crime in Europe: Offers That Can't Be Refused*. Aldershot: Dartmouth.

Sapone, M. 1999. "Have Rifle with Scope, Will Travel: The Global Economy of Mercenary Violence." *California Western International Law Journal* 30 (fall): 1–43.

Schwendinger, H., and J. Schwendinger. 1975. "Defenders of Order or Guardians of Human Rights?" In *Critical Criminology*, ed. I. Taylor, P. Walton, J. Young, 113–46. London: Routledge and Kegan Paul.

Shapiro, S. P. 1990. "Collaring the Crime, Not the Criminal: Reconsidering the Concept of White-Collar Crime." *American Sociological Review* 55 (3): 346–65.

Shiva, V. 1997. *Biopiracy: The Plunder of Nature and Knowledge*. Boston: South End Press.

Silverstein, K. 1997. "Privatizing War: How Affairs of State Are Outsourced to Corporations beyond Public Control." *The Nation* (digital edition). http://www.thenation.com.

Silverstein, K. 1999. "Millions for Viagra, Pennies for Diseases of the Poor." *The Nation*. July 19. http://past.thenation.com/cgi-bin/framizer.cgi?url=http://past.thenation.com/issue/990719/990719silverstein.shtml.

Silverstein, K., and A. Cockburn. 1995. "Major U.S. Bank Urges Zapatista Wipe-Out: 'A Litmus Test for Mexico's Stability.'" *Counterpunch* 2 (3). Available at http://www.hartford-hwp.com/archives/46/025.html.

Simpson, S. S. 2002. *Corporate Crime, Law, and Social Control*. Cambridge: Cambridge University Press.

SMR Research Corp. 1997. *The Personal Bankruptcy Crisis*. Hackettstown, NJ: SMR.

Snider, L. 1993. *Bad Business: Corporate Crime in Canada*. Scarborough: Nelson Canada.

Stone, C. D. 1975. *Where the Law Ends: The Social Control of Corporate Behavior*. New York: Harper and Row.

Sutherland, E. H. 1949. *White Collar Crime*. New York: Dryden.

Sutherland, E. H. 1983. *White Collar Crime: The Uncut Version*. New Haven: Yale University Press.

Szasz, A. 1986. "Corporations, Organized Crime, and the Disposal of Hazardous Waste: An Examination of the Making of a Criminogenic Regulatory Structure." *Criminology* 24 (1): 1–27.

USDA. 1990. *Foreign Agricultural Service GSM 102 and 103 Programs Tobacco Export Sales.* Audit Report 07099-2-At. Washington, DC: U.S. Department of Agriculture.

Vallette, J., and D. Wysham. 2002. *Enron's Pawns.* Washington, DC: Sustainable Energy and Economy Network/Institute for Policy Studies.

Vogel, J., ed. 1997. *Crapped Out: How Gambling Ruins the Economy and Destroys Lives.* Monroe, ME: Common Courage Press.

Warde, I. 1998. LTCM: "A Hedge Fund above Suspicion." *Le Monde Diplomatique.* November.

Watkins, K. 1997. *Globalisation and Liberalisation: Implications for Poverty, Distribution, and Inequality.* Occasional Paper 32. New York: U.N. Development Program.

Wells, L. 1998. "A Wolf in Sheep's Clothing: Why Unocal Should Be Liable under U.S. Law for Human Rights Abuses in Burma." *Columbia Journal of Law and Social Problems* 32 (fall): 35–71.

Yeager, P. C. 1995. "Law, Crime, and Inequality: The Regulatory State." In *Crime and Inequality,* ed. J. Hagan and R. D. Peterson, 247–76. Stanford, CA: Stanford University Press.

Yeoman, B. 2000. "Steel Town Lockdown." *Mother Jones.* May–June, 38–47.

Zarate, J. C. 1998. "The Emergence of a New Dog of War: Private International Security Companies, International Law, and the New World Disorder." *Stanford Journal of International Law* 34 (winter): 75–162.

2

The Cigarette Industry

Richard A. Daynard

The Industry

The American cigarette industry has for the past fifty years consisted almost exclusively of the same companies: Philip Morris, R. J. Reynolds, Brown and Williamson, American Tobacco (now part of Brown and Williamson), Lorillard, and Liggett. These cigarette companies *are* the tobacco industry in the United States because their products account for nearly 95 percent of retail tobacco sales.[1] The industry yields approximately $45 billion in domestic sales, led by Philip Morris, with a more than 45 percent market share, and followed by R. J. Reynolds (30 percent share), Brown and Williamson (20 percent share), and Lorillard and Liggett (a combined 7 percent share).[2] Philip Morris's Marlboro brand accounts for about one-third of all U.S. cigarette sales.[3]

Internationally, tobacco sales generate more than $275 billion, showing 1–2 percent growth each year.[4] China consumes approximately 30 percent of all cigarettes produced; Europe, Asia (excluding China and Japan), and the United States account for roughly 10 percent each; and Japan smokes more than 5 percent.[5] On the power of its Marlboro brand, Philip Morris commands approximately 15 percent of the world market. Brown and Williamson's parent company, British American Tobacco, and Japan Tobacco, which recently purchased R. J. Reynolds's international operations, each have an estimated 10 percent international market share.[6] Other foreign cigarette manufacturers account for the rest of the international cigarette market.[7]

The Problem

The international cigarette industry is without peer in terms of the harm it causes. Each year, its products kill more than 400,000 Americans[8] and more than 4 million people worldwide.[9] Each year, the cigarette industry's products cause premature deaths in the United States that steal more than five million years of potential life.[10] About 100 million people were killed by tobacco products (mostly cigarettes) during the twentieth century; if current trends continue, about 1 billion people will be killed during the current century.[11]

On an individual basis, this means that a man who smokes is twenty-two times more likely to die from lung cancer and ten times more likely to die from bronchitis and emphysema than a nonsmoker is.[12] A woman who smokes is nearly twelve times more likely than a nonsmoking woman to die from lung cancer and more than ten times more likely to die from bronchitis and emphysema.[13] For a middle-aged man or woman, smoking triples the risk of dying from heart disease.[14]

Disease and death caused by cigarette smoking is not limited to lung cancer, bronchitis, and emphysema. Instead, smoking causes an extraordinary range of diseases, only some of which are fatal. A jury in the *Engle* class-action case found that cigarettes cause aortic aneurysms; cancers of the bladder, cervix, kidney, lung, oral cavity, pancreas, stomach, and throat; chronic bronchitis and emphysema; various types of heart disease, including heart attacks; miscarriages; peripheral vascular disease; and strokes.[15] In the United States, the fatal diseases or their complications cause the death of half of all lifetime smokers.[16] As a result, smokers die on average seven years before nonsmokers.[17]

Cigarettes directly injure nonsmokers as well. In the United States, about fifty thousand nonsmokers die each year from the health effects of inhaling toxins from other people's cigarettes.[18] Another thousand die from cigarette-caused fires.[19]

Addiction itself is a massive problem, involving a significant loss of freedom and causing people to buy and use a product even though they would rather not do so. Human dignity and happiness is reduced when individuals are constrained from realizing their choices and objectives by the physiological and psychological effects of addictions. The problem is exacerbated by the fact that the addiction itself is generally acquired unwittingly. With few exceptions, almost every cigarette smoker starts smoking before the age of eighteen, and a large percentage of those begin at the age of ten or eleven years old[20]—hardly an age that lends itself to making informed decisions about the long-term health effects of lighting up. In fact, despite decades of education regarding and media attention to the health risks of smoking, a survey of eighth-graders shows that only half of the children interviewed believed that smoking a pack or more of cigarettes a day could be harmful.[21] Interestingly, a recent report by the Society for Research on Nicotine and Tobacco shows that adolescents can become addicted to nicotine in as little as four weeks after smoking their first cigarette without even smoking every day.[22] Adding to a potential smoker's uninformed decision to start smoking has been the cigarette industry's long-standing denial that nicotine is addictive and aggressive marketing campaigns targeted at children.

Despite its public statements, the cigarette industry has long known of the addictive nature of nicotine. Disclosed insider documents reveal that cigarette manufacturers financed research by the Battelle Memorial Institute laboratory in Geneva, Switzerland, from the late 1950s through 1967 that showed nicotine to be addictive. In "A Tentative Hypothesis on Nicotine Addiction," Battelle researchers reported that "chronic intake of nicotine tends to restore the normal physiological functioning of the endocrine system [for smokers], so that ever-increasing dose levels of nicotine are necessary to maintain the desired action."[23] This impact on the endocrine system, concluded the Battelle researchers, creates an "unconscious desire [that] explains the addiction of the individual to nicotine."[24]

The Battelle research forced one industry lawyer to conclude, "Nicotine is addictive. We are, then, in the business of selling nicotine, an addictive drug."[25] The industry lawyer's words are an understatement of nicotine's addictive nature: the chances of becoming addicted to nicotine for smokers are greater than their chances of becoming dependent by using crack or cocaine intravenously.[26] Although the cigarette industry had publicly promised to report its research findings to health officials, it was "disturbed at [the Battelle research's] implications [regarding] cardiovascular disorders" and found submission of the report to the surgeon general "undesirable."[27]

The cigarette industry's public denials of nicotine's addictive nature in light of the industry's private knowledge shows its complete disregard for the public's health. Even worse, the cigarette industry then proceeded to market and advertise its addictive and deadly product to children. In 1950, a U.S. Tobacco Journal article noted that a "massive potential market still exists among women and young adults, [the] cigarette industry leaders agreed, acknowledging that recruitment of these millions of prospective smokers comprises the major objective for the immediate future and on a long term basis as well."[28]

The cigarette industry wasted little time or scruples in pursuing its major objective of recruiting young smokers. Cigarette manufacturer Philip Morris's marketing research documents, disclosed in litigation, show that children as young as twelve years old were included in marketing research that focused on teenage consumption. This was not an isolated practice within the industry, as Philip Morris's research found that "the data from [its] study [were] consonant with the findings of other such studies, both at Philip Morris and without."[29] R. J. Reynolds, for its part, set increasing its share of fourteen- to twenty-four-year-old smokers as one of its "marketing goals" for 1975 because "as they mature, [they] will account for key market share of cigarette volume for next 25 years."[30] Reynolds thereupon launched its Camel brand ad campaign, featuring the cartoon character Joe Camel. This campaign was so effective at reaching children that one study published in the *Journal of the American Medical Association* found six-year-olds to be nearly as familiar with Joe Camel as with Mickey Mouse.[31] A final revelation of the cigarette industry's approach to enticing children to smoke comes from discovered documents that show the industry tolerated trademark infringement and granted confectioners permission to market candy cigarettes in packs with designs similar to those of major cigarette brands.[32]

Since most smokers start smoking as children, since nicotine is highly addictive, and since the cigarette industry has publicly lied about its product while targeting children with marketing and advertising, the industry's familiar argument that smokers exercise free will and assume the health risks of smoking by choosing to smoke is inherently fallacious. Furthermore, the contention that smokers must perceive a net benefit from smoking or they wouldn't choose to do it is doubly false, since addiction both explains their behavior and frustrates their current choices. Our society prohibits the sale of heroin and cocaine because of the costs to society of these addictive drugs, yet there is no such prohibition on the cigarette industry profiting from the scourge of nicotine addiction and its attendant societal costs.

The human devastation caused by the cigarette industry is not limited to life, health, and freedom. In the United States alone, cigarette smoking costs at least $50 billion each year in health care costs and another $50 billion in lost productivity (the money that smokers and nonsmokers would be making if they were not sick, dying, or dead from cigarette-caused diseases).[33] The noneconomic but nonetheless very real costs in terms of pain and suffering and of grief and loss of companionship experienced by smokers' family members cannot even be factored into the final sum.

The costs imposed by the cigarette industry are not needed to support employment or public finances. In non-tobacco-growing states, cigarette revenues are exported: ending cigarette use would actually increase employment there.[34] On balance, employment would rise in the United States if cigarette smoking stopped.[35] Similarly, lost cigarette tax revenues would be offset by reductions in health care and other costs incurred within the jurisdiction, while alternative forms of taxation are always available. And, federal funds that currently go to support tobacco farmers and other tobacco-related activities—more than $48 million in 1997 alone—could be removed from the federal budget or put to more constructive uses.[36]

Indeed, the economic benefit of an activity may be measured by its ability to produce profits after it has internalized the costs it imposes. In the United States, it has been estimated that with its existing cost structure, the cigarette industry could, by charging the profit-maximizing price, realize profits of about $52 billion per year. Given that it imposes quantifiable economic costs for health care and lost productivity of more than $100 billion per year as well as substantial additional nonquantifiable costs, the cigarette industry imposes on society a huge net economic cost. On a per pack basis, it is estimated that these costs equal $3.90 in smoking related health care expenses for each pack of cigarettes sold—costs borne entirely by the American public.[37]

The industry nonetheless remains in business because the legal system, which could require the industry to internalize these costs by holding it legally responsible for them, has—with one major exception—not yet done so. The exception involves settlements reimbursing the states for their cigarette-caused health care costs, which shift about $10 billion per year of these costs to the industry. Even with this exception, the failure of the legal system to impose liability on the industry for the great majority of cigarette-caused costs amounts to more than a $100 billion annual subsidy paid by the rest of society to the cigarette industry. Furthermore, the subsidy is not paid equally by all members of society. Cigarette smoking and exposure to cigarette smoke occur disproportionately among poorer citizens; so, of course, do the resulting diseases. Cigarette addiction, disease, and death thus behave like a regressive tax.

Finally, the cigarette industry creates another pressing set of problems on an entirely different dimension. The public has been treated to the spectacle of the seven cigarette company chief executive officers lying under oath to a congressional committee in 1994 and subsequently escaping prosecution. More generally, the notorious ability of the cigarette industry in the United States and elsewhere to subvert the governmental processes that are supposed to protect citizens from preventable pandemics of addiction, disease, and death contributes to a corrosive public cynicism about "democratic" government. This cynicism itself further weakens government's responsiveness to citizens' needs when these needs conflict with the interests of moneyed and influential corporate predators like the cigarette industry.

Why Hasn't the Problem Been Corrected?

If someone today were to propose marketing a product that fulfills no pre-existing need, is highly addictive, and kills half of all its users (who continue to use it until contracting their fatal illnesses), he would immediately be sent to the local psychiatric hospital for examination. But it didn't happen that way. In the early 1950s, when the public first heard about studies showing that cigarette smoking caused lung cancer, most American men smoked cigarettes.[38] At that time, the problem was recategorizing as an addictive killer something that had been taken for granted as a slightly sinful but otherwise innocuous part of American life and culture.

The cigarette industry was determined to prevent that recategorization and allowed neither cost nor moral scruples to get in its way. On December 15, 1953, the presidents of the five U.S. cigarette companies met at New York's Plaza Hotel, where they devised a strategy to neutralize the impact of the emerging scientific research on the public's understanding of the dangers of cigarettes.

The strategy was to create a false controversy about the science, a public impression that the facts about smoking-caused diseases were merely theories. To that end, the cigarette industry organized and funded a phony "independent" research organization to investigate the potential danger of tobacco use and report its results to the public. To quote internal industry documents, this supposed research organization, which became the Council for Tobacco Research (CTR), was actually "organized as a public relations effort" that enabled the industry "to give quick responses to new developments in the propaganda of the avid anti-smoking groups."[39]

One CTR researcher, Dr. Theodor Sterling, received more than $5 million in funding between 1973 and 1990 for his work in studying the "constitutional hypothesis" of disease (that is, genetic factors rather than smoking cause cancer).[40] Sterling was well funded not only for his research but also for his "ability to respond quickly to new scientific developments" and publicly attack research that found tobacco use to be harmful.[41]

Although the CTR was created as a public relations instrument, cigarette industry lawyers quickly realized its potential to shield the industry from legal responsibility for its product and took direct control of the CTR's "special projects" research. The lawyers directly oversaw the expenditure of more than $14 million in funding for CTR special projects aimed at refuting the mounting evidence that tobacco use was harmful to health.[42] An additional benefit of creating the CTR and funding scientific research was that the cigarette industry found protobacco scientists and medical doctors who could serve as witnesses in lawsuits and before legislative bodies.

The cigarette industry's other main method of creating a controversy about the health impact of tobacco was adamantly to deny that cigarettes cause any disease at all. The best-known example of this strategy in action was the image of cigarette industry executives swearing before a 1994 U.S. Senate hearing that they did not believe cigarettes to be harmful despite the decades of contrary evidence. Industry documents, however, tell a very different story.

As early as 1946, cigarette industry scientists were aware of evidence that compounds produced by burning tobacco and tested on animals showed "definite carcinogenic properties."[43] While research linking smoking and lung cancer was becoming public in the 1950s and 1960s, the cigarette industry was conducting private research and reviewing existing tobacco studies. Industry scientific reports exposed through litigation show that as early as 1953, the cigarette industry's researchers were of the opinion that "studies of clinical data tend to confirm the relationship between heavy and prolonged tobacco smoking and incidence of cancer of the lung."[44]

Although the cigarette industry was publicly stating that it accepted "an interest in people's health as a basic responsibility, paramount to every other consideration in [its] business" and that it was "pledging aid and assistance to the research effort,"[45] discovered documents show that cigarette makers were privately more concerned about the health of business. In an internal report prepared by a researcher at R. J. Reynolds, the scientist raised the question of how publicly denying the link between tobacco and cancer while the company's research confirmed that link might "affect adversely the company's economic status" in potential litigation.[46] The cigarette industry's solution to this threat to its business was to discontinue funding of potentially damaging research and to suppress any negative research results. This action was necessary, to quote one industry lawyer warning of the dangers of a proposed tobacco research program, because "no matter what our explanation happened to be the fact of the red light [a positive test for cancer] in our own hands would be serious burden to the tobacco industry if it came out in legislative hearings or in litigation."[47]

The final piece of the cigarette industry's strategy to create a controversy about the impact on health was to spend massive amounts of money on advertising. A 1997 government report shows that cigarette companies spend more than $5 billion a year on advertising and promotion.[48] This amount is even more incredible when one considers that the industry has spent no money on television advertising since the practice was banned in 1971.

Where does the money go? Aside from heavy print and billboard advertising[49] and sports sponsorship, the cigarette industry spent money in Hollywood on product placement in major motion pictures and television to perpetuate a positive image of smoking. One interesting find in the millions of cigarette industry documents made public in the last couple of years is a 1983 letter from actor Sylvester Stallone in which he promised to "use Brown & Williamson tobacco products in at least five feature films. It is my understanding," wrote Stallone, who created such American heroes as Rocky Balboa and Rambo, "that Brown & Williamson will pay a fee of $500,000" in return for the product placement.[50] Furthermore, Philip Morris paid $350,000 to have cigarettes featured in the James Bond movie *License to Kill*.[51] Perhaps these expenditures help explain why current movie stars are three times more likely to smoke on screen than average real-life Americans.[52]

Given the weight of the legitimate scientific research showing the unprecedented devastation cigarettes cause, the industry's disinformation campaign has had remarkable success. Public awareness of the nature and extent of smoking's dangers has trailed the truth by decades. The confusion has provided necessary cover for a compliant Congress (well greased with tobacco money) to refrain from passing any effective regulatory measures while immunizing the industry from some forms of state regulation and legal liability. The confusion has permitted the industry to continue to market cigarettes to successive generations as a sophisticated, slightly sinful, but not really dangerous entrée into adult society and pleasures. The confusion has allowed the industry to fool smokers into believing that filtered cigarettes and later "low tar" cigarettes would adequately remove whatever risks cigarettes might present. (In fact, the industry knew that smokers would smoke more or differently to maintain their accustomed nicotine dosages and secretly designed the new cigarettes to facilitate this "compensation".)[53] And the confusion has tempered the efforts of governmental bodies at all levels to protect the health of nonsmokers after the scientific evidence of the dangers of smoking began to emerge.

Disinformation and financial contributions have helped the cigarette industry control the American political process. The industry contributed $32.6 million in political action committee and soft money between 1989 and 1999 and has spent an additional $120 million on federal lobbying activities from 1997 to 1999.[54] The fact that tobacco growing is important in several states has also given the industry important bargaining chips, since "their" senators and representatives will support the projects and concerns of other legislators if and only if these other legislators vote "correctly" on tobacco issues.

The industry's political agenda has also been helped by "Astroturf" organizations (like the industry-funded National Smokers Alliance) and by the "Smoke Ring"—the media, suppliers, recipients of industry charity, the hospitality industry, and other credible and apparently independent individuals and organizations who believe their fortunes to be tied to the cigarette industry and exercise their influence accordingly.[55] One example among many is the American Civil Liberties Union, which receives large cigarette industry contributions, has set up a special unit to protect the "rights" of smoking employees, and publicly downplays the dangers of cigarette smoke to nonsmokers.[56]

That money is the mother's milk of politics is well known. Less well known is the power of money in the legal process. Yet the cigarette industry has been able to discourage all but a few lawsuits against it through a scorched-earth litigation strategy, as described in an internal memo: "The way we win these cases, to paraphrase Gen. Patton, is not by spending all of [cigarette manufacturer R. J.] Reynolds' money, but by making the other son of a bitch spend all of his."[57] This involved listing dozens of expert witnesses when only a handful would be called, deposing more than a hundred acquaintances of the plaintiff, filing endless motions on issues important and trivial, refusing to settle any cases, and otherwise making sure that plaintiffs' attorneys' costs would always exceed expected fees.

The cigarette industry has also been very effective in immunizing itself from tobacco litigation by secretly lobbying for "tort reform" legislation at the state level. Documents discovered in litigation reveal that the industry, along with other manufacturers of dangerous products and chemicals as well as insurance companies, secretly created and funded with millions of dollars political action committees with names such as Citizens against Lawsuit Abuse.[58] Posing as grassroots organizations of concerned citizens, these front groups lobbied state legislatures to weaken tort law to stop "out-of-control" and "frivolous" litigation.

What Is to Be Done?

U.S. Supreme Court Justice Louis D. Brandeis once said that "sunlight is the best disinfectant."[59] It is certainly true that the cigarette industry does its best work in the dark. Front groups lose most of their credibility when the curtain is pulled, revealing the strings. Tobacco executives' assertions of Cartesian doubt ("We do not believe nicotine is addictive"; "Smoking has not been *proven* to cause lung cancer") appear fraudulent rather than merely quixotic when juxtaposed against decades-old internal documents in which these leaders' admit both addiction and causation.

To the extent that the cigarette industry impeded the public recategorization of cigarettes as an addictive and deadly product, the industry itself had to be recategorized to remove the impediment. As long as the cigarette companies were seen as mere purveyors of an agricultural good to satisfy a preexisting demand, the disinformation they generated seemed genuine and caused the intended confusion. Once manufacturers were exposed as liars who disbelieved their own propaganda and as greedy and amoral pushers of highly engineered nicotine devices to kids, the "controversy" and the benign image of the cigarette largely disappeared.

The change in image for the cigarette industry and its product has been reflected in the results of tobacco liability cases. Until 1994, plaintiffs generally lost: juries viewed the cases as involving individuals who chose to smoke, with adequate knowledge of the risks. Since 1994, when millions of pages of incriminating documents have became available from whistle-blowers as well as from formal legal discovery proceedings, juries that have been allowed to see the documents have viewed the cases as involving a rogue industry that deceived its customers, including the plaintiffs, about its deadly and addictive products.

Nonetheless, the cigarette industry continues to recruit new generations of smokers in undiminishing numbers. More than 40 million Americans continue to smoke, with 1 percent of them dying prematurely each year of cigarette-caused diseases. With the exception of the end of cigarette billboards and taxi-top advertising pursuant to the industry's settlement with the states, cigarettes continue to be promoted and marketed as before. With the exception of the recent law requiring cigarettes sold in New York after 2003 to be fire-safe, cigarettes continue to be as toxic and deadly as before. The recategorization of cigarettes and cigarette manufacturers in the minds of much of the public obviously has not solved the problem. So what is to be done?

I have three suggestions. First, the recategorization must be reinforced and extended to segments of society where it has not yet penetrated. Funds from the states' settlement with the cigarette industry can and should be used for this purpose. California, Massachusetts, and Florida have developed effective media campaigns, and a national television campaign has dramatized the effect of smoking by featuring body bags being dropped off outside a major tobacco headquarters. Widespread grassroots involvement and advocacy is needed to spread, reinforce, and solidify the transformation of the images of smoking and the tobacco industry.

Second, litigation against the industry needs to proceed full bore. The promise of tobacco litigation is still what I outlined in 1988: (1) forcing the price to reflect a larger proportion of the industry's full social cost, thereby reducing smoking, especially among younger people; (2) dramatizing the dangers of smoking to real people (not just statistics); (3) developing incriminating material from the industry's files and employees, thereby undermining its political power; (4) making money available for the health care system and for tobacco control; and (5) forcing cigarette executives to reconsider their more egregious behavior and perhaps to make concessions to regulatory demands to avoid or reduce punitive damages.[60]

Third, strong measures must be enacted at the local, state, and national levels to (1) eliminate involuntary exposure to cigarette smoke; (2) raise taxes to discourage smoking; (3) eliminate marketing techniques used to recruit new smokers; and (4) regulate cigarette design to minimize the product's toxicity and lethality.

There is, of course, a chicken-and-egg problem here. These suggestions are not practicable to the extent that the cigarette industry is seen as invulnerable. Conversely, the industry seems invulnerable to the extent that the suggestions are not being carried out. We need somehow to break into this closed cycle. Fortunately, we have already begun.

NOTES

The author wishes to thank Northeastern University School of Law students Jeffrey Daley and Daniel Fox for their assistance with this chapter.

1. J. Grey, "Tobacco Industry, 2000," http://www.hoovers.com/industry/snapshot/0%2c2204%2c43%2c00.html.

2. Ibid.

3. Ibid.

4. Ibid.

5. Ibid.

6. Ibid.

7. Ibid.

8. M. J. Thun, L. F. Apicella, and S. J. Henley, "Smoking vs. Other Risk Factors as the Cause of Smoking-Attributable Deaths," *Journal of the American Medical Association* 284 (6) (August 9, 2000): 706–12.

9. G. H. Brundtland, "Achieving Worldwide Tobacco Control," *Journal of the American Medical Association* 284(6) (August 9, 2000): 750–53.

10. Centers for Disease Control and Prevention, "Smoking-Attributable Mortality and Years of Potential Life Lost—United States, 1990," *Morbidity and Mortality Weekly Report* 42 (33) (1993): 645–48.

11. P. Jha and F. J. Chaloupka, "The Economics of Global Tobacco Control," *British Medical Journal* 321 (5) (August 2000): 358–61.

12. Centers for Disease Control and Prevention, "Smoking-Attributable Mortality."

13. Ibid.

14. Ibid.

15. *Engle v. R. J. Reynolds Tobacco Co.*, 14.3 Tobacco Products Litigation Reporter 2.101 (July 1999).

16. American Cancer Society, "Cancer Facts and Figures 1998: Tobacco Use," http://www.cancer.org/statistics/cff98/tobacco.html.

17. Centers for Disease Control and Prevention, Office on Smoking and Health, Tobacco Information and Prevention Source, Fact Sheet, "Cigarette Smoking–Related Mortality" (1994), http://www.cdc.gov/tobacco/mortali.htm.

18. California Environmental Protection Agency, *Health Effects of Exposure to Environmental Tobacco Smoke, Final Report* (Sacramento: California Environmental Protection Agency, September 1997).

19. Centers for Disease Control and Prevention, Office on Smoking and Health, Tobacco Information and Prevention Source, Fact Sheet, "Cigarette Smoking–Related Mortality."

20. American Heart Association, AHA Medical/Scientific Statement, "Active and Passive Tobacco Exposure: A Serious Pediatric Health Problem" (1994), http://www.americanheart.org/Scientific/statements/1994/119401.html.

21. American Cancer Society, "Tobacco and Cancer: Facts about Children and Tobacco Use" (January 6, 1999), http://www.cancer.org/tobacco/facts.html.

22. S. Adler, "Young Teens Hooked Quickly," ABCNews.com, February 16, 2000, http://abcnews.go.com/sections/living/DailyNews/teensmoke000216_feature.html.

23. C. Haselbach and O. Libert. A Tentative Hypothesis on Nicotine Addiction (London: BAT, 1963), reprinted in part in Stanton A. Glantz, John Slade, Lisa A. Bero, Peter Hanauer, and Deborah E. Barnes, The Cigarette Papers (Berkeley: University of California Press, 1996), 68–69.

24. Ibid.

25. A. Yeaman, "Implications of Battelle Hippo I and II and the Griffith Filter," memo, July 17, 1963; reprinted in part in Glantz et al., Cigarette Papers, 72–74.

26. American Cancer Society, "Tobacco and Cancer."

27. Cable sent by A. Yeaman, general counsel for Brown and Williamson, to A. D. McCormick, research and development executive at British American Tobacco, July 3, 1963, reprinted in Glantz et al., Cigarette Papers, 73.

28. P. J. Hilts, Smokescreen—The Truth behind the Tobacco Industry Cover-Up (New York: Addison Wesley, 1996), 66, 76–77.

29. Philip Morris Marketing Research Department, "Incidence of Smoking Cigarettes," May 18, 1973 (Minnesota Trial Exhibit 11,801).

30. R. J. Reynolds, "Domestic Operating Goals," November 26, 1975 (Minnesota Trial Exhibit 12,377).

31. Quoted in T. Houston, P. Fischer, and J. Richard Jr., "The Public, the Press, and Tobacco Research," Tobacco Control 1 (2) (1992): 118–22.

32. E. Ross, "Candy Cigarette Conspiracy?" ABC News, August 4, 2000, http://more.abcnews.go.com/sections/living/dailynews/candycigs000804.html.

33. Centers for Disease Control and Prevention, "Medical-Care Expenditures Attributable to Cigarette Smoking—United States, 1993," Morbidity and Mortality Weekly Report 43 (26) (1994): 469–72.

34. K. E. Warner and G. A. Fulton, "The Economic Implications of Tobacco Product Sales in a Nontobacco State," Journal of the American Medical Association 271 (10) (1994): 771–76.

35. K. E. Warner, G. A. Fulton, P. Nicolas, and D. R. Grimes, "Employment Implications of Declining Tobacco Product Sales for the Regional Economies of the United States," Journal of the American Medical Association 275 (16) (1996): 1241–46.

36. American Heart Association, "Federal Support for Tobacco: AHA Advocacy Position," 2000, http://www.americanheart.org/heart_and_stroke_A_Z_ Guide/ftpb.html.

37. American Cancer Society, New England Division, "Advocating for a Tobacco-Free Campus" (2001), http://www.cancer.org/downloads/Advocating _For_ A_Tobacco-Free_Campus.doc.

38. J. Slade, "Tobacco and Other Addictions," in *Tobacco and Health*, ed. Karen Slama (New York: Plenum Press, 1995), 319.

39. Memo from Ernest Pepples, vice president of Brown and Williamson Tobacco, to J. A. Edens, chairman and chief executive officer of Brown and Williamson Tobacco, April 4, 1978, reprinted in Glantz et al., *Cigarette Papers*, 44.

40. Glantz et al., *Cigarette Papers*, 296.

41. Letter from William Shinn, outside counsel for the tobacco companies, to the companies' inside counsel, February 4, 1981, reprinted in Glantz et al., *Cigarette Papers*, 297.

42. Glantz et al., *Cigarette Papers*, 289.

43. D. Campbell, "Revealing Documents Discuss Nicotine Levels and Marketing to Teens," *Greensboro News and Record*, June 28, 1998, D1.

44. C. Teague, "Survey of Cancer Research with Emphasis upon Possible Carcinogens from Tobacco," February 2, 1953, http://tobaccoducuments.org/rjr/ 501932947–2968.html.

45. Tobacco Industry Research Committee, "A Frank Statement to the Public by the Makers of Cigarettes," January 4, 1954, http://www.tobacco.neu.edu/ box/BoekenBox/Boeken%20Evidence%20PDF/0363.pdf.

46. A. Rodgman, (R. J. Reynolds Tobacco Company Chemical Research Department), "The Smoking and Health Problem—A Critical and Objective Appraisal," 1962, p. 13, http://www.rjrtdocs.com/rjrtdocs/frames.html.

47. Memo from Ernest Pepples, vice president of Brown and Williamson Tobacco, to A. Yeaman, general counsel for Brown and Williamson Tobacco, March 10, 1977, reprinted in Glantz et al., *Cigarette Papers*, 288.

48. *Federal Trade Commission Report to Congress for 1997, Pursuant to the Federal Cigarette Labeling and Advertising Act* (Washington, DC: U.S. Government Printing Office, 1999), 18.

49. As part of the 1998 Master Settlement Agreement with state attorneys general, the cigarette industry has agreed no longer to use billboard advertising.

50. Letter from Sylvester Stallone to Bob Kovoloff, Associated Film Promotion, April 28, 1983, reprinted in Glantz et al., *Cigarette Papers*, 366.

51. Action on Smoking and Health, "Clouds of Smoke Hang over Academy Awards," http://ash.org/oscars.html (October 24, 2000).

52. Ibid.

53. "Chronology of Brown and Williamson Smoking and Health Research" (1988), http://tobaccodocuments.org/Ness/8878.html.

54. "Paying the Price: How Tobacco, Gun, Gambling, and Alcohol Interests Block Common Sense Solutions to Some of the Nation's Most Urgent Problems," *Follow the Dollar Report* (Common Cause), June 2000, 4.

55. Peter Taylor, *The Smoke Ring: Tobacco, Money, and International Politics* (New York: Pantheon, 1984).

56. Morton Mintz, "The ACLU's Tobacco Addiction: American Civil Liber-

ties Union Receives Donations from Tobacco Industry; Abstract," *The Progressive*, December 3, 1998.

57. Quoted in *Haines v. Liggett Group, Inc.*, 814 F. Supp. 414 (D.N.J. 1993).

58. Center for Justice and Democracy, "The CALA Files: The Secret Campaign by Big Tobacco and Other Major Industries to Take Away Your Rights, Executive Summary," http://www.citizen.org/congress/civjus/consumer/calaexecsum.htm (October 23, 2000).

59. L. Brandeis, *Other People's Money, and How the Bankers Use It* (1933), 62.

60. R. A. Daynard, "Tobacco Products Litigation as a Cancer Control Strategy," *Journal of the National Cancer Institute* 80 (1988): 9.

3

Externalities of the Arms Trade

Loretta Bondi

Overview

During the 1990s, global arms trade and military transfers became less a function of foreign policy than a government-sponsored commercial race to occupy lucrative market niches abroad. Scant consideration was given to the detrimental effects that such virtually unrestrained competition might engender in areas affected by chronic political instability, gross violations of human rights, sluggish economic growth, and widespread corruption. This trend is not likely to subside.[1]

A look at the arms-supplying countries in the aftermath of the Cold War reveals a military-industrial complex that has been distorted by years of massive government investment and bloated to overcapacity and whose survival depends heavily on new outlets outside of domestic procurement. With overall demand dropping after 1987 and never resuming the robustness of preceding decades, the arms trade assumed and still maintains the characteristics of a buyer's market. In this configuration, buying countries dictate conditions that drive prices down and facilitate access to ever-more-sophisticated weaponry. This, in turn, triggers parallel efforts among regional rivals to import previously unavailable technology to build up arsenals and/or domestic production. Ultimately, the establishment and maintenance of a home-grown industrial base in countries eager to join the arms-producers club not only engenders further arms proliferation but is often achieved at the expense of pressing needs of economic development and good governance.

In this changing environment, the U.S. arms industry has responded to the new challenges with, on the one hand, a retrenchment that has paved

43

the way to consolidation through a spate of mergers and acquisitions. On the other hand, industry keeps production lines open by exporting what it cannot sell in the United States. Overseas sales are helped by a mixture of incentives for buyers, which include the transfer of technology and equipment for the manufacture of military goods abroad. Rejecting critics' concerns, industry in the United States and in other supplier countries has successfully argued that these strategies permit economies of scale that, in turn, preserve national military prowess, readiness, and capacity for innovation. Another industry rationale to justify such methods intones, "If we don't do it, somebody else will." This logic, which in fact is at the very core of today's conventional arms proliferation and which potentially undercuts the much heralded post–Cold War peace dividends, nonetheless has been persuasive in policy-making circles in Washington and elsewhere.

The aftermath of the Cold War has already spurred often overlooked and nefarious and unforeseen externalities. After the fall of the Berlin Wall in 1989, for example, the downsizing of military forces in former Warsaw Pact countries unleashed a cascade of excess weapons to warring parties in Africa and elsewhere. In their quest for hard currency and market shares, former Eastern Bloc governments and private sellers were less than fastidious about buyers' human rights credentials. For their part, buyers accepted weaponry that, while hardly state-of-the-art, was efficient, cheap, and abundant.

Consequently, commercial considerations have consistently taken precedence over the need to discipline a trade that, by its international nature, has increasingly chipped away at governments' ability to control exports of military equipment and technology as well as to verify the bona fide credentials of these goods' recipients and the exported articles' end use. If anything, the United States and other major arms producers have demonstrated a degree of willingness to abdicate such responsibility and demolish some of the barriers that might be regarded as impediments to the global arms trade. By contrast, norms of self-restraint in arms transfers that major producers claim to embrace or abide by, such as codes of conduct on exports, continue to fail the many reality checks and eventually yield to the profit-making opportunities presented by the world's conflicts.

Government neglect is particularly evident at the low end of the arms race, which has engendered a proliferation of small and light weapons in areas of conflict around the world and in countries that can least afford it. The effects of this diffusion have long been both underreported and difficult to calculate. One thing is certain, however: the spread of small arms among the many belligerents of today's wars has contributed to the privatization of conflict, resulting in nonstate suppliers and recipients acquiring prominence, wealth, and firepower. Tragically, the victims of these wars have also been predominantly nonstate actors, as civilians became the favorite targets of ruthless armed forces and irregular militia.

Although these circumstances are likely to persist, countervailing influences have also emerged. The successful International Campaign to Ban Landmines showed in 1997 that eliminating conventional weapons responsible for such massive destruction and suffering is possible and feasible. A similar worldwide movement, the International Action Network on Small Arms (IANSA), is currently trying to replicate the land mine campaign's success by calling on the international community to curb and eventually prevent the proliferation and misuse of small arms. United Nations' initiatives and civil-society-led efforts have also placed on various governments' agendas norms of self-restraint in the transfer of weapons and military assistance. Although practical applications of these norms have been disappointing, the pressure of public opinion on governments to achieve a higher standard of responsibility and more transparency will not subside.

Big Chill, Hot New Wave

The end of the Cold War in 1991 triggered a decline in defense spending by major weapons suppliers and consequently a steep downturn in national procurement. Between 1989 and 1992 overall major weapons procurement dropped by more than 21 percent in the United States and 23 percent in Europe.[2] An even greater downward movement affected Warsaw Pact countries. For example, between 1990 and 1999 the Soviet Union's and then Russia's expenditure declined at an average of 16.7 percent per annum, while Bulgaria's dropped by an average 12.2 percent per year over the same period.[3]

This sharp spending decline left the military-industrial complex of major suppliers bloated to overcapacity by the procurement binge of the preceding decades, with production capacity standing at levels far in excess of domestic absorption. Against this backdrop and with few incentives to convert the industry to civilian use, the stage was set for successive, massive export drives.

The changed international landscape, however, also resulted in a contraction of overseas arms markets. From 1985 to 1995, the international arms trade dropped by a steady 11.2 percent per year. On average, between 1991 and 1995 the total value of exports accounted for an estimated $32.3 billion per annum, or 45 percent of the 1985 volume, with the former Soviet Union bearing the brunt of the decline. Sales regained some momentum in the mid-1990s but stabilized at lower levels than in the previous ten years. Throughout this period, the United States maintained pole position among competitors.[4]

Despite the U.S. dominance of the arms trade and military superiority firmly established during and after the 1991 Gulf War, the shrinking arms market invigorated fierce competition within the U.S. defense establishment. As a result, the 1990s witnessed a race to meet the dollar bottom line, which crowded out any lofty rhetoric of a U.S.-led new world order and thus mirrored the less visionary European commercial ethos.[5]

This energetic trade drive was eagerly promoted by President George H. W. Bush. In 1992, for example, his administration gave the green light to a sale of forty-eight top-of-the-line McDonnell Douglas F-15E "Strike Eagle" fighter planes to Saudi Arabia. Lora Lumpe, an arms trade analyst, noted that the sale was motivated largely "by the aggressive Jobs Now Campaign waged by the manufacturer." This deal involved "the most sophisticated combat aircraft the United States had ever exported—until a year and a half later, when the Clinton administration and Congress agreed to give Israel 21 F-15E [fighters] with enhanced capabilities." The rationale for this latter arms sale, Lumpe concluded, was to maintain Israel's "qualitative military edge over Saudi Arabia."[6]

Similarly, U.S. weapons are fueling the long-standing regional rivalry of two North Atlantic Treaty Organization (NATO) allies, Greece and Turkey. In 1998, for example, Greece acquired frigates, destroyers, and Hellfire antitank missiles, thereby prompting Turkey to stock up on frigates and Harpoon antiship missiles.[7] Such competitive upgrading of arsenals in volatile regions might have been highly desirable for an industry profitability but might also undermine long-term U.S. foreign policy objectives and international peace and security.

These latter considerations did not resonate with the Clinton administration, which endorsed the Saudi deal and which sold nearly $4.9 billion in weaponry to Turkey between 1993 and 1998.[8] Moreover, in 1995, the administration brought the trade drive full circle with a policy review for conventional arms transfers, Presidential Decision Directive 41, which set this new "salesman's ethos" in stone.[9] The directive for the first time explicitly incorporated concerns about the economic viability and main-tenance of the U.S. military industry as an integral part of and weighty fac-tor in decisions pertaining to conventional arms-transfer policy. Overall, as a 1999 U.S. General Accounting Office report stated, one of the gov-ernment's objectives in giving the green light to an aggressive export drive was to reduce the cost of weapons procurement by the Department of Defense, though the report points out that it was questionable whether costs really decreased as expected.[10]

The new administration's position raised a number of red flags, not least with the Presidential Advisory Board on Arms Proliferation Policy, which in 1996 reported that "the best solution for [industrial] overcapacity . . . is to reduce supply rather than increase demand." The board further main-tained that economic considerations should be de-coupled from arms exports to avoid unleashing arms proliferation.[11] Such criticism remains unheeded to this day.

Rising to the Task

The arms industry responded to the challenge by first putting its own house in order. The leaner and meaner 1990s triggered a retrenchment through an unprecedented scale of mergers and acquisitions emboldened by government subsidies.[12] Consolidation of large companies allowed diversification of portfolios and, arguably, maximization of research and development investment, the cost of which, it was envisioned, could be partly absorbed by foreign customers picking up the tab for big-ticket con-ventional weaponry.

Although the arms trade accounts for a small share of total exports—roughly 3.4 percent of U.S. and 2.2 percent of the six major European pro-ducers' gross domestic products—the weapons industry successfully argued that expanding its outreach would achieve vital domestic and foreign pol-icy objectives.[13] A rationale often repeated on national interest grounds was that trade would not only provide an outlet for the new muscle of U.S. corporate giants but would also allow state-of-the-art production lines to remain open and viable in the event of war. Trade, with its beneficial repercussions in the balance of payments, would mean job preservation or creation and increased domestic income. In addition, familiarity with U.S. weapons would secure future orders for U.S. products. In turn, the use of U.S. weapons would ensure interoperability among U.S. allies. Moreover, reliable and technologically advanced supplies would encourage a perpetuation of U.S. influence as well as trading partners' dependence on spare parts and the benevolent bestowing of newly developed U.S. fighting technology. Aside from the companies' hefty profits, the benefits to the general public of this trade drive remain in dispute.

By way of an example, a Lockheed executive testified before Congress that the United States had to make a multibillion-dollar investment for the heavily taxpayer subsidized development of the F-22 jet fighter. He argued that the new plane was required to maintain superiority over foreign arsenals that had previously been stocked with top-of-the-line U.S.-made F-16s and F-15s.[14]

The bitter irony of such a rationale was not lost on the industry's critics and arms control advocates, who described this phenomenon as "indiscriminate exporting" of conventional weaponry, noting that U.S. taxpayers continued to shore up the cost of the aircraft.[15] As analyst William D. Hartung observed,

> More than half of U.S. weapons sales are now being financed by taxpayers instead of arms purchasers. During fiscal year 1996 . . . the government spent more than $7.9 billion to help U.S. companies secure just over $12 billion in agreements for new international arms sales. The annual $7.9 in subsidies includes taxpayer-backed loans, grants, and government promotional activities that help U.S. weapons makers sell their products to foreign customers. Also the provision of low-cost facilities and extensive subsidies for research and development . . . fosters a "risk-free" environment in which weapons makers have little economic incentive to produce effective systems at affordable prices.[16]

Above all, critics also noted that such deals hardly factored in human rights considerations, respect for humanitarian law, regional stability, international peace and security, and good governance.[17]

To be sure, human rights concerns were not on the radar screen of the U.S. Department of Commerce, which argued in 1995, when seeking to promote arms sales to Indonesia,

> Instances of human rights abuses have given rise to concerns in the U.S. from time to time, the most significant being the decision of Congress to suspend military training assistance [to Indonesia] in 1992, but the overall relationship provides opportunities for U.S. defense companies to benefit from the pace of economic growth and concomitant defense needs of the Armed Forces of the Republic of Indonesia.[18]

While Indonesia was involved in the violent repression of East Timor, signs of the widespread corruption that ultimately brought down the Suharto regime in 1997 were conspicuously evident. However, these hard facts—as hard as any commercial interest—had been conveniently dismissed by Commerce Department strategists.

Another illustration of such disregard is offered by the so-called Onyx Program, which has allowed Turkey to build, under a coproduction agreement with the U.S. Lockheed Corporation, one of the largest assembly lines for the F-16 fighter aircraft.[19] Turkey then used these aircraft against the country's Kurdish insurgents. In 1995, Human Rights Watch reported,

> Turkish fighters, including F-16s, have been used to attack villages and kill civilians in violation of international humanitarian law. In other instances, the planes have been used deliberately to destroy civilian structures, contributing to the general process of forced dislocation.[20]

Despite mounting criticism, defense lobbyists continued to dominate the debate and win the day by arguing that if the U.S. defense apparatus were to withdraw from the export competition, someone else would fill that vacuum. A "do or die" logic underscores this argument. As Joel Johnson, a representative of the Aerospace Industry Association, put it in reference to a 1989 tank deal with Saudi Arabia, "If we can knock the Brits [the competitors] out of the box . . . that leaves us with no real competitors in the world tank business."[21] In other words, the battle in the narrow but lucrative environment of market niches would be fought with only one survivor outstripping all others.

Winner Takes All?

Greater policy latitude, superior weaponry, and aggressive corporate strategies established the U.S. industry's primacy in the arms trade, but this situation hardly represented the winner-takes-all scenario that Johnson envisaged. Almost all other major competitors of the United States joined the race to conquer promising market niches through the transfer of weapons (at times top-of-the-line products), know-how, and a multiplicity of coproduction and military cooperation agreements and licensed ventures as well as through a varied range of incentives to buttress buyers' resolve. Buyers' increasing involvement in the production process fosters their ties with a list of preferred and reliable suppliers. In turn, such a strong collaboration allows recipients to replenish and upgrade their arsenals at lower cost and acquire the resources and information to foster the growth and capacity of their domestic military industries.

Third World countries became the primary "beneficiaries" of this selling spree. In August 2000 a Congressional Research Service report, *Conventional Arms Transfers to Developing Nations, 1992–1999*, concluded that over that period, the developing world had absorbed $166 billion in arms deliveries, or 68.3 percent or the total. The United States maintained its overall dominance in total volume of deliveries to developing nations in 1999 ($11.4 billion, or 50.15 percent of the total) and continued to lead in terms of new agreements with the developing world, capturing $8.1 billion in sales, or 39.2 percent of the total. The report also found that Russia had increased its share of new arms orders from 13.4 percent in 1998 to 19.9 percent ($4.1 billion) in 1999, with Germany's 9.7 percent of new agreements following in a distant third place.[22]

While the Middle East, supported by its oil revenues, maintains the lion's share of arms demand, transfers of equipment and know-how to sub-Saharan Africa are of particular concern. As reported by the UN secretary-general, in 1996 alone that part of the world was the theater of fourteen conflicts, accounting for more than half of all war-related deaths worldwide.[23]

The role of Belgium in contributing to further destabilization of the East African powder keg, for example, came under attack in 1996 when it was discovered that the largest arms manufacturer in Belgium, the Fabrique Nationale d'Armes de Guerre, in partnership with the Kenyan government, had built an ammunition factory in the western Kenyan town of Eldoret.[24] According to parliamentary records, allegations were made in 1996 that the factory was supplying the Burundian Hutu militia, in contravention of Belgium's stated policy of proscribing weapons transfers to Burundi.[25]

The record of America's Cold War rivals, Russia and China, is equally alarming. In 1998, Russia reportedly signed an agreement with Angola—a country involved in a brutal civil war—that included a five-year plan for the construction of an arms factory there. The factory allegedly was to service the entire region and repair and upgrade Russian-manufactured military equipment.[26]

For its part, China built a facility in Nakasongola, northern Uganda, for the production of weapons, including ammunition and land mines, that reportedly catered to the warring Burundian government and Tutsi militia. Although the Ugandan government, which was itself fighting indigenous rebellions, insisted that the factory output was meant exclusively for domestic consumption, doubts persist about the real end users of the facility's production.[27]

The glut of weapons and the multiplicity of supplying countries allowed recipients to play eager suppliers against one another and extract concessions previously frowned on by arms producers. Such concessions have been variously defined as offsets, spin-offs, or countertrade. In essence, offsets or their variants represent the means by which the cost to recipients of purchasing defense goods is offset by other deals consummated with the supplier.[28]

For example, in December 1999 South Africa signed deals to buy ships, submarines, and aircraft worth $5 billion from European arms producers. These procurement agreements include a commitment by international arms suppliers to generate $17.3 billion in "countertrade" investments, exports, and local sales for South African industries. Observers noted that South Africa would not reap these benefits for at least a decade, if ever.[29] However, this massive acquisition program has already sparked the undesirable side effect of suspected corruption. In January 2000, South African parliamentarian Patricia de Lille delivered a voluminous package of documents to a commission appointed to investigate corruption allegations connected with awarding tenders to foreign companies involved in the procurement drive. The commission acknowledged the sensitivity and impact of these documents.[30]

On the supply side, the notion that offsets are economically sound has been challenged not only by advocates of human rights and good governance but also by government agencies. A 1997 study by the U.S. Department of Commerce, for example, noted that the value of offset arrangements negotiated by U.S. companies that year amounted to 81 percent of the actual value of the contracts in question, with agreements in Europe totaling 104 percent of export contracts.[31] One analyst concluded, "With the value of offsets approaching 100 percent of the value of the arms sale for many large sales, the overall balance-of-payment impact becomes ambiguous." A subsequent report by the U.S. Department of Commerce valued at $19 billion the total U.S. offset agreements attached to contracts worth $35 billion, an average offset ratio of 54.3 percent. The report noted that between 1993 and 1997, more countries were moving toward 100 percent offset requirements. This report further observed, "Offset contacts are becoming more complex and lengthy and impose a major burden on the prime contractor in terms of cost, time, and labor."[32] It has also been observed that since offsets may require the transfer of entire production lines overseas, domestic jobs are negatively affected.[33] In light of these findings, the claimed overall beneficial impact in terms of an arms exporter's ability to create new jobs, generate income, and economic efficiency at home needs to be seriously reappraised.

Policy and Practice: The Top Ten Exporters

The many flaws in policy and significant negative effects that the arms trade drive exposed has never hindered efforts by representatives of the defense industry in the United States and elsewhere to weaken existing export controls and bypass norms of self-restraint in arms transfers.

In the United States, defense companies have complained for years that, due to long delays in processing export license applications, post–Cold War export controls represented not only a barrier to competitive trade but also an obstacle to technological progress and military prowess of the country and its allies.[34] U.S. controls are regarded as the most stringent in the world, providing for congressional scrutiny as well as periodic reviews of individual and cumulative sales and the impact these may produce.[35]

As the U.S. defense manufacturing base concentrated and trade became more globalized, defense contractors' efforts to weaken and short-circuit such controls gathered momentum. NATO intervention in Kosovo in 1999, which had exposed shortcomings in the allies' capabilities, force projection, and interoperability offered the industry a golden opportunity to drive the point home. Johnson observed,

> The Kosovo experience crystallized the problem in the minds of senior Defense Department officials. They saw just how the arms export system affected our relations with our allies and how it affected the allies' ability to work with us in the battlefield.[36]

Remarks such as Johnson's did not fall on deaf ears. Responding to defense establishment pressure and in collaboration with it, the Clinton administration designed a new, industry-friendly policy, the Defense Trade Security Initiative (DTSI), which was unveiled in July 2000. The DTSI envisages "fast-track" export licensing and will be implemented following a revision to the International Trafficking in Arms Regulations. Overcoming some resistance within her department, on May 24, 2000, U.S. Secretary of State Madeleine Albright explained how the seventeen-step proposal would expedite export procedures.[37]

The new policy, among other provisions, would allow staunch U.S. allies such as Britain and Australia to obtain U.S. defense items license free, provided that the countries put in place export controls consistent with U.S. law. However, similar exemptions, previously granted to Canada, had backfired when it was discovered that Canadian firms had transferred sensitive technology to China and Iran, two banned destinations under U.S. law. In addition, the DTSI would now allow the retransfer of U.S. military goods by NATO allies, as well as Japan and Australia, despite the risk that such goods might be later diverted to improper destinations. This risk stems from weak export controls by some alliance members and their inability to monitor recipient (or end-user) compliance with the terms under which military articles are transferred.[38] In light of these facts, it is noteworthy that not a single component of the DTSI has been advanced in the specific interest or spirit of strengthening existing export controls.

A concomitant barrier-reduction movement was afoot in the European Union (EU). On July 27, 2000, France, Germany, Italy, Spain, Sweden, and the United Kingdom—the six largest arms producers in Europe— signed the Framework Agreement Concerning Measures to Facilitate the Restructuring and Operation of the European Defense Industry. True to its intent, the agreement took stock of the strong regional drive to consolidate the EU defense-industrial complex, which reflected similar dynamics occurring across the Atlantic. The agreement was also aimed at counterbalancing the muscle of the U.S. conglomerates and competing with them on stronger terms.[39]

The binding framework agreement includes provisions to streamline trade among signatories as well as new procedures to draw a list of acceptable destinations for weapons produced by European multinational defense firms and joint ventures. In formulating such a multilateral export policy, the six parties have pledged to take into consideration the parameters established by the European Code of Conduct on Arms Exports, an EU-wide nonbinding political commitment that is, in essence, a body of self-restraint norms and a transparency-enhancing instrument regulating EU arms transfers. The code was approved in June 1998 and includes a strong human rights plank as well as consideration of such factors as risk of diversion and the impact on regional stability when determining decisions on arms exports.

Critics of the framework agreement, however, have pointed out that not all is well with the signatories' commitment to respect the code. For starters, the white list of acceptable recipients need not be submitted to parliamentary and public scrutiny, thereby curtailing progress in transparency measures achieved under the code, which requires a consolidated annual report by EU exporters. In addition, such white lists would be negotiated en bloc, eliminating the case-by-case decisions and timely adjustments to changing security concerns envisioned by the code. The hidden dangers of this approach have been noted by trade analysts who observed that while the agreement provides for the removal of a country from a list of permitted destinations,

> decisions about the white lists will be made years in advance of a sale and there is no systematic process for reviewing those lists. It is up to the participant countries themselves to raise objections to export destinations. Further, such an action is only envisaged in the event of major developments, such as "full scale civil war" and only after a lengthy consultation process among partners.[40]

Critics' overall concern is that the framework agreement may contain a bias to drop export standards to the lowest denominator as countries with strong controls and traditionally prudent arms-export policies would be hard-pressed to restrain their more freewheeling partners when the momentum to sell builds up.

As discussions on codes of conduct proceed by fits and starts in the West, China and Russia, two other major arms producers, have chosen to isolate themselves from the debate altogether. Both countries have elaborated policies that purportedly incorporate norms for responsible arms transfers. In 1995, the Chinese government published a white paper that reportedly outlines China's policies regarding arms control, arms exports, and disarmament. The white paper maintains that China exercises a strict control over its military transfers. The export of Chinese weapons, the document continues,

> should help the recipient nation increase its appropriate defense capacity. The transfer must not impair peace, safety or stability regionally or globally. China does not use trade in weaponry to interfere in sovereign states' internal affairs.[41]

Two years later, China issued new "Regulations on Export Controls of Military Items," and in 1998 the country further elaborated its policy in a white paper, *China's National Defense,* which stated that China "is concerned about the adverse effects on world security and regional stability arising from excessive accumulation of weaponry."[42]

For its part, Russia established the "Principles of Official Policy in the Field of the Military-Technical Cooperation of the Russian Federation and Foreign States" in 1998. Without offering any specifics, this set of norms refers to the "observance of the international commitments" made by Russia in the field of export controls and nonproliferation and disarmament.[43]

In practice, both China and Russia have displayed an alarming disregard for the application of the norms by which they claim to abide. The two nations have armed some of the most egregious human rights abusers in the world, at times in violation of arms embargoes, and transferred weapons to states engulfed in internal conflict and/or at war with their neighbors (see the following section).[44]

At another latitude, postapartheid South Africa, the tenth-largest arms producer in the world and sector leader on the African continent, has also shown an inclination to interpret creatively its stringent parameters for arms exports. In August 1995, the government of Nelson Mandela established new, ethical arms-transfers policies and export controls that spelled out the principles and criteria governing the national arms trade. The policy commits South Africa to exercising restraint in the transfer of conventional weapons by taking into account factors such as the human rights record and the internal and regional security situation of the recipient country in light of existing tensions or armed conflicts and regional stability.[45]

Over time, however, such principled policy has been progressively weakened by realpolitik and profit-making considerations—so much so that in December 1999, the Commonwealth Human Rights Initiative, a nongovernmental organization, reported that five of the top ten destinations for South African arms exports between 1996 and 1998 (India, Colombia, Pakistan, Congo-Brazzaville, and Algeria) had experienced some form of conflict during that period. The report noted that the

> disturbing record of arms sales since April 1994 has fed the perception, domestically and internationally, that the ANC Government's foreign policy is haphazard and that South Africa has failed to become a restrained and responsible arms trader. It went on to add that recent

arms deals "suggest that maintaining jobs in the arms industry, and other economic considerations, are more important than the Government's stated commitment to human rights principles." The group noted that the net returns from South Africa's arms exports are relatively insignificant, especially once the cost of subsidies for the defense industry are taken into account.[46]

Brave New World

The race to sell new and technologically advanced weaponry, the lowering of export barriers, and the sprouting of industrial capacities in developing countries often overshadow another dubious outcome of the new world order: the global dumping of excess and obsolete arsenals. In 1996, the Federation of American Scientists reported that between 1990 and 1995 the United States gave away or sold at greatly reduced prices arms originally valued at $8.7 billion.[47]

The primary beneficiaries of this U.S. excess-weapons bonanza had been NATO allies. Since the end of the Gulf War in 1991, Middle East and North African states as well as former Warsaw Pact countries have received free U.S. surplus hardware, as have South American and Caribbean countries engaged in counternarcotics operations.[48]

The infusion of obsolete and excess weapons into areas of violent conflict has been driven, to a large extent, by former Warsaw Pact countries, which, throughout the 1990s, were downsizing their military forces and seeking to modernize their arsenals. Arms at times hemorrhaged from these sources in violation of international or regional arms embargoes.[49] In the quest for hard currency, market share, and influence, official and private sellers have not been fastidious about buyers' human rights records. Buyers, in turn, have accepted weaponry that was hardly state-of-the-art but that could do the job and was cheap and plentiful. These suppliers, many of which have now become either new NATO partners or allies, as well as countries associated with the EU and members of the Organization for Security and Cooperation in Europe, were never held accountable by these organizations for deals carried out in disregard of international agreements and norms.

Ironically, this trend was set in motion with the 1990 Treaty on Conventional Forces in Europe, which established weaponry limits for the signatory countries' arsenals. The treaty sought to reduce the threat of war in

Central Europe, but one of its effects was to exacerbate conflict elsewhere through the supply of excess weapons. At the time the treaty entered into force in 1992, state parties were able to set aside any equipment declared to be awaiting export, which was not counted toward their initial reduction obligations.[50]

Between 1992 and 1995, for example, Germany disposed of five hundred tanks, fourteen hundred armored combat vehicles, and four hundred artillery pieces inherited from the former East Germany. One of the buyers was Turkey, which, as noted earlier, has been responsible for persistent patterns of abuse. Others have also taken advantage of the market niche for excess weapons kept wide open by a seemingly insatiable demand. Investigations conducted by Human Rights Watch researcher Kathi Austin discovered that in July 1995, a Ukranian company had reportedly sold weapons in eastern Zaire to the genocidal Rwandan exiled forces in violation of the May 1994 United Nations arms embargo.[51] Ukrainian dealers and mercenaries have reportedly been involved in trafficking and in the provision of military services to embargoed rebels in Angola and Sierra Leone as well as to Colombian insurgents.[52]

Russia and Bulgaria allegedly were reliable arms suppliers to Burundian forces and Angolan rebels, who were under a 1996 regional arms embargo and a 1993 international weapons ban, respectively.[53] In 1998, Poland reportedly blocked a shipment of fifty T-55 tanks to Sudan only after strong U.S. protests. Since 1996, Sudan has been under an EU arms embargo. A year later Poland proceeded to sell Yemen two installments of the same tanks, which the U.S. suspected would be diverted to Sudan. When the United States gave Poland a slap on the wrist, Warsaw halted the second delivery of the hardware. Shortly thereafter, however, the Czech Republic—which, along with Poland, had recently joined NATO—cleared delivery of ninety-six excess tanks to Yemen, blatantly disregarding Warsaw's warning regarding U.S. displeasure.[54] In 1998, however, both the Czech Republic and Poland pledged to adhere to the principles of the EU Code of Conduct on Arms Exports, which proscribes sales to embargoed destinations.[55]

Bulgaria carefully calculated the incentives to seek clients in conflict-ridden areas, estimating that destroying excess tanks and selling them for scrap could fetch a meager profit of just two thousand dollars each. Selling them, however, would bring thirty thousand dollars apiece into the cash-strapped Bulgarian treasury. In December 1998 Bulgaria proceeded to sell 140 surplus tanks to Uganda and Ethiopia, both of which were involved in conflicts with their neighbors.[56] In this instance Bulgaria was in the good company of other former Warsaw Pact allies—the Czech Republic, Russia, Slovakia, and the Ukraine, all of which had supplied weapons for the war in Ethiopia and Eritrea. Although such deals were reportedly completed before the United Nations imposed a mandatory arms embargo on both belligerents in May 2000, these five countries had defiantly ignored previous nonbinding calls to stop arming Ethiopia and Eritrea made by the UN and the Wassenaar Arrangement for Export Controls over Conventional Arms and Dual-Use Goods.[57] In an unprecedented move, U.S. officials publicly reprimanded the five during the Wassenaar group consultations in May 2000. This "name and shame" tactic was met with denials or silence.[58]

Under pressure from nongovernmental organizations, NATO began to recognize the need to provide security and accountability for the excess arsenals of its partners and allies. To this end, in March 1999 the NATO Euro-Atlantic Partnership Council created an ad hoc working group tasked with addressing one of the scourges of contemporary conflicts, the proliferation of small and light weapons flowing from allies' and partners' arsenals.[59] Although this action represents a step in the right direction, there is no visible evidence that this tardy recognition and the work of the group has prevented or stopped vintage Warsaw Pact weapons from reaching abusive forces around the world.

Small Arms

The fall of the Berlin Wall generated worldwide optimism regarding the prospects for international peace and security. Events in recent years have crushed these expectations. As noted previously, in place of increased security, virulent internal conflicts accompanied by unprecedented civilian casualties, and gross violations of human rights have emerged at an alarming rate. The local roots and causes of conflict are numerous and diverse. However, in nearly all of today's conflicts, the diffusion of weapons has played a decisive role in intensifying such escalation. Small arms now pose one of the gravest threats to human security.

Conflicts and the ensuing humanitarian crises are sustained and extended particularly because of uncontrolled flows of large quantities of small arms and light weapons. It is estimated that 500 million of these arms are in circulation today. Large quantities of these weapons represent a legacy of the proxy wars fought by the superpowers during the Cold War.

Such hardware continues to cascade from conflict to conflict, joining with newly produced arms to fuel wars.[60] According to a study of 101 conflicts fought between 1989 and 1996, small arms and light weapons were the belligerents' weapons of preference and often the only weapons used in those hostilities.[61] Increasingly throughout the wars of the 1990s, armed aggressors have deliberately targeted civilians, as conflicts in Rwanda, the former Yugoslavia, East Timor, and Sierra Leone attest. In addition, the proliferation of light and easy-to-use small arms has meant the widespread recruitment of child soldiers in these conflicts.[62] As scholar Michael Klare has observed, in violent confrontations from Angola to Sierra Leone and from Colombia to Haiti,

> Young men (and some women) equipped solely or primarily with AK47 [assault rifles] and other "light" weapons have produced tens of thousands—and sometimes hundreds of thousands—of fatalities. Most of the casualties in these conflicts are non-combatants. Civilians constituted only five percent of the casualties in World War I, but they constitute about 90 percent of all those killed or wounded in more recent wars.[63]

While big-ticket items such as jet fighters, frigates, helicopters, and tanks are transacted mainly among governments and are subject to some form of control, guns and light weapons are no longer the exclusive preserve of military and police forces but have fallen into the hands of an array of non-state actors. As warlords and rebel leaders became able to arm their followers with readily available cheap weapons, their bid to seek power or control over natural resources has produced devastating and drawn-out conflicts such as those in Angola, Burundi, and Sierra Leone.[64]

The ideological motives of rebel leaders, citizen militia, sectarian gangs, paramilitary forces, and death squads around the world are often murky or simply expedient. A World Bank study described such armed rebellions as a large-scale "predation of productive economic activities" and calculated that when abundant natural resources are up for grabs in weak states, the feasibility of such predation and the consequent financial viability of rebel organizations become a reliable predictor of conflict. Although these rebel organizations develop a behavior akin to organized crime, this study chillingly concluded,

> Unlike a mafia, the rebel group must expect sometimes to confront substantial government forces, and so will need to protect itself. Rebel groups, therefore need to be much larger than mafias. Typically, rebel organizations have in the range of 500–5,000 fighters, whereas mafias

are generally in the range of 20–500. It is because rebel organizations need to be large and to confront government forces in order to function as predators that conflicts can produce cumulative mortality in excess of 1,000 and so qualify empirically as civil wars.[65]

As ruthless nonstate actors increasingly joined the ranks of belligerents and acquired weapons, arms supply lines also became more and more privatized. An enduring legacy of the Cold War is the mushrooming of private traffickers who were recruited to carry out covert deals on behalf of governments. The pipelines thus activated remain operational, attract resourceful newcomers to the business, and are also employed in the illicit trade in endangered animal species and products, precious gemstones, minerals, and other valuable commodities.[66] Such operators often act on their own, but they also have continued to offer their services to governments and official agents.

Governments have therefore been reluctant to stem under-the-counter deals that may serve commercial, geopolitical, or national security interests but do not directly expose the governments, thereby enabling them to plausibly deny any role in illegal or questionable transactions. Given these powerful interests, it is not surprising that far too little energy and resources have been invested in understanding the manner in which arms pipelines and international arms traffickers operate in conflict zones and how small arms keep falling into the hands of abusive forces despite international prohibitions such as UN mandatory bans.

As discussed earlier, arms traffickers throughout the world can easily access obsolete weapons of Warsaw Pact vintage. Such commerce is also facilitated by the proliferation of small arms manufacturers. According to one study, at the turn of the twenty-first century, three hundred producers in more than seventy countries offered small arms at competitive prices.[67] Above all, throughout the 1990s, traffickers took full advantage of weak and patchy laws to freely ply their lethal commerce, even in violation of international arms embargoes.[68]

In general, governments have been reluctant to support global measures to stem such trafficking, even though it is patently clear that the spread of deadly weapons does not stop at national borders. Preoccupied with the proliferation of weapons of mass destruction, states as well as the arms control community have for too long neglected the problem of small arms, considering it the "poor relation" in proliferation debates. To justify their inertia, officials have also argued that weapons are tools rather than a cause of violence and have claimed impotence in controlling the traffickers. Although a direct causality can not be firmly established, mounting evidence points to the role of light weapons as a stimulus to conflict and a harbinger of massive human rights abuses and humanitarian crises.[69]

Slow Awakening: A Brief Review of Arms Control Initiatives

Acting Small . . .

The prevalence of small arms in today's wars and the human toll their indiscriminate use exacts have prompted a growing recognition of the need to curb such proliferation. Invigorated by the success of the International Campaign to Ban Landmines, a new movement has emerged to address the catastrophic problem of the diffusion and misuse of small arms. This movement is led by a loose coalition of United Nations agencies, like-minded national governments, and nongovernmental organizations that have set their sights on disciplining the legal trade and curtailing illicit trafficking in weapons.[70] To date, nongovernmental organizations have submitted blueprints for treaties offering principles for arms exports, as well as regulations concerning arms brokering and the marking and tracing of weapons.[71]

Institutional Progress

The United Nations, which reported that small arms proliferation and misuse affected virtually every part of the UN system, has undertaken several groundbreaking initiatives. In July 2001, the United Nations held the first global consultation on this matter, the Conference on the Illicit Trade in Small Arms and Light Weapons in All Its Aspects. After mammoth negotiations, the conference wrapped up with a consensus document, the *Programme of Action to Prevent, Combat, and Eradicate the Illicit Trade in Small Arms and Light Weapons in All Its Aspects*, heavy in rhetoric and light in actual commitments from the 150 participant states.[72]

The document incorporates concerns relating to the human dimension of the problem. It devotes language to the protection of those most vulnerable (women and children). It includes provisions for reintegration of combatants into civil communities and destruction of surplus weapons that would otherwise continue to cascade from conflict to conflict. It fails, however, to make the connection between human rights abuses and availability of arms and to spell out the criteria that would prevent weapons from falling into the wrong hands. Moreover, calls for negotiations on international treaties regulating the activities of brokers and on arms marking and tracing have been significantly toned down. Similarly, states carefully trimmed all references to new infusions of cash to sustain the stated goals of the *Programme*.

The primary merit of the conference outcome resides in the fact that the dangers posed by the proliferation and abuse of small arms were put on all governments' radar screens. Indeed, the strongest legacy of this process is that, for the first time, an issue that was long neglected and considered a minor disarmament topic has been framed beyond the confines of arsenal reduction and destruction. The debate now embraces a wide spectrum of concerns, from intrastate conflict to the devastation of communities and sexual violence.

This is probably one of the reasons that induced countries to negotiate the *Programme of Action*, a political document, with the same fervor, attention to semantics, and rigidity of parameters that are usually reserved for treaties and agreements legally binding in nature.

A case in point was offered by the U.S. delegation, which drew and fiercely defended five so-called redlines, or thresholds that the United States would not allow the conference to trespass. The final document, the United States insisted, should not include:

1. Any definition encompassing any nonmilitary-style weapons or lethal weapons of war.
2. Any restriction on civilian possession of arms.
3. Any clause banning transfers to nonstate actors.
4. Any calls for negotiations on legally binding international instruments.
5. Any fixed review process.

Participants saw the articulation of this position as strident and arrogant. In the horse-trading that ensued, the United States gave way on the fifth redline in exchange for acquiescence on the second, which was most actively supported by the U.S. progun lobby. Other countries resented the notion that the narrow interests of a U.S. progun minority view should prevail at an international forum and supersede global concerns. After all, at stake here was not the infringement of a constitutional prerogative, as the United States claimed, and certainly not a blanket ban on civilian possession of arms, but the establishment of criteria for such possession, many of which were consistent with norms in place in several jurisdictions in the United States. In the end, however, this reasonable position was defeated.

On this and other accounts the United States wrested acquiescence from other countries and in so doing ensured short-run success for what will placate larger-than-life domestic constituencies. In the long run, however, what the United States has really achieved remains to be seen. To be sure, the United States managed to isolate itself from its closest allies and alienate many delegations from the developing world and civil society. It was also singled out as the one country that more than any other had prevented a more successful outcome of the conference. Sad to say, this interpretation was only partially correct, since several other delegations had taken cover behind the combative vociferousness of the United States and had been equally obstructionist.

Other delegates, for example, shared U.S. misgivings on a ban on arms transfers to "nonstate actors" that African countries fiercely fought for. The United States maintained that such a clause would prevent freedom fighters from receiving weapons needed to defend themselves against tyranny. The counterargument held that, in today's conflicts, massively abusive rebel forces such as those in Sierra Leone and Angola would continue to benefit from a lack of restrictions. In addition, as the UNITA rebels in Angola and the mujahidden in Afghanistan have proved, the U.S. clients of yesterday could become the U.S. foes of today. In view of the vagaries of politics and its alliances, critics of the United States concluded it would be prudent not to inject more weapons into volatile regions, which would only enhance the lethal power of ferocious forces accountable to no one.

A biennial meeting mandated by the UN conference to assess progress on the *Programme of Action* took place in New York July 7–11, 2003. Asked to appraise the outcome of this meeting, its chairperson, Ambassador Kuniko Inoguchi, observed that UN members

> have seen progress in institutional building, in the development of national action plans, as well as in the creation of legislation where legal frameworks were missing. While it is true that we have not yet seen the emergence of legally binding international instruments to address the threat of small arms proliferation, the national laws are closing important gaps.[73]

In a parallel process to the conference the UN Economic and Social Council negotiated a firearms protocol attached to the UN Convention on Transnational Crime. Although legally binding for all signatories, this instrument covers only commercial transfers of certain categories of small arms.

Some of the most innovative steps in small arms control have occurred at the regional level and have produced binding rules disciplining the international small arms trade in areas most affected by the spread of these weapons. The first occurred with the passage of the 1997 Inter-American Convention against the Illicit Manufacturing of and Trafficking in Firearms, Ammunition, Explosives, and Other Related Materials. In 1998, under the visionary leadership of Mali, the Economic Community of West African States adopted an unprecedented three-year moratorium on the import, export, and manufacture of small arms and light weapons.

Civil Society Initiatives

As noted previously, civil society and nongovernmental organizations have been the avant-garde, spearheading a series of initiatives aimed at bringing greater attention to the problem of proliferation and misuse of light weapons and small arms that culminated with the launch of the International Action Network on Small Arms (IANSA) in May 1999. By 2003, IANSA had become a network of more than five hundred nongovernmental organizations from all over the world. At the local level, from Kenya to Nicaragua, a number of civil society organizations, many of them IANSA members, have advocated and promoted action to mop up weapons in these heavily affected communities.[74]

Civil society has two sides, however, and efforts to contain and respond to the risks posed by small arms have come under sustained attack from an array of mostly U.S.-based progun organizations, publications, and politicians. The most prominent champion of this countervailing position is the U.S. National Rifle Association (NRA), which has compared international efforts to regulate the small arms trade to a "war" against the U.S. Constitution's Second Amendment, which, the NRA contends, guarantees Americans the right to bear arms. The NRA regards these initiatives by the UN and civil society as a conspiracy of gun snatchers and reportedly hopes to scare U.S. gun owners and in the process raise money and enlarge the organization's membership.[75] Outside the United States, the NRA has allegedly subsidized sport shooters and gun clubs, contributed money to progun political candidates as far afield as Australia and New

Zealand, and supported public campaigns against attempts at gun regulation in Canada, Japan, South Africa, the United Kingdom, and elsewhere. The NRA has formed such proxy groups as the World Forum on the Future of Sport Shooting Activities to bog down efforts at tackling small arms at the United Nations and other forums.[76] The NRA argues that gun control will benefit only "Third World dictatorships."[77] But logic suggests that rogue states, militias, and insurgents are most likely to find common ground with the progun lobby's campaign to foil international small arms control.

Despite these and other obstacles that the movement for small arms control has encountered, its activities have placed the issue on the international community's agenda, where it is bound to remain for years to come.

. . . Thinking Big

While some policymakers have been actively engaged in the small arms debate, governments and defense establishments have resisted proposals to extend to all arms-trading practices the same level of scrutiny and self-restraint they pledge on small arms transfers, fearing that the ability to trade in major conventional systems and extend military assistance to clients could thus be curtailed. Despite this stumbling block, there are encouraging signs that the debate on small arms might provide a sort of Trojan horse and be the catalyst to modify governments' discourse (and hopefully their outlook) regarding irresponsible arms trading practices in general.

Even before such a debate gathered momentum, in 1995, Dr. Oscar Arias, former president of Costa Rica, invited his fellow Nobel Peace laureates to join him in developing the International Code of Conduct on Arms Transfers and providing moral leadership for the code campaign. The group drafted the text of a code that would require governments to uphold internationally recognized standards of democracy, human rights, and peaceful international relations in determining who is entitled to receive weapons.[78] Arias subsequently led a group of nongovernmental organizations, including Amnesty International, Saferworld, and Oxfam, to develop the idea of the code into a Framework Convention on International Arms Transfers.[79] Similarly, a model convention to regulate the activities of arms brokers was submitted by the Fund for Peace and drafted by a group of international lawyers of Clifford Chance—led by Jeremy Carver and Loretta Bondi.[80] A third model convention on marking and

tracing weapons was presented by the Groupe de recherche et d'information sur la paix et la sécurité. As mentioned earlier, the EU agreed on its
own Code of Conduct on Arms Exports in 1998. This decision was stimulated only in part by the activism of nongovernmental organizations. The
European weapons industry rightly saw the code as a vehicle for watching
over each other's shoulders and for facilitating the consolidation of the EU
military complex through a set of common rules. Following that decision
and after years of debate, the U.S. Congress also issued a mandate for the
country to negotiate a code at an international forum.

In terms of transparency measures, in 1992 the United Nations created
the Register of Conventional Arms Transfers, which covers seven major
weapons categories. Although contributions to the register are voluntary,
this instrument constitutes an important confidence-building locus.[81] In
1998, China was the only major supplier that did not report to the register, and that nation refused to do so primarily because of a squabble with
the United States regarding arms sales to Taiwan.[82]

Experiences in Afghanistan, the former Yugoslavia, Haiti, Iraq,
Panama, Sierra Leone, and Somalia—where U.S. and other peacekeepers
faced their own weapons in combat—demonstrate that involvement in
internal conflict may very well become a permanent feature in the operations of alliances such as NATO or regional groups such as the Organization for Security and Cooperation in Europe. The fact that belligerents
may be armed with the same weaponry used by peacekeepers should escape
neither public consciousness nor public debate.

NOTES

1. Research for this chapter was conducted between June and September
2000.

2. John Lovering, "Which Way to Turn? The European Defense Industry
after the Cold War," in *Arming the Future: A Defense Industry for the Twenty-first
Century*, ed. Ann R. Markusen and Sean S. Costigan (New York: Council on Foreign Relations, 1999), 337–40. In 1998, defense spending in the United States
amounted to $270 billion, while the combined expenditure of the six European
major producers was estimated at $147 billion (*The Military Balance: 1999–2000*
[London: International Institute of Strategic Studies, 2000], 20–103).

3. SIPRI Military Expenditure Database, http://first.sipri.org:7020/ milex
_retrieve.

4. David Gold, "The Changing Economics of the Arms Trade," in *Arming the Future*, ed. Markusen and Costigan, 249–50.

5. William W. Keller, *Arms in Arm: The Political Economy of the Global Arms Trade* (New York: Basic Books, 1995), 91. Between 1995 and 1999, the United States has been the biggest arms supplier and delivered almost as much as all other suppliers combined. See Stockholm International Peace Research Institute, *SIPRI Yearbook 2000: Armaments, Disarmament, and International Security* (Oxford: Oxford University Press, 2000), 339–67.

6. Lora Lumpe, "Negative Consequences of Surplus Arms Production and Trading," in *Arming the Future*, ed. Markusen and Costigan, 289.

7. Tamar Gabelnick, William D. Hartung, and Jennifer Washburn, "Arming Repression: U.S. Arms Sales to Turkey during the Clinton Administration," in *A Joint Report of the World Policy Institute and the Federation of American Scientists* (October 1999), 25–32.

8. Ibid., 6.

9. William Hartung observed that the like-mindness of the two U.S. presidents on this topic became clear during the presidential campaign: "In the nine weeks from September 1992 until election day, the Bush administration announced over $20 billion in new overseas arms deals. In just two months, George Bush rushed through the equivalent of a year's worth of weapons exports." Hartung continued, "This reckless exercise in 'pork barrel proliferation' should have been an inviting target for the Clinton/Gore campaign. . . . Unfortunately, the debate never happened. Not only did Bill Clinton fail to challenge Bush's election-year arms binge, he openly supported the most controversial sale of all— the export of seventy-two F-15 fighter planes to Saudi Arabia" (*And Weapons for All: How America's Multibillion-Dollar Arms Trade Warps Our Foreign Policy and Subverts Democracy at Home* [New York: HarperCollins, 1995], 276–77).

10. U.S. General Accounting Office, *Defense Trade: Department of Defense Savings from Export Sales Are Difficult to Capture*, GAO/NSIAD-99-191 (September 1999).

11. Janne E. Nolan et al., "Report of the Presidential Board on Arms Proliferation Policy," http://fas.org/asmp/resources/govern/advisory_board.html.

12. The decade reshaped the configuration of the top ten defense contractors in the United States, leading to the megamergers of, for example, Grumman and Northrop in 1994 and Lockheed and Martin Marietta in 1995. For a discussion of the government-subsidized incentives for these mergers, see William D. Hartung, "Corporate Welfare for Weapons Makers: The Hidden Cost of Spending on Defense and Foreign Aid," *Policy Analysis*, no. 350 (August 12, 1999), 17–19. Such subsidies included special compensation packages for defense industry executives and board members. The workforce did not fare as well, however; by 1994, the top twenty-five defense contractors had cut 608,000 jobs, or almost one-fourth of the 1989 workforce. One observer noted that "employment reductions far outstripped real sales decline" (Michael Hoden, "Restructuring the Defense Industrial Base," in *Arming the Future*, ed. Markusen and Costigan, 86). Citing the trade journal *Defense Mergers and Acquisitions*'s semiannual review, Chris Helmann noted that during the first part of 1999, completed or announced mergers broke

new records, with deals reaching almost $60 billion, surpassing the $49 billion record set in 1997 ("Defense Mergers at All-Time High," *Weekly Defense Monitor* [Center for Defense Information] 3 [26] [July 8, 1999]).

13. Quoted in Kathleen Miller and Theresa Hitchens, "European Accord Threatens to Lower Export Controls," *Basic Paper*, no. 33, August 2000.

14. *Arms Sales Monitor* (Federation of American Scientists), no. 28, February 15, 1995, http://www.fas.org/asmp/library/asm/asm28.htm.

15. Lumpe, "Negative Consequences," 289.

16. Hartung, "Corporate Welfare," 1.

17. Lumpe, "Negative Consequences," 289–90.

18. U.S. Department of Commerce, *Pacific Rim Diversification and Defense Market Assessment: A Comprehensive Guide for Entry into Overseas Markets* (Washington, DC: U.S. Department of Commerce, November 1994), 21, quoted in Hartung, "Corporate Welfare," 14, 15.

19. Gabelnick, Hartung, and Washburn, "Arming Repression," 15–17.

20. Human Rights Watch Arms Project, *Weapons Transfers and Violations of the Laws of War in Turkey* (New York: Human Rights Watch, 1995), 31.

21. Quoted in Hartung, *And Weapons for All*, 162.

22. Richard F. Grimmet, *Conventional Arms Transfers to Developing Nations, 1992–1999* (Washington, DC: Congressional Research Service, Library of Congress, 2000).

23. *Secretary-General's Report to the Security Council on the Causes of Conflict and the Promotion of Durable Peace and Sustainable Development in Africa*, A/52/871-S/1998/318 (April 16, 1998), 3.

24. Oral question by Geert Bourgeois, member of Parliament, to Philippe Maystadt, minister of foreign trade, Belgian Senate, Plenary Session, March 28, 1996.

25. Public Meeting, November 26, 1996, Chamber of People's Representatives of Belgium, 49th Session, 1995–96, in GZ-Handelingen-COM 27.11.1996, 11–15.

26. Human Rights Watch, *Angola Unravels: The Rise and Fall of the Lusaka Peace Process* (New York: Human Rights Watch, 1999), 101.

27. Human Rights Watch, *Stoking the Fires: Military Assistance and Arms Trafficking in Burundi: Case-Study: China* (New York: Human Rights Watch, December 1997).

28. Bernard Udis and Keith E. Maskus, "Offsets as Industrial Policy: Lessons from Aerospace," *Defence Economics* 2(1991): 151.

29. Stockholm International Peace Research Institute, *SIPRI Yearbook 2000*, 354–55.

30. "Heath to Quiz People about Arms Corruption Claims," *Sapa*, January 11, 2000.

31. Bureau of Export Administration, U.S. Department of Commerce, *Offsets in Defense Trade: Executive Summary* (Washington, DC: U.S. Department of Commerce, 1997), quoted in Gold, "Changing Economics," 254–55.

32. Ibid. See also Bureau of Export Administration, Office of Strategic Industries and Economic Security, U.S. Department of Commerce, *Offsets in Defense*

Trade: Fourth Annual Report to Congress (Washington, DC: U.S. Department of Commerce, 1999).

33. Gabelnick, Hartung and Washburn, "Arming Repression."

34. U.S. export controls fall primarily under the Arms Export Control Act (AECA), a comprehensive law enacted in 1976 that regulates most activities related to the export of weapons. The law is enforced by the Office of Defense Trade Controls of the Department of State under the International Traffic in Arms Regulations, a set of implementing regulations that correspond to specific AECA provisions.

Under the AECA, Congress authorizes the president to control the import and export of defense articles and defense services. The act requires that all those involved in the export and import of defense articles and services register with the U.S. government and obtain an export license for each transaction in which they participate. Licenses may be prohibited if the export of the article will (1) contribute to an arms race; (2) aid in the development of weapons of mass destruction; (3) support international terrorism; (4) increase the possibility of the outbreak or escalation of conflict; or (5) prejudice the development of bilateral or multilateral arms control or nonproliferation agreements or other arrangements. The Foreign Assistance Act of 1961 governs the overall provision of economic and military assistance to foreign governments. Government-negotiated arms sales fall under the purview of the Department of Defense, while the Department of State has jurisdiction over industry direct commercial sales. For a comprehensive overview of U.S. arms trade laws, see Lora Lumpe and Jeff Donarski, *The Arms Trade Revealed: A Guide for Investigators and Activists* (Washington, DC: Federation of American Scientists Arms Sales Monitoring Project, 1998).

35. Congress is entitled to review and block all proposed arms sales valued at or in excess of $14 million for major defense equipment and $50 million for all other transfers and has thirty days (fifteen days for NATO members) to review cases before licenses are granted and deals concluded. Such prior scrutiny on the part of lawmakers is unique in the world. Congress has been negligent or unwilling to exercise this prerogative, however.

36. Colin Clark, "U.S. Export License System Broken, Say Allies," *Defense News*, April 24, 2000.

37. Miller and Hitchens, "European Accord."

38. Ibid.

39. This drive culminated in 1999 and 2000 with consecutive mergers of DaimlerChrysler Aerospace AG (Germany), the Lagardere Group (France), Constuccionnes Aeronautics (Spain), and Alenia Aerospazio (Italy), which led to the launch of the European Aeronautic Defense and Space Company. This new giant is Europe's largest aerospace company and the second-largest worldwide, with revenues of $33.17 million. By comparison, the revenues of the world's largest firm, Boeing, amount to $58 million. Ibid.

40. Ibid.

41. Text provided to Xinhua news agency (Beijing) by the Information Office of the State Council of the People's Republic of China and reproduced in "Xinhua

Runs Text on Arms Control," FBIS-PRC, serial OW1611081795, November 16, 1995.

42. Evans S. Medeiros and Bates Gill, *Chinese Arms Exports: Policy, Players, and Process* (Carlisle, PA: Strategic Studies Institute, 2000), 24–27.

43. "Principles of Official Policy in the Field of the Military-Technical Cooperation of the Russian Federation and Foreign States," http://projects.sipri.se./expcon/natexpon/Russia/rusframes.htm.

44. Kathi Austin, interviews by author, July–December 1997. Between 1994 and 1996, Austin documented eighteen shipments of weapons carried out under the aegis of a Chinese-Tanzanian joint-venture, the SINOTASHIP, which were unloaded at the port of Dar es Salaam and intended for embargoed recipients in Rwanda and Burundi. China's export of M-11 missiles to Pakistan in the early 1990s and ongoing exports of missile-related technologies to Iran and Pakistan also came under attack. See Medeiros and Gill, *Chinese Arms Exports,* 25.

45. *Guide to the Terms of Reference of Conventional Arms Control in South Africa* (Pretoria: Directorate for Conventional Arms Control Office of the Secretary of Defence, May 1, 1996), 1–5.

46. Anthony Stoppard, "Disarmament—South Africa: Stained Arms Record Hard to Shake," InterPress Service, December 20, 1999. See also Commonwealth Human Rights Initiative, "Over a Barrel: Light Weapons and Human Rights in the Commonwealth," paper presented at the Commonwealth Heads of Government Meeting, Durban, South Africa, November 12–15, 1999.

47. Paul Pineo and Lora Lumpe, *Recycled Weapons: American Exports of Surplus Arms, 1990–1995* (Washington, DC: *Federation of American Scientists,* 1996): 16–17.

48. Lumpe and Donarski, *Arms Trade Revealed,* 14–15.

49. See Human Rights Watch, *Arsenals on the Cheap: NATO Expansion and the Arms Cascade: A Human Rights Watch Short Report* (New York: Human Rights Watch, April 1999); Loretta Bondi, "Arms Embargoes Implementation and Enforcement," paper presented at the Conference on Smart Sanctions, The Next Step: Arms Embargoes and Travel Sanctions, Bonn, Germany, November 21–23, 1999.

50. The treaty required signatory countries to destroy excess stocks or to dispose of them by exceptional means such as conversion to nonmilitary use or use for target practice. Some heavy equipment in excess of treaty limits was indeed destroyed (Dorns Crawford, *Conventional Armed Forces in Europe [CFE]: A Review and Update of Key Treaty Elements* [U.S. Arms Control and Disarmament Agency, January 1999]).

51. Kathi Austin graciously provided references to this author for these examples. On the role of the Ukranian company, see interview with Kenyan and expatriate airport personnel, Nairobi, February 27, August 19, 1996, and a series of telephone interviews with an arms trader involved in the deal, Kampala, September 18, 19, 1996, and by phone, Prague, December 1995–January 1996.

52. Human Rights Watch, *Angola Unravels,* 110–11; United Nations Security Council, "Letter Dated 10 March 2000 from the Chairman of the Security Council Committee Established Pursuant to Resolution 864 (1993) Concerning the

Situation in Angola Addressed to the President of the Security Council," S/2000/203, March 10, 2000. See also Alain Lallemand, "The 'Blood Diamonds,'" *Le Soir* (Brussels), August 30, 2000; Claudia Rocio Vasquez, "Defense Minister: Yes, There Was a Report Made to the CIA," *El Tiempo* (Bogotá), August 27, 2000.

53. Russia provided Burundi with ammunition, mortars, and armored vehicles: see Kathi Austin's interviews with a Burundi representative to the Arusha talks, Nairobi, August 14, 1996; with Burundian military officers, Bujumbura, March 5, 18, 1996; and with a pilot and cargo industry personnel, Kampala, September 18, 1996; Human Rights Watch, *Angola Unravels*, 113; United Nations Security Council, "Letter Dated 10 March 2000."

54. Author's interview with U.S. officials, August–September 1999. See also E. Blanche, "Czech Republic to Sell Upgraded MBTs to Yemen," *Jane's Defence Weekly* 32 (13) (September 29, 1999).

55. This principle is enshrined in the first criterion of the code, which pledges, "Respect for the international commitments of EU member states, in particular the sanctions decreed by the UN Security Council and those decreed by the Community, agreements on non-proliferation and other subjects, as well as other international obligations." The full text of the code is available at http://www.basicint .org/eucode.htm.

56. Human Rights Watch, *Bulgaria: Money Talks: Arms Dealing with Human Rights Abusers: A Human Rights Watch Short Report* (New York: Human Rights Watch, April 1999), 17, 21.

57. The Wassenaar Arrangement was established in July 1996 by representatives of thirty-three states. Members are expected to provide information semiannually on exports to non-Wassenaar countries of weapons and "sensitive" dual-use goods included in the regime's two control lists: the Munitions List and the Dual-Use Goods and Technology List.

58. Author's interview with a U.S. official present during these discussions, Washington, DC, June 6, 2000.

59. Human Rights Watch, *Arsenals on the Cheap*, 7–8.

60. Michael Renner, *Small Arms, Big Impact*, World Watch Paper (October 1997), 19.

61. P. Wallensteen and M. Sollenberg, "Armed Conflicts, Conflict Termination, and Peace Agreements, 1989–1996," *Journal of Peace and Research* 34 (3).

62. Human Rights Watch, *World Report 2000* (New York: Human Rights Watch, 2000).

63. Michael Klare, "The Kalashnikov Age," *Bulletin of the Atomic Scientists*, January–February 1999.

64. Human Rights Watch, *World Report*.

65. Paul Collier, *Economic Causes of Civil Conflict and Their Implications for Policy* (Washington, DC: World Bank, June 15, 2000).

66. See United Nations Security Council, "Letter Dated 10 March 2000."

67. Peter Abel, "Manufacturing Trends: Globalising the Source," in *Running Guns: The Global Black Market in Small Arms*, ed. Lora Lumpe (London: Zed Books, 2000), 81–100. Between 1980 and 1990, eighty-nine new manufacturers entered the market, twelve of them in Africa.

68. Since Iraq's invasion of Kuwait, the United Nations has declared twelve mandatory arms embargoes, which have been observed mainly in the breach. For violations pertaining mainly to small arms trafficking, see Bondi, "Arms Embargoes." See also Human Rights Watch, *Rearming with Impunity: International Support to the Perpetrators of Rwanda's Genocide: A Human Rights Watch Short Report* (New York: Human Rights Watch, May 1995); United Nations Security Council, "Letter Dated 18 November 1998 from the Secretary-General Addressed to the President of the Security Council," S/1998/1096, November 18, 1998; United Nations Security Council, "Letter Dated 10 March 2000."

69. International Committee of the Red Cross, *Arms Availability and the Situation of Civilians in Armed Conflict: A Study by the International Committee of the Red Cross* (Geneva: International Committee of the Red Cross, 1999). See also Klare, "Kalashnikov Age."

70. The broader nature and scope of the small arms proliferation poses a variety of problems for those who wish to replicate the land mine campaign's success, including for example, the nature of the weapons, which is not per se indiscriminate, as well as the crossover between legitimate use in self-defense and, in the United States, the right to ownership.

71. See Loretta Bondi, *Expanding the Net: A Model Convention on Arms Brokering* (Washington, DC: Fund for Peace, 2001), and Loretta Bondi, James Bourke, Jeremy Carver, Rae Lindsay, and Richard Winfield, *A Model Convention on the Registration of Arms Brokers and the Suppression of Unlicensed Arms Brokering* (Washington, DC: Fund for Peace, 2001). See also the Framework Convention on International Arms Transfers, available at http://www.controlarms.org, and the GRIP Draft Convention on the Marking, Registration, and Tracing of Small Arms and Light Weapons, available at http://www.grip.org/bdg/pdf/g4040.pdf.

72. For a discussion of the conference and its outcome, see Loretta Bondi, "Disillusioned NGOs Blame the United States for a Weak Agreement," *SAIS Review* 22 (winter–spring 2002).

73. Ambassador Kuniko Inoguchi, interview by Loretta Bondi, director, Center for Transatlantic Relations, Cooperative Security Program, *Shoulder to Shoulder: Views from Government and Civil Society on Cooperative Security* 1 (3) (July–August 2003).

74. A comprehensive library of documents on this subject appears at http://www.iansa.org.htm.

75. "NRA's Extremism Goes Global," *Atlanta Journal and Constitution,* November 14, 1996, p. 22A. The editors quoted from a NRA alert sent to members attacking the UN Panel of Governmental Experts on Small Arms. The Panel, said the NRA, was proof that "the White House has chosen foreign policy as its weapon of choice in the war on our [Second Amendment] rights." When queried about the use of language, former NRA spokeswoman Tanya Metaska replied, "We had members concerned about what was going on at the United Nations."

76. Despite its name, the NRA has long engaged in international activism. In 2000, the NRA produced a series of infomercials in one of which the NRA executive vice president warned, "At the United Nations and around the world, the movement against your gun rights is gaining money and momentum fast. Their

target is the United States. Their objectives are international gun registration, global gun confiscation, and an end to your right to keep and bear arms" (Kathi Austin, "The Second Amendment, Going Global," *Washington Post*, March 26, 2000).

77. Adam Buckmann, "Infomercial with a Bang: NRA Buys Airtime on Ch. 9 to Recruit New Members," *New York Post*, February 8, 2000. The infomercial alleged that "Third World dictatorships are plotting—through the UN—to eliminate your Second Amendment."

78. The full text of the code and information on its background are available at http://basicint.org.

79. The American Friends Service Committee, Amnesty International, the Oscar Arias Foundation, BASIC, the Federation of American Scientists, Oxfam, Project Ploughshares, and Saferworld, Framework Convention on International Arms Transfers, available at http://www.armslaw.org.

80. See Bondi, *Expanding the Net*.

81. Over the years, the number of countries reporting has fluctuated but has ultimately risen. For example, in 1999, ninety-nine states provided information about their arms imports and exports; in 1998, eighty-four; and in 1997, ninety-eight.

82. Human Rights Watch, *World Report*, 409.

4

Firearms

Another Peculiar American Institution

Tom Diaz

Introduction

The United States is the last great civilian firearms market in the world. A 1994 survey by the Police Foundation, sponsored by the U.S. Department of Justice, estimated about 192 million guns, a third of them handguns, owned by civilians.[1] These firearms are not uniformly distributed: only about one-quarter of the adults in the United States own any firearm, and about one in six owns a handgun.[2]

The size of the U.S. civilian firearms market and the permissive legal and regulatory regimen in which it operates notwithstanding, the gun industry has serious problems. The most significant is that it is a mature market, one that industry officials and observers regularly describe as "saturated" or "stagnant." The entrepreneurial steps the gun industry has taken over the past four decades to overcome this market inertia—primarily firearm design innovations—have radically changed the nature and product mix of firearms sold in the United States. That change in the kinds of guns sold, often overlooked in a public debate focused on political rights, lies at the heart of the problem of firearms death and injury in the United States.

That problem can be only roughly grasped in the statistics of death and injury. In 1997—a fairly representative but not record year—32,436 Americans were killed with firearms.[3] Nearly three times as many people each year receive treatment in emergency rooms as a result of firearms injuries.[4] Firearms are the second-leading cause of traumatic death related to a consumer product in the United States (after motor vehicles) and are the second-most-frequent cause of death overall for Americans ages fifteen to twenty-four.[5] This record is unique in the world: A 1997 study by the Centers for Disease Control and Prevention analyzed firearms deaths for children less than fifteen years old in twenty-six countries and found that 86 percent of the deaths occurred in the United States.[6] A 1998 study in the *International Journal of Epidemiology* found that the overall rate of firearms death in the United States is eight times higher than the firearms death rates of twenty-five other high-income countries combined.[7]

The Rise of the Modern Gun Industry

The American gun culture is often discussed as if it were a uniform phenomenon throughout the country's history in terms of the kinds of guns sold and the people who owned them. In other words, it is assumed that such rates of death and injury are an inevitable outgrowth of a long-standing "gun culture." In fact, there is a substantial difference between the early gun industry and its markets (through roughly the nineteenth century) and the mature modern industry and its markets (latter half of the twentieth century).

The Early Industry

The history of the early or premodern U.S. gun industry is significant more for its effect on the mythology of guns in the United States than for its relevance to the problem of firearms violence today. America's current romance with guns is intertwined with nostalgic—but more often than not fictional—images of the frontier and the Wild West. However, the actual source of America's gun violence problem lies not in the effects of a lingering colonial and cowboy gun culture but in deliberate changes the industry made after World War II. Almost half of the guns (46 percent) made available to civilians between 1899 and 1993 were produced between 1947 and 1993, and 80 percent of all guns in private hands in 1994 had been acquired since 1974. Moreover the product mix is radically different today than it was in all of the years before World War II.

The modern gun trade is a far cry from the preindustrial gun trade that existed from the colonial era to the turn of the nineteenth century. Guns throughout that period were either imported from abroad or handmade by gunsmiths, who passed their skills down within the family or through apprentices in a typical craft system.[8] Design innovation was leisurely.

This situation began to change by the mid-1840s, as evolving technology afforded American gun makers higher productivity. Monumental events such as the Mexican War, the Civil War, and westward expansion also gave the firearms industry the impetus to innovate and expand to support military adventures. The most ambitious, successful, and ultimately influential of this generation of arms makers was Samuel Colt, who patented the first of his revolvers in 1835. The significance of the advent of the mass-produced, reliable, and affordable handgun can hardly be overstated. The handgun has little practical use other than killing another person at close range. The modern handgun designed by Colt and soon mimicked by others introduced ready portability to firearms—one now could conveniently carry reliable killing power on one's person. This development changed American life in the nineteenth century; most importantly, however, it laid the seeds for the gun violence problems of the twentieth and twenty-first centuries, when mass marketing of handguns has really taken off.

The Modern Industry

The firearms industry changed structurally after World War II. New manufacturing enterprises were founded, many in states such as California and Florida, far from the traditional northeastern manufacturing base of Connecticut and New York's "Gun Valley" but offering less costly production. A number of these new companies introduced products like so-called Saturday night specials and various forms of military-type semiautomatic assault weapons that were later adopted and adapted for the mainstream by larger companies. Foreign gun manufacturers also discovered the vast American civilian market and devised strategies to penetrate it. Civilian gun imports grew dramatically between 1978 and 1994, the peak year so far for gun imports. During that period, 20,462,605 guns were imported for the American civilian market.[9]

But changes in the modern gun industry's design and marketing strategy have had more impact on public health and safety than have structural changes in the industry. In fact, the structure of the industry has followed marketing-driven design. Beginning in the mid-1960s, the gun industry started heavily marketing handguns and military weapons adapted for civilian sale, in preference to the previous long-term staples of the civilian gun market, long guns (shotguns and rifles) used for hunting and target sports. This change in the kind of firearms sold in America—the industry's response to the inertia of its stagnant markets—dramatically affected the gun violence problem.

The Problem of Stagnation

Unlike many other consumer industries, which grow along with population growth or rely on product obsolescence or deterioration to induce continued demand, the firearms industry in the United States for at least the past twenty-five to thirty years has faced saturated, declining markets.[10] This stagnation is the cumulative effect of a number of factors.

One factor is the durability of the product. Given reasonable care, modern firearms simply do not wear out. In the words of *Shooting Industry* writer Massad Ayoob,

> Who owns their grandfather's icebox or 1950 Plymouth? However, many of us have inherited our grandparents' firearms. These are durable goods in the truest sense—gifts that truly "last forever."[11]

In short, there is hardly ever a substantial utilitarian reason to replace a modern firearm unless it has been seriously abused, lost, or stolen.

Social, cultural, and economic factors have also combined to curtail or impede gun industry sales. For example, recreational hunting has declined because of suburban growth into hunting land, competing recreational outlets, and growing social disapproval. The impact of this decline on gun markets goes far beyond lost sales to hunters. Hunting has traditionally been an important means by which young people have been exposed to firearms and introduced to the gun culture in a positive way. The decline of hunting means, in the words of a Glock vice president, that "grandpa or dad isn't taking the kid out into the field to teach him to shoot anymore."[12] This reduces gun sales beyond hunting, because the single-most important factor in determining whether an adult buys a firearm is exposure to firearms in the home as a child.[13] The end of the military draft, another important means by which interest in guns was transmitted from one generation to another, has had a similar negative effect. Many young men who would otherwise have been drafted and learned to use firearms now grow into adulthood without ever having touched a gun.

In addition, there are fewer places even for current gun owners to shoot: urban growth has restricted various forms of target shooting as well as hunting. The explosion of other recreational outlets, from television to the Internet, and growing social disapproval of firearms have made them less attractive options for leisure time. Some mass market retailers, like K-Mart, Wal-Mart, and Target, have also opted either to limit gun sales or to drop them entirely. This eliminates what has been a convenient entry point into the gun culture for would-be first-time buyers, who may feel uncomfortable visiting a "real" gun shop, where their novice status and comparative ignorance would be quickly apparent.[14] (The gun culture highly values technical literacy about firearms.)

The net effect of these impediments has been markets in which, according to one industry observer, "more and more guns [are] being purchased by fewer and fewer consumers."[15] This does not mean that the gun industry is selling more guns overall, even though it does have the occasional boom year, but rather that a dwindling proportion of the population is buying guns. Thus, 74 percent of gun owners own more than one gun, and those who own at least four guns (about 10 percent of the nation's population) hold 77 percent of the total stock of guns.[16]

Breaking out of this ever-tightening coil of concentrated ownership has been the modern industry's principal challenge. Since people do not *need* more guns, some means must be devised to make them *want* more guns.

The Industry Response—Innovation

Like many other consumer product industries, the gun industry quite logically has used innovation in product design to counter the effects of these factors and to stimulate markets. "Convincing people they need more guns is the job of innovation," a panel of industry experts reported in a 1993 *Shooting Industry* forum.[17] The nature of this persuasive innovation and its importance to the gun industry's survival was described in 1993 by Andrew W. Molchan, publisher and editor of *American Firearms Industry*, a magazine catering to federally licensed retail gun dealers:

> Without new models that have major technical changes, **you eventually exhaust your market.** You get to the point where 90% of the peo-

ple who might want one **have one already.** This is the fundamental problem with the classic rifle and shotgun market.

Handguns during the last twenty years have sold better than long guns, mainly because of the innovation. A lot of 1993 handguns are very different from what was around in 1933. This innovation has driven the handgun market.[18]

The nature of that innovation, and especially its emphasis on handguns, is crucial to understanding its effects on public health and safety. Although to many people, a gun is a gun is a gun, the fact is that the design of a firearm directly affects the likelihood that it will be used in some form of violence and the consequences of that use.[19]

The Elements of Lethality

Before examining the specific design changes that the modern gun industry has introduced, it will be useful to describe the relationship between certain firearm design features and lethality, which is here defined to mean the cumulative effect of (1) the likelihood that a firearm will be used against a human being and (2) the likelihood that use will result in death or serious injury. (It is not necessary to pretend that this definition can be reduced to a mathematical formula to confirm its obvious utility.)

All firearms are capable of killing human beings, and virtually all firearms are designed to do so. But not all firearms are capable of killing with equal efficiency. Lethality is directly affected by specific design features regarding (1) the gun's availability for use, (2) its ammunition capacity, and (3) the caliber of its bullets. These factors may make it more likely that the gun will be on hand for use in an inappropriate way, as for example in a moment of anger or depression, that the wounds it inflicts will be more numerous, that those wounds will be more serious, or all of the above. For example:

- Differences in ammunition capacity (the number of rounds a gun can hold at one loading) and caliber (bullet size) translate into greater or less capability to deliver lethal force in terms of the number of wounds and their seriousness. A person shooting a gun with twenty rounds of ammunition has a greater chance of hitting his target—and hitting it more often—than a person shooting six rounds. Because the principal wounding effects of bullets are crushing and tearing tissue and damaging organs, bigger bullets do a more effective job. "Of the bullets which attain desired penetration depth, those of larger diameter are the most effective, crushing more tissue," wrote the authors of a comparative study of police ammunition.[20]

- Differences in handling characteristics, such as the operation of the "action" (firing mechanism), affect the ease with which a given gun may be fired or reloaded. For example, it is more difficult to fire accurately and quickly a handgun that requires the user to exert relatively heavy force by hand (to do the mechanical work of loading, cocking, and firing) than it is to fire a handgun that uses recoil forces to operate a system of springs and levers to do the same work.

- Differences in firearm size affect the likelihood that a gun will be carried concealed on the person or kept conveniently at hand in a drawer or glove box and thus available in the event of confrontation or emotional crisis. It is simply harder to carry conveniently—and certainly to conceal—a rifle or shotgun than a handgun.

- Ammunition design, beyond the size of the bullet, affects the wounding potential of any given shooting. Some bullets, for example, are designed to expand on impact or to project clawlike cutting edges to increase the wounding effects.

All of the most significant design changes that the modern gun industry has introduced or emphasized to stimulate its markets have increased lethality by enhancing one or more of these factors. These design changes include (1) the rise of handguns to dominance over long guns, (2) the rise of semiautomatic pistols to dominance over revolvers, (3) the growth in ammunition capacity, (4) the increased manufacture of higher-caliber handguns, (5) the diminution in the size of handguns, (6) the proliferation of "defensive" ammunition designed to inflict maximum injury, and (7) the introduction into the civilian market of nonsporting military and military-style firearms, such as semiautomatic assault weapons and sniper rifles. Taken together, these amount to realization of what National Rifle Association (NRA) official Gary Anderson described at an internal industry seminar as the "Rambo factor": "American shooting activities place a *predominant emphasis on large caliber arms that can be fired rapidly*. If you look at the key words in arms and ammunition advertising, they are not skill, accuracy or marksmanship. The key words are 'power,' 'speed' and 'firepower.'"[21]

Deadly Changes in the Civilian Gun Market

The following brief survey of the evolution of the modern U.S. civilian gun market illustrates the most significant innovations and lays the foundation for a discussion of growing lethality that has inevitably followed the gun industry's marketing of the "Rambo factor."

(1) *The Rise of Handguns to Dominance over Long Guns.*   This has been the most striking change in the U.S. civilian firearms market since the end of World War II. Long guns dominated the civilian market throughout the first half of the twentieth century. In 1946, handguns accounted for only 8 percent of firearms available for sale.[22] Beginning in the mid-1960s, however, the firearm product mix changed significantly. Handguns rapidly rose to dominate the civilian market and, with the exception of a brief resurgence of long guns in the mid-1970s, have continued to do so. Handguns accounted for 54 percent of domestic firearm production in 1994, a peak year, and 46 percent in 1997.[23]

(2) *The Rise of Semiautomatic Pistols to Dominance over Revolvers.*   A somewhat more recent but extraordinarily important trend has been the emergence of semiautomatic pistols over revolvers as the dominant handgun in the United States civilian market. Generally speaking, many more rounds (eight to seventeen) can be fired from a semiautomatic pistol, with less effort, than from a revolver (six rounds), and an empty pistol can be reloaded more quickly than an empty revolver. This is especially true of the more modern "double column" or "double stack" high-capacity pistols, so called because their ammunition magazines (clips) are designed to hold two columns of ammunition instead of one, totaling between thirteen and twenty rounds, stacked in a zigzag or staggered pattern within the magazine.

As pistol production increased, revolver production plummeted in the early 1980s, and in 1987 the two trend lines crossed. Domestic pistol production surpassed revolver production and now leads the handgun market by a wide margin. At a single stroke, the emergence of the semiautomatic pistol increased the ammunition capacity of commonly available handguns by two to three times.

(3) *Growth in Caliber.*   Another trend within the handgun market has been an increase in the volume of pistols manufactured in the upper range

of commercial handgun calibers. The shift to higher handgun caliber is reflected both in firearm manufacturing data and in survey data about handgun ownership. Handguns acquired in 1993 or 1994 were less likely to be of small caliber (.32 or less) than those acquired prior to 1993.[24] The caliber of bullets involved in shootings seen in a number of trauma centers has also been increasing.[25]

One interesting aspect of this trend to bigger bullets is that one of the hottest items in terms of sales is semiautomatic pistols in an entirely new caliber, the .40 Smith and Wesson. This caliber was introduced to the civilian market as a by-product of industry competition to develop a more powerful gun for the Federal Bureau of Investigation (FBI), which perceived a need for more firepower after a shootout in Miami in which several of its agents were killed or wounded.[26] This is an example of the civilian gun industry's practice of adapting to the civilian market weapons and ammunition originally developed for military or police use. As *American Firearms Industry* put the matter,

> Anything in small arms manufacturing that is developed and adopted by the military, always ends up in one form or another at the civilian consumer level. You, as a dealer, have to know what the government contract [research and development] departments are producing, because it's just a matter of time before sporting arms manufacturers incorporate new methods, ideas and materials into the products they produce and an even shorter period of time before your customers start asking about them.[27]

(4) *Reduction in Size.* Just as handgun caliber has been increasing, handgun size has been shrinking. New materials have made it possible to design much smaller handguns in higher calibers, a combination of size and power that would have been impossible to make or dangerous to the user in earlier generations of handguns.[28] This technological possibility has been realized in the widespread marketing of so-called subcompact handguns, also known as pocket rockets. These guns have the effect of increasing not only the availability of more concealable and portable handguns but also the size and number of bullets likely to be fired. This trend was summarized in 1997 by Bob Rogers, editor of *Shooting Sports Retailer*, a prominent gun business magazine: "Firepower is increasing. So is the killing potential as guns shrink in size and concealibility."[29]

(5) *Emergence of Military-Style Weapons*. A final phenomenon has been the appearance of two classes of military-style firearms: semiautomatic assault guns and sniper rifles.

Semiautomatic assault weapons are distinguished by their high ammunition capacity and by design features that facilitate rapid "spray" firing. They have virtually no sporting use. Most are merely modified versions of military weapons designed to deliver a high rate of fire over a less-than-precise killing zone, a procedure often called hosing down an area.[30]

A more recent development has been the marketing of military sniper rifles. These are not merely off-the-rack hunting rifles with telescopic sights but are "purpose-designed" military weapons fielded by armies in conflicts around the world. These include such pieces as the Barrett M82A1 .50 caliber sniper rifle, used by U.S. forces during the 1991 Gulf War to destroy Iraqi light armored vehicles, missiles, and artillery pieces at very long range.[31] Jane's *International Defense Review* has concluded that "from an operational standpoint, the closest parallel weapon to a 0.50-calibre rifle is probably the 60mm mortar."[32] Although not likely often to be used in ordinary crime, these weapons are ideal tools for terrorism and assassination.

The Sales Benefits

Marketing lethality has proven to be good business for the gun industry. Although the industry is for the most part privately held and quite secretive, so that details of sales and profit are not available, a clear picture of the more profitable trends and the hot products can be derived from industry publications and occasional public interviews by industry officials.

For example, the overall change in the nature of firearms, and its relation to what sells, was described in 1997 by industry expert Ayoob, who writes a regular column for *Shooting Industry*, the premier gun industry business magazine:

> I recently was leafing through an issue of *Shooting Industry* from 1971. Talk about a blast from the past! A quarter century later, things have changed dramatically. In SI back then, it appeared that shotguns and .22s were the mainstay of the firearms business. A firearms retailer today knows that . . . that type of shooting market is stagnant at best. The guns

that are selling during the sales trough in the industry are defensive firearms, particularly handguns thanks to reformed "shall issue" concealed-carry rules in several states.[33]

The shift to high-capacity semiautomatic pistols in the mid-1980s is an example of a moneymaking dynamic described by William Ruger, the president of Sturm, Ruger, and Company, the most successful and only publicly held American gun manufacturer. Ruger told *Forbes* magazine in 1992, "We have a little moneymaking machine here. All we have to do is keep introducing the correct new products. . . . We operate on a philosophy that you have to have new stuff, and you have to have it annually."[34] Among the "new stuff" on which Ruger relied during the 1980s was the high-capacity semiautomatic pistol it described in a 1989 filing with the Securities Exchange Commission:

> From 1986 to 1989, unit sales of firearms products increased significantly due in part to the successful introduction of new products such as the P85 nine-millimeter semiautomatic pistol.[35]

"Pocket Rockets"

The record on pocket rockets provides a rare glimpse into another dimension, the profitably symbiotic relationship between the gun industry and the powerful gun lobby.

Gun manufacturers have never hesitated to promote the concealability of such small handguns but until recently were constrained by the fact that concealed carrying was illegal in most states. Then, during the 1990s, the NRA kicked off a successful campaign to change state laws to allow persons with permits to carry concealed firearms. The NRA's former chief lobbyist, Tanya Metaksa, claimed credit in a 1996 *Wall Street Journal* interview for thereby generating new gun industry sales: "The gun industry should send me a basket of fruit—our efforts have created a new market."[36]

The gun industry agreed. *Firearms Business* reported in 1995 that the new laws and the related demand for small pistols were "turning into an economic windfall in both gun sales and in classes required to obtain [concealed-carry] permits."[37] The marketing vice president for Interarms, a major gun importer, called concealed-carry laws "the most important star on the horizon."[38] A 1997 headline put the matter more bluntly: "More Gun Permits Equal More Gun Sales."[39]

Sniper Rifles

The civilian sniper rifle market is the latest example of how the gun industry transfers lethal technology developed specifically for the military to civilian markets. Although it impossible to get accurate sales figures, recent industry advertising and articles have made clear that this niche is responding well to heavy marketing efforts, such as those described in a 1998 book on sniping rifles:

> Demand for sniper rifles has encouraged many firearms manufacturers to produce long range tactical rifles. Competing for rifle sales has kept pricing reasonable. Just like the target rifle did in the past, sniper rifle demand is directly responsible for much of the changes in stock designs, improved barrel quality, improved scope sights, improved ammunition and components, and much more. As a result, the entire firearms industry, including the shooter, has benefitted.[40]

The Exploitation of Fear

The industry has used "fear marketing" as the fuel with which to drive most of its innovation marketing, especially the sale of handguns. In an article on "'Trend Crimes' and the Gun Dealer," Ayoob bluntly described how the industry uses fear to sell more guns on "impulse":

> Customers come to you every day out of fear. Fear of what they read in the newspaper. Fear of what they watch on the 11 o'clock news. Fear of the terrible acts of violence they see on the street. Your job, in no uncertain terms, is to sell them confidence in the form of steel and lead.[41]

GunGames publisher Wally Arida expressed a slightly different spin on how retailers should follow up to sell more guns:

> We scare them to buy one gun. Now let's get these people shooting their guns and educate them to buy more guns. We should tell them, "Now you have your defense gun, now you need to buy a gun to shoot this sport and another one to shoot this other sport."[42]

The gun industry exploits fear by describing its products as tools for "selfdefense." In 1997, Shooting Industry said that "concealment handguns and other defensive firearms are the bright spots in gun retailing," telling retailers, "It's time to jump in on the defensive handgun market if you haven't already."[43] In 1995, 75 percent of Smith and Wesson's pistol sales were reported to have been to people who bought them mainly for personal protection,[44] and a Beretta executive that said 20 percent of the company's $120 million in 1994 sales came from the personal defense market, the fastest-growing segment of the company's business.[45]

The steady growth in handgun sales reflects the effects of this intensive fear marketing. Three-quarters of long-gun owners report that they own their weapons primarily for sporting purposes, such as hunting or target shooting. But 63 percent of handgun owners report that they own their guns for protection against crime—self-defense.[46]

The Lethal Consequences

If innovation has been good for the gun industry, it has been disastrous for society in general. These changes in the mix of firearms available in the civilian market have increased the deadliness of armed encounters in the United States by enhancing the three specific factors identified earlier as contributing to the likelihood of death or serious injury by firearm—availability, capacity, and caliber.

(1) *Availability.*   The rise of handguns and the emergence of subcompact pistols in particular have increased dramatically the availability of firearms for use in potentially violent encounters, whether criminal, unintentional, or suicidal. The purpose of the handgun is to allow it to be carried on the person, and the purpose of the subcompact gun is to make it easier to conceal. On average, handguns are used in nearly 70 percent of firearm suicides[47] and 80 percent of firearm homicides.[48] Of all firearm-related crimes in 1993, 86 percent involved the use of a handgun.[49] More than two out of three of the 1 million Americans who died in firearm-related homicides, suicides, and unintentional shootings between 1962 and 1997 were killed with handguns.[50]

The lethality of handguns is put in sharper relief when one considers their distribution in the population. Rifles and shotguns outnumber handguns two to one. Only a distinct minority own handguns. Yet handguns account for the vast majority of killings, injuries, and gun crimes.

It is no exaggeration to say that the United States has not so much a

gun violence problem as a handgun violence problem and that this problem is directly traceable to gun industry fear marketing since the mid-
1960s.

(2) *Capacity*.   The ammunition capacity of firearms bought in the U.S.
civilian market—especially handguns and military-style assault weapons—
has increased because of the design changes and marketing initiatives
described earlier. The greater ammunition capacity of firearms affects the
outcome of armed encounters. Although most handgun shootings occur at
close range, the stress of a lethal force encounter is so great that most bullets fired, even by trained law enforcement officers, miss their targets.[51] For
example, FBI agents are reported to have fired at least seventy rounds at
two assailants in a fierce 1986 firefight in Miami, but only eighteen rounds
hit the criminals.[52] Therefore, the more rounds a gun can fire quickly, the
more likely that a given shooting will result in at least one hit and probably multiple wounds. More wounds increase the likelihood of death or serious injury in a given incident.[53]

The high-capacity danger of assault weapons first became evident during the 1980s because police complained increasingly that the guns were
showing up in the hands of criminals, especially drug gangs. "The real issue
is the safety of our officers," the Prince George's County, Maryland, police
chief said of assault weapons in 1988. "In my opinion, they should not be
sold in the United States."[54] If police were alarmed, the general public
became outraged as mass shooting incidents with assault weapons became
a frightening national phenomenon. In July 1984 James Huberty—armed
with an Uzi, a handgun and a shotgun—went "hunting for humans" at a
San Isidro, California, McDonald's. He killed twenty-one and injured
nineteen. In April 1987, William B. Cruse killed six and injured ten with
a Ruger Mini-14 at a Palm Bay, Florida, shopping center. And on January
17, 1989, Patrick Purdy walked onto a Stockton, California, schoolyard
with an AK-47 assault rifle and opened fire on nearly four hundred students who were outside for recess. Purdy emptied a one-hundred-round
magazine and thirty-round magazine and then took his own life. Five children were left dead and thirty others were wounded.

(3) *Caliber*.   The shift to higher handgun caliber is reflected in
increasing mortality in shooting incidents. The dynamics of wound ballistics involve a complex set of variables. But all other things being equal,
bigger bullets cause more serious wounds.[55] It is no surprise then that one

consequence of the gun industry's lethal marketing shift is that trauma centers are seeing an increase in bullet caliber[56] and that the fatality rate is higher for persons shot by large-caliber handguns than for those shot with small-caliber handguns.[57] This is especially true when the bullets are "defensive rounds," specially designed to inflict maximum trauma and cause incapacitating injury.[58]

Although not strictly a matter of size, bullet design can enhance wounding potential within any given caliber. The most significant design variable is between "hollow-point" and "ball" ammunition. A hollow-point bullet "has a hole in the nose which causes the bullet to rapidly expand in diameter upon impact with an object"; ball ammunition "has a solid or fully jacketed bullet which does not expand significantly on impact with an object."[59] The mushroom-like expansion of the bullet in effect increases its caliber.

Detailed data about types and amount of ammunition produced and marketed is not available simply because manufacturers and sellers are not required to report such information. However, there is a fair amount of evidence in a wide range of sources, including gun press articles and advertising, that indicates that a substantial increase has occurred in the design and marketing of various types of expanding handgun ammunition.[60] As one gun press expert wrote in 1995, "Each of the major manufacturers has its own proprietary jacketed hollowpoint bullet painstakingly designed to expand reliably to a certain point to create a large wound channel, while still holding together for deep penetration."[61]

Effects on Law Enforcement Armament

A collateral and more specialized consequence of the design changes in the civilian arms market has been an escalation in the lethality of law enforcement armament. The gun industry devotes attention to police agencies partly because the law enforcement community is a considerable market in itself. The United States has more than 17,000 state, local, and federal police agencies employing 700,000 full-time and more than 40,000 part-time sworn officers.[62] More importantly, supplying police departments or federal law enforcement agencies with a given gun enhances the image of both the manufacturer and the gun, which in turn boosts sales in the far bigger and more lucrative civilian market.

Austrian gun maker Gaston Glock, who formerly made door hardware and trenching tools, entered the gun business in the mid-1980s. He imme-diately and quite successfully went after the U.S. law enforcement market. Glock candidly told an interviewer that his pursuit of law enforcement agencies was a deliberate strategy to gain prestige; he would then use that cachet to sell to civilians: "It was a conscious decision to go after the law enforcement market first," Glock said. "In marketing terms, we assumed that, by pursuing the law enforcement market, we would then receive the benefit of 'after sales' in the commercial market."[63]

The company's strategy worked so successfully that by 1995 the com-pany was downplaying advertising and products were chronically back ordered.[64] An industry analyst described a similar benefit for Italian pistol maker Beretta, noting that its M9 pistol's top "selling points" included "being the military's choice" and proving "highly popular among the nation's police."[65]

Gun manufacturers go out of their way, therefore, to create and main-tain special ties with law enforcement agencies. One common approach is to hire former police officials to work in "law enforcement sales" posi-tions—in effect, to lobby former colleagues to buy the manufacturers' guns and other products. For example, Beretta appointed a twenty-five-year FBI veteran, Ron Kirkland, to be its law enforcement sales manager in 1994. Kirkland had served as a supervisory agent at the FBI's National Academy. As the manager of the FBI's domestic and international police training, Kirkland's position gave him unparalleled personal access to police officials all over the world, an incomparable asset that he brought to Beretta.[66]

This type of attention from pistol manufacturers has had dramatic results. Through the 1970s, the overwhelming majority of U.S. law enforcement agents carried six-shot revolvers. That changed with the appearance on the civilian (and, hence, criminal) market of high capacity 9mm semiautomatic pistols in the early 1980s. "Law enforcement officers then found themselves on the short end of the perception scale as the feel-ing grew that they were 'outgunned' by the criminal element."[67]

Law enforcement agencies reacted to their position on the "perception scale" in two waves. In the first wave, they switched from the six-shot revolver to the high-capacity semiautomatic pistol, predominantly in 9mm, with the consequent increase in ammunition capacity. In the sec-ond and still continuing wave, they are increasing the caliber of their handguns from 9mm to .40 Smith and Wesson or .45 ACP, thereby increasing bullet size.

Several incidents during the late 1990s illustrated the tensions that increased police firepower can raise in the communities they serve. These are cases in which police have killed suspects after firing a quantity of rounds unlikely to have been possible with the older service revolvers. Notable examples include the fatal shooting of an unarmed West African immigrant, Amadou Diallo, by New York City police in February 1999[68] and the Riverside, California, police's shooting of a nineteen-year-old student in January 1999.[69]

In the New York case, four officers reportedly fired a total of forty-one bullets, nineteen of which hit Diallo. Two officers emptied their sixteen-round-capacity semiautomatic pistols, one fired five times, and one fired four times.[70] A shooting report prepared for the district attorney stated that a total of twenty-three rounds were fired by four officers in the Riverside case—one officer fired eight rounds, one fired seven, one fired six, and one fired two.[71]

The number of rounds fired in both incidents inspired charges of excessive force, often accompanied by allegations of racism and deliberate brutality.[72] Putting aside the contested merits of the individual officers' conduct, such incidents raise fundamental questions. For example, how effective can police be in suppressing gun violence in a community in which the police themselves are seen as overarmed and inordinately inclined to shoot? Because a number of similar but less highly publicized multiple-round shooting cases have been reported throughout the United States in recent years,[73] we may assume that these and other questions related to escalation in police armament will continue to be raised.

Toward Harm Reduction

It is wildly unrealistic to suggest that firearms be completely eliminated from American society. However, it is not unrealistic to believe that the extent of death and injury they inflict can be reduced.

As has been demonstrated, product design is at the core of gun death and injury in the United States, especially the developments that have resulted in the ubiquity and enhanced lethality of the handgun: from 1962 through 1994, some 992,388 people in the United States died from firearm injuries. The thirty-three-year period saw a low of 16,720 such deaths in 1962 and a high of 39,595 in 1993.[74] However complex the causes of interpersonal violence may be, it can be no coincidence that this explosion in gun violence occurred almost exactly during the period in which the gun industry was busy reinventing itself by heavily marketing killing power. This is all the more apparent when comparisons are made to countries that strongly regulate private firearms ownership with an emphasis on minimizing access to handguns. For example, in 1995 the U.S. firearms death rate was 13.7 per 100,000; in Canada 3.9 per 100,000; in Australia 2.9 per 100,000; and in England and Wales it was 0.4 per 100,000.[75] Contrary to a common rationalization, the United States is not especially violent relative to other "older" cultures; in fact, as Western Europe grows more violent, the United States becomes less so.[76] The main difference between those nations and our own is that we have more than 60 million handguns. The lesson to be learned from this is, as one public health researcher stated, "People without guns *injure* people; guns *kill* them."[77]

Ironically, there is a well-established body of knowledge and experience in harm reduction in the context of virtually every other consumer product, such as motor vehicles, power tools, children's toys and clothing, pesticides, and so forth. Unfortunately, however, other inherently dangerous consumer products do not share the gun's intensity as an ideological and cultural symbol, whether pro or con. And none enjoys the firearm's maddeningly obscure, certainly tenuous, but nonetheless real constitutional status. There is, for example, no serious body of argument that tobacco or automobiles enjoy special constitutional protection from government health and safety controls. Conversely, many well-meaning gun control advocates simply do not know or bother to learn the intricacies of firearms design, the details of firearms epidemiology, or the demonstrable relationships between these factors.

As a result, discussions about the problem of gun violence in America—indeed, whether there is a problem and what to do about it—have invariably been more emotional than informed or useful. They are often characterized by rhetorical exchanges in which both sides use facts only as selected ammunition intended to make points grounded in broader ideological views. Two examples of such rhetoric suffice: At the NRA convention held in 2000, the association's president, actor Charlton Heston, closed his speech by holding a musket over his head and repeating a slogan often seen on bumper stickers: "From my cold dead hands!"[78] Only weeks earlier, ads sponsored by the so-called Million Mom March for gun control offered the platitudinous goal, "We all want safe kids."[79] Neither of these slogans advances the debate very far.

The history of gun control reflects this studied obliviousness to fact, cause, and effect. From the first federal firearms law, the War Revenue Act of 1919, to the Brady Law of 1993, legislation has attempted to keep guns out of the "wrong hands" by limiting access to firearms to "law-abiding people." As apparently reasonable as that goal sounds, the fact is and the record demonstrates that most of the nation's firearms violence is committed by "law-abiding" persons, caught up in the moment but with easy access to firearms. That is to say, the real problem is the ubiquity of certain specific types of guns, particularly handguns.

Proposals for new gun control laws continue to almost always target the gun owner rather than focusing upstream on the gun industry and its products. The perennial and currently favorite solutions in gun control circles are licensing and registration, neither of which has much logical relation to preventing the kind of gun violence this country suffers. Creating a paper trail of handguns and the people who own them may serve a useful after-the-fact law enforcement purpose, such as facilitating gun tracing, but it will have little prophylactic effect on suicides, acquaintance homicides, and unintentional shootings.

The symbol of a license to buy a handgun is very compelling. The argument is frequently heard, "You need a license to drive a car, why not a license to own a gun?" Unfortunately, the car analogy does not hold up under close scrutiny. State systems to license drivers have been in place since 1903, and all states required vehicle registration by 1948. They were in no way responsible, however, for the sharp reductions we have seen in motor vehicle death and injury over the past thirty years. In fact, the dramatic rise witnessed in motor vehicle death and injury during the 1950s and 1960s came at a time when all cars were registered and all drivers were licensed. It was only after the creation of the National Highway Traffic Safety Administration in 1970, implementation of comprehensive regulations regarding vehicle crashworthiness, and changes in the driving environment (breakaway lampposts, guard rails, and so on) that deaths resulting from motor vehicle crashes began to decline.

Advocates of a U.S. system of licensing and registration often point to such systems in other nations with lower levels of gun death and injury. However this argument fails to acknowledge that lower gun death rates in foreign countries do not result from licensing or registration per se but from far lower rates of gun ownership—and most notably handgun ownership—per capita and that many nations implemented such systems at a time when their gun populations, especially handgun populations, were relatively low.

Proposals to require providing trigger locks are also popular among politicians and gun control advocates. Of course effective trigger locks are a good thing. The ultimate benefit of such a requirement is often wildly inflated, however. Considering that there were only 581 unintentional shootings out of the 32,000 firearm deaths in 1997 and that many of these were cases of adults handling their own guns, the universe of lives likely to be saved or injuries avoided boils down to just several hundred a year. Because most of these victims are small children, there is no question that strong, functional safety locks are a good thing. But that leads to the second problem in many such proposals, which is the complete absence of product standards to ensure that the locks work as they are supposed to. I have personally dismantled models of one of the most popular—and, not surprisingly, cheapest—handguns with such common tools as paper clips or common scissors. The same model can be easily destroyed with a sharp blow from a hammer. It is fatuous to believe that trigger locks will discourage adults intent on doing in their spouses, unbalanced persons setting out to do mass murder by shooting up a public place, or common criminals.

A Promising Approach

Is there a way out of this morass? One promising approach, the public health and safety model, has been gathering support. It moves the debate away from purely ideological grounds for all but the hardest of the hard core and invites much more rigorous analysis of the effects—the costs and benefits—of firearms in society.

The public health community, gun control advocates, and public policymakers have come to understand that the same techniques that have reduced deaths and injuries from motor vehicles, pesticides, and flammable clothing can be applied to guns. Ironically, gun experts also frequently compare handguns to other consumer products. "Think of your gun as a power tool," writes Bill Clede, author of *The Practical Pistol Manual*.[80] Another author writes, "A gun is a tool, but like a car, it can do a lot of damage if not used correctly and treated with respect."[81]

Nevertheless, Congress has failed to enact legislation—such as the Firearms Safety and Consumer Protection Act introduced by Senator Robert Torricelli and Representative Patrick Kennedy—that would subject firearms to federal consumer product health and safety regulation, just like power tools and cars.

The key question the public health and safety approach asks of any con-sumer product is what the product's relative risks and benefits are. If a product inflicts more harm than good, the inquiry is whether the cause of harm is a defect in design or some factor inherent in the nature of the product. If the source of harm is a design defect, like a motor vehicle with a tendency to roll over on curves, it may be possible to correct the design. However, some products, like highly toxic pesticides, are so inherently dangerous that no amount of design tinkering can make them reasonably safe. In such cases, the product may either be restricted to specific persons, such as licensed applicators, or banned outright.

The federal government is the only entity in America capable of doing this job in terms of firearms. The shortcomings of control measures at the state level are obvious. Because firearms move in interstate commerce and any measure adopted by a state necessarily stops at the state line, federal controls setting a regulatory floor are essential (although a given state might implement stronger measures if it chooses). To succeed, any such product regulation must at a minimum

- adequately and effectively regulate firearms as consumer products;
- restrict the availability of weapons shown to cause an unreasonable risk of injury; and
- ensure that products developed by the firearms industry do not pose a threat to public safety or present an unreasonable risk of injury or death to consumers.

The first step toward such a rational regimen is to recognize firearms for what they are—inherently dangerous consumer products. The second is to design a comprehensive, workable regulatory framework.

The most extensive body of expertise and knowledge concerning firearms currently resides in the Bureau of Alcohol, Tobacco, and Firearms (ATF). But the agency has limited powers and has rarely shown the incli-nation or the imagination to use what powers it does have to take on the gun industry. This could be changed. Meaningful regulation of the manu-facture, distribution, and sale of firearms, firearms-related products, and ammunition could come about through comprehensive legislation giving the ATF regulatory tools like those used every day by other federal health and safety agencies to protect Americans from unreasonably dangerous and defective products.

All of this can be accomplished while still allowing the public to have access to guns with legitimate sporting purposes. There is a national con-sensus that some firearms should remain available to the civilian popula-tion. It is possible to create a regulatory system that acknowledges this consensus and controls firearms, just as we currently control other poten-tially dangerous consumer products. Just as regulation of pesticides did not lead to an outright ban on their use, neither would expanding ATF's authority result in a gun-free America.

It could, however,

- reduce the availability of specific categories of weapons to criminals, minors, and others currently prohibited from purchasing weapons;
- place controls on an industry that today is free to manufacture and sell firearms or related products without any consideration of the consequences to the public health and safety; and,
- protect purchasers and owners of firearms from products that present a serious risk of injury because of a hazardous design characteristic or manufacturing defect.

Ironically, the only protection gun owners now have against poorly designed firearms is the possibility of a lawsuit after someone has been injured or killed.

It may make sense to split ATF into two entirely separate agencies or into two relatively autonomous divisions, one focused on criminal enforcement and the other on product regulation. In any case, existing regulatory models suggest ways to give an enhanced ATF meaningful authority over firearms.

In sum, it may well be true that simply passing more gun control laws will do nothing to alleviate our gun violence problem if they are simply more of the same. What is needed a direct strike at the precise root of the problem—the industry and the nature of the products it designs, markets, and sells.

NOTES

1. U.S. Department of Justice, *Guns in America: National Survey on Private Ownership and Use of Firearms* (May 1997), 6–7.

2. Philip Cook and Jens Ludwig, *Guns in America* (Washington, DC: Police Foundation, 1996), 14, 33.

3. Donna L. Hoyert, Kenneth D. Kochanek, et al., "Deaths: Final Data for 1997," *National Vital Statistics Reports* 47 (19) (June 30, 1999).

4. Darci Cherry, Joseph L. Annest, et al., "Trends in Nonfatal and Fatal Firearm-Related Injury Rates in the United States, 1985–1995," *Annals of Emergency Medicine* 32 (1) (July 1998).

5. Kimberly D. Peters, Kenneth D. Kochanek, et al., "Deaths: Final Data for 1996," *National Vital Statistics Reports* 47 (9) (November 10, 1998).

6. "Rates of Homicide, Suicide, and Firearm-Related Death among Children—26 Industrialized Countries," *Morbidity and Mortality Weekly Report* 46 (5) (February 7, 1997).

7. E. G. Krug, K. E. Powell, et al., "Firearm-Related Deaths in the United States and 35 Other High- and Upper-Middle-Income Countries," *International Journal of Epidemiology* 27 (1998).

8. For a description of this system at its latter end, see Merritt Roe Smith, "The Craft Origins of Production, 1798–1816," in *Harpers Ferry Armory and the New Technology: The Challenge of Change* (Ithaca: Cornell University Press, 1977), 52–68.

9. Import data from ATF and Foreign Trade Division, U.S. Bureau of the Census, in author's files.

10. See, e.g., "In the Market for Guns, The Customers Aren't Coming Back for More," *Wall Street Journal*, October 26, 1999, p. A1.

11. Massad Ayoob, "Presentation Guns Make Ideal Gifts while Increasing Sales," *Shooting Industry*, February 1996, 14. For the most part, Ayoob's "Lethal Force" column advises gun dealers on how to boost sales through emphasizing the "self-defense" market.

12. "The Four-Gun Family in Their Sights: U.S. Gunmakers Are on the Offensive," *Financial Times*, March 2, 1996, 7.

13. U.S. Department of Justice, *Guns in America*, 2.

14. See, e.g., "Running Scared: The Pressures That Forced America's Largest Discounter to Quit Stocking Handguns," *Shooting Sports Retailer*, July–August 1994, 12.

15. "Doing Business in the Golden Age of the Consumer," *Shooting Industry*, February 1997, 29.

16. Cook and Ludwig, *Guns in America*, 14.

17. "The Industry White Papers: Expert Intelligence on the State of the Industry: The Future of the Gun Industry," *Shooting Industry*, July 1993, 40.

18. "Industry Insights," *American Firearms Industry*, February 1993, 74.

19. See G. J. Wintemute, "The Relationship between Firearm Design and Firearm Violence," *Journal of the American Medical Association* 275 (22) (June 12, 1996): 1749; M. D. McConigal, J. Cole, C. W. Schwab, D. R. Kauder, M. F. Rotondo, and P. B. Angood, "Urban Firearm Deaths: A Five-Year Perspective," *Journal of Trauma* 35 (4) (October 1993): 532.

20. D. B. Dean and K. D. Powley, "Comparative Performance of 9mm Parabellum, .38 Special and .40 Smith & Wesson Ammunition in Ballistic Gelatin," *Wound Ballistics Review* 2 (3) (1996): 9. See also M. L. Fackler, "Gunshot Wound Review," *Annals of Emergency Medicine* 28 (2) (August 1996); "USSOCOM Calls for .45-cal 'Offensive Handgun,'" *International Defense Review*, December 1, 1990, 1401 (describing Dr. Fackler's emphasis on the wounding effect of the permanent

cavity as equating to "the bigger the bullet, the bigger the hole, the more rapid the incapacitation due to circulatory collapse").

21. International Association of Fish and Wildlife Agencies, *Proceedings of the First National Shooting Range Symposium* (1990), 89.

22. Unless otherwise noted, the production figures in this section are based on data from U.S. Department of the Treasury, Bureau of Alcohol, Tobacco and Firearms, "Civilian Firearms—Domestic Production, Importation and Exportation," in author's files.

23. *Shooting Industry*, July 1999, 38.

24. National Institute of Justice, *Guns in America*.

25. R. P. Caruso, D. I. Jara, and K. G. Swan, "Gunshot Wounds: Bullet Caliber Is Increasing," *Journal of Trauma: Injury, Infection, and Critical Care* 46 (3) (March 1999): 462.

26. See "Trends in Law Enforcement Handguns," *American Guardian*, July 1999, 31–32. *American Guardian* is the official journal of the National Rifle Association.

27. "Ceramic Gun Barrels," *American Firearms Industry*, September 1992, 6.

28. "Trends in Law Enforcement Handguns," 33.

29. "Headache Cure #2000," *Shooting Sports Retailer*, January 1997, 6.

30. See, e.g., *The Gun Digest Book of Assault Weapons*, 3d ed. Northbrook, IL: DBI Books, (1993), 41 ("one could not afford to waste even one round climbing over their heads when you were hosing them down").

31. See, e.g. "A Tale of Two Fifties: 0.50-Calibre Sniper Rifles Gain Popularity," *International Defense Review*, June 1, 1994, 67.

32. Ibid.

33. Massad Ayoob, "The Defensive Market Today," *Shooting Industry*, February 1997, 20.

34. Joel Millman, "Steady Finger on the Trigger," *Forbes*, November 9, 1992, 188.

35. Quoted in "Gun Firms Spur Market; Stronger Weapons, Arms Sales Coincide with More Violence," *Boston Globe*, December 19, 1993, p. 1.

36. "Tinier, Deadlier Pocket Pistols Are in Vogue," *Wall Street Journal*, September 12, 1996, p. B1.

37. "CCW Bills Positive Direction for Industry," *Firearms Business*, June 15, 1995, 1.

38. "Companies Eye Gun Carry Laws," *Firearms Business*, April 15, 1995, 7.

39. "More Gun Permits Equal More Gun Sales," *Shooting Industry*, February 1997.

40. Mike R. Lau, *The Military and Police Sniper: Advanced Precision Shooting for Combat and Law Enforcement* (Manchester, CT: Precision Shooting, 1998), 71.

41. Massad Ayoob, "'Trend Crimes' and the Gun Dealer," *Shooting Industry*, March 1993, 18.

42. "GunGames Publisher Wants Change in Industry," *Firearms Business*, July 1, 1995, 3–4.

43. "Shot Show Indicates Defense Guns on the Roll," *Shooting Industry*, April 1997, 16.

44. "Baby with a Bark," *American Firearms Industry*, June 1995, 78.

45. "Beretta Keeps Going Great Guns," *Baltimore Sun*, May 1, 1995, p. 6C.

46. Cook and Ludwig, *Guns in America*, 37–38.

47. G. J. Wintemute, S. P. Teret, et al., "The Choice of Weapons in Firearm Suicides," *American Journal of Public Health* 78 (7) (1988): 824–26; Stephen W. Hargarten, Trudy A. Karlson, et al., "Characteristics of Firearms Involved in Fatalities," *Journal of the American Medical Association* 275 (1) (1996): 42–45.

48. FBI Supplementary Homicide Report data, 1978–97.

49. M. Zawitz, *Guns Used in Crime: Firearms, Crime, and Criminal Justice—Selected Findings* (Washington, DC: Bureau of Justice Statistics, 1995).

50. "Fatal Firearm Injuries in the United States: 1962–1994," in *Violence Surveillance Summary Series*, no. 3 (Atlanta: National Center for Injury Prevention and Control, 1997); Robert N. Anderson, Kenneth D. Kochanek, et al., "Deaths: Final Data for 1995," "Report of Final Mortality: Statistics, 1995," *Monthly Vital Statistics Report* 45 (11), suppl. 2 (June 12, 1997); Peters et al., "Deaths: Final Data for 1996"; Hoyert et al., "Deaths: Final Data for 1997."

51. "The Internet Pathology Laboratory: Firearms Tutorial," Department of Pathology, University of Utah, available at http://medstat.med.utah.edu/WebPath/TUTORIAL/GUNS/GUNINTRO.html. Accessed August 30, 1999.

52. "The Miami Shootout: What Really Happened!" *Handguns*, August 1999, 66, 80.

53. Wintemute, "Relationship," 1749 ("Reports from major cities document a contemporaneous increase in the overall severity of firearm-related injuries. The transition from revolvers to pistols is considered a key factor by many observers"); McConigal et al., "Urban Firearm Deaths," 532 ("Changes in [Philadelphia] handgun usage [from predominance of revolvers and lower-caliber pistols to predominance of higher-powered pistols,] had a marked effect on survival").

54. "Arms Race Escalates," *Washington Post*, February 23, 1988, p. B5.

55. Wintemute, "Relationship," 1749, 1750 ("higher wounding potential of their more powerful ammunition"; see also table on p. 1751); for a comprehensive review of the elements that contribute to the wounding potential of various types of ammunition and firearms, see Fackler, "Gunshot Wound Review," 194.

56. See Caruso, Jara, and Swan, "Gunshot Wounds," 462 (trend to larger-caliber bullets used in unintentional shootings, suicides, and homicides over a sixteen-year period, 1981–97).

57. A. L. Kellermann, "Do Guns Matter?" *Western Journal of Medicine* 161 (6) (December 1994): 614, citing F. E. Zimring, "The Medium Is the Message: Firearm Calibre as a Determinant of Death from Assault," *Journal of Legal Studies* 1 (1972): 97–124.

58. "Internet Pathology Laboratory" ("Tissue destruction can be increased at any caliber by use of hollowpoint expanding bullets"); Fackler, "Gunshot Wound Review," 194 ("Wounding potential is also determined to a great extent by a bullet's physical characteristics. . . . For example, an expanding soft-point or hollowpoint bullet causes more tissue disruption than a similar but nonexpanding one"); G. M. McCormick II, D. B. Young, and J. C. Stewart, "Wounding Effects of the

Winchester Black Talon Bullet," *American Journal of Forensic Medicine and Pathology* 17 (2) (1996).

59. National Law Enforcement and Corrections Technology Center (Rocky Mountain Region), Informational brief, "Hollow Point vs. Ball Duty Ammo," May 1997. Available at http://www.nletc.org/nlectrm/ammo.html. Accessed (August 17, 1999).

60. See, e.g., "Defensive Handgun Ammo," *Shooting Industry*, January 1996, 29.

61. "Update: Stopping Power: A Look at the Latest in High-Performance Handgun Ammunition," *Guns and Ammo*, July 1995, 58.

62. U.S. Department of Justice, Bureau of Justice Statistics, *Sourcebook of Criminal Justice Statistics 1996*, table 1.25; "Law Enforcement Statistics" (April 6, 1998).

63. "The Marketing 100: Gaston Glock, Glock," *Advertising Age*, June 26, 1995, 830.

64. Ibid.

65. "Beretta's M9 Anniversary Will Help You Sell This Semi-Auto," *Shooting Industry*, October 1995, 24.

66. "Beretta Appoints Top Managers," *Shooting Industry*, April 1994, 2; see also "Smith and Wesson Increases Sales Staff," *Shooting Industry*, March 1996, 12 (former South Dakota state trooper named director of law enforcement sales); "Marx Moves to Michaels," *Shooting Sports Retailer*, November–December 1992, 46 (former Chicago police officer moves from top law enforcement marketing job at Smith and Wesson).

67. "Trends in Law Enforcement Handguns," 31.

68. "Officers in Bronx Fire 41 Shots, and an Unarmed Man Is Killed," *New York Times*, February 5, 1999, p. A1.

69. "A Confusing Police Shooting Kills a Teenager," *Newsweek*, January 11, 1999, 32.

70. "Officers in Bronx."

71. "Tactical Analysis," *Press-Enterprise* [Inland Southern California], May 7, 1999, p. E6.

72. See, e.g., "Fatal Judgment: The Police Shooting of Tyisha Miller, 19, Tears a California City Apart," *People*, October 11, 1999, p. 143; "The Scales of Injustice: Police Brutality and a Flawed Criminal Justice System Help Keep Racial Tensions High," *Emerge*, May 31, 1999, 49; "Jesse Jackson: Police Abuse Terrorism of Highest Order," *Gannett News Service*, February 25, 1999.

73. See, e.g., "Phoenix, Buchanans Settle Suit," *Arizona Republic*, March 18, 1999, p. B1 (eighty-nine shots fired at suspect); "Pair Shot as Chase Ended Sue Police," *Providence Journal-Bulletin*, February 25, 1999, p. 1C (seventy-one rounds allegedly fired at car); "Lawyer: Race May Not Have Been a Factor," *Providence Journal-Bulletin*, February 28, 1998, p. 3A (forty rounds allegedly fired at driver after traffic stop); "Knife-Wielding Boy Was Riddled with Bullets," *Arizona Republic*, November 19, 1996, p. A1 (twenty-five rounds allegedly fired at sixteen-year-old); "DA Releases Tapes in Truax Case," *Denver Post*, May 4, 1996, p. B1 (twenty-five rounds allegedly fired at vehicle).

74. "Fatal Firearm Injuries in the United States: 1962–1994."

75. L. A. Fingerhut, C. S. Cox, et al., "Comparative Analysis of Injury Mortality," in *Advance Data* (Hyattsville, MD.: National Center for Health Statistics, 1998).

76. Patrick A. Langan and David P. Farrington, *Crime and Justice in the United States and in England and Wales, 1981–1996* (Washington, DC: Bureau of Justice Statistics, 1998).

77. Susan P. Baker, "Without Guns, Do People Kill People?" *American Journal of Public Health* 75 (June 1985): 588.

78. "NRA Leaders Make Gore the Day's Primary Political Target," *Charlotte Observer*, May 21, 2000, p. 1A. The implication of this slogan is that committed gun owners will resist to the death any government attempt to confiscate their firearms.

79. "Marching Moms Hope to Recast Gun Debate," *Washington Post*, May 10, 2000, p. A1.

80. Bill Clede, *The Practical Pistol Manual* (Ottawa, IL: Jameson Books, 1997), 1.

81. Chris Bird, *The Concealed Handgun Manual: How to Choose, Carry, and Shoot a Gun in Self-Defense* (San Antonio: Privateer Publications 1998), 91.

Leashing the "Dogs of War"

Herbert Howe

"Mercenaries" are social pariahs to most of civilized society. Many critics would prefer to outlaw soldiers who may display only temporary and purchasable loyalty, act inhumanely against civilian populations, introduce more efficient methods of killing, and limit hopes for peaceful resolution. As such, these critics argue, private security undermines the nation-state system and the rules of civility that govern everyday behavior. This chapter uses *mercenary* to apply to those unregulated private individuals or groups that offer military services to a foreign cause for remuneration that exceeds normal living expenses.[1]

Yet private security has been attracting renewed interest and some support during this post–Cold War era, as African militaries cannot counter rising threats, as Western nations refuse to intervene militarily into unstable countries, and as large numbers of skilled ex-soldiers offer themselves for hire.

The shift from state to private security has been dramatic but difficult to quantify. *Equitable Securities Research* suggests that worldwide revenues were $55.6 billion in 1990 and should climb to $202 billion by 2010.[2] The greatest amount of this was for domestic security—for example, security guards and bodyguards. This chapter, however, refers to *private security* only as it operates in foreign countries. Between 1992 and 2000, Halliburton, through its Brown and Root subsidiary, won more than $2 billion in contracts supporting U.S. peacekeeping efforts abroad.[3] Defence Systems Limited (DSL) had 130 contracts worldwide with 115 clients (private and government) in twenty-two countries by early 1999.

Mercenary is a pejorative label, somewhat akin to *terrorist*, that can foreclose serious discussion about a growing trend that needs analysis. This chapter argues that private security that operates overseas has both legitimate and illegitimate actors and that any "antimercenary" legislation should recognize this division. Established private security companies can serve the interests both of the host state (the United States or Britain, for example) and of the recipient state—if appropriate safeguards are applied. Yet unregulated soldiers for hire certainly threaten international stability, and the international community should apply much more control than now exists.

A short history of private security begins this chapter, suggesting that Africa's current demand for private security stems from complex political and security problems that, if not corrected, will continue to attract foreign soldiers, regardless of regulations.[4] The next section places traditional antimercenary arguments (notably those of nonaccountability and brutality) in the context of recent African developments, arguing that well-regulated private security can assist state development and human rights protections. However, mercenaries have undeniably had an ugly past and can easily pose serious international threats in the absence of strong national and international regulations.

History

Prostitution may be the world's oldest profession, but private soldiering cannot be far behind. In 401 B.C., Xenophon wrote about the service of ten thousand mercenaries to Cyrus, pretender to the Persian throne. Private armies became a common military instrument in the fifteenth century, with condottieri commanders hiring "free companies." With the growth of nation-states following the Thirty Years' War (1618–48) and the subsequent spread of nationalism following the French Revolution, national armies replaced private forces as the primary military organization.

Yet private security continued, albeit on a smaller scale. The British East African Company and the British South African Company employed adventurers to gain land and mineral concessions from African rulers. Idealistic Americans fought for England and France in World War I and for Canada in World War II prior to the U.S. entry into those conflicts. Foreigners composed the International Brigade to fight Spanish fascism in the mid-1930s, and American pilots of the Flying Tigers supported China against Japan in the late 1930s (whether foreigners fighting largely for ideals rather than solely for profit are "mercenaries" is examined later).

Africa generally has not seen widespread private soldiering for much of the past century. Colonial militaries held a virtual monopoly on military force until the 1960s. Newly independent Africa saw a brief resurgence of foreign soldiers, as handfuls of Europeans fought for secessionist movements in the Congo and Nigeria (Mike Hoare's 5 Commando for Katanga and Rolf Steiner's 4 Commando for Biafra, respectively).[5] Activity during the 1970s and 1980s centered on racist southern African regimes; perhaps a thousand South Africans, Europeans, and Americans fought for Rhodesia during the 1970s.

The Cold War stabilized some otherwise insecure regimes, whereas its ending often induced both greater insecurity and a growing demand for skilled foreign personnel.[6] Until 1990, many African states were but "juridical" entities, or "lame leviathans," with unprofessional militaries and dependent on external financial and military support.[7] Foreign financial aid provided the new regimes with budgetary and patronage powers, while military assistance (troop intervention, advisers, and equipment) helped the states to maintain the balance of military coercion. Between 1960 and 1989, only two sub-Saharan states (Chad and Uganda) were overthrown directly by insurgencies or invasions. France was the leading intervener, dispatching its military forces some twenty times to provide support to threatened regimes.

Africa became more unstable after 1990. Declines in foreign aid sped the collapse of several Western and Soviet client states, including Samuel Doe's Liberia, Siad Barre's Somalia, and Mengistu Haile Mariam's Ethiopia. The post-Somalia reluctance (the "Somalia Syndrome") of non-African states to rescue embattled states also lessened state stability. Significant downsizing of Western militaries—the United States nearly halved its personnel and budget between 1989 and 1998, for example—further discouraged Western intervention in noncritical wars. Eastern European nations contributed to the instability by selling surplus weaponry to insurgencies at bargain-basement prices, and demobilized European and South African soldiers offered themselves as mercenaries.

The nature of the African state contributed to its military insecurity. Undemocratic, neopatriarchal rule continued to dominate many African states after independence, weakening national militaries. African rulers knew well the coup threat that operationally capable militaries posed; some ninety-five military coups had occurred by the late 1990s. Hence, many rulers weakened the operational effectiveness of their national security forces, either by "ethnicizing" them or by creating parallel forces answerable only to the ruler himself. Ethnicization removed trained officers belonging to ethnic groups opposed to the current ruler and replaced them with often unskilled but ethnically correct personnel. Presidential guards siphoned supplies, budget, and manpower from the national militaries.

These growing threats to state stability produced barbaric behavior throughout the 1990s. The Revolutionary United Front (RUF) in Sierra Leone has severed the arms or legs of perhaps thirty thousand civilians and has forced unknown numbers of girls into sexual slavery (and has smuggled overseas about half a billion dollars worth of the country's diamonds). The Lord's Resistance Army in northern Uganda has committed numerous abominations against the country's civilian population.

African governments, not wanting to empower militaries of dubious loyalty, sometimes hired private security groups during the 1990s. Angola contracted with the South African–based Executive Outcomes (EO) between 1993 and late 1995 to fight against the UNITA (Union for the Total Independence of Angola) insurgency. Sierra Leone also hired EO from 1995 to early 1997 to counter the RUF threat. The late Mobutu Sese Seko hired the so-called White Legion of Eastern Europeans in 1997 as a last-ditch and unsuccessful attempt to repulse a coalition opposition. (Insurgencies also have hired mercenaries, usually in far fewer numbers.)

The results of these mercenary actions have stoked both sides of the debate over whether to proscribe the private security industry. For example, EO soldiers, most of whom had served with the former South African Defence Force, helped to repulse UNITA in Angola and RUF in Sierra Leone. The South African Defence Force had defended the morally bankrupt ideology of apartheid but also created a top-notch army and air force that accepted civilian supremacy over the military. As a result, EO practiced generally correct behavior toward civilians, did not attempt military coups, and left the two countries when requested by its regime employers. Conversely, the White Legion, a hastily created force, proved both militarily ineffective against insurgents and sometimes brutal when dealing with civilians.

The Case for Proscription

Machiavelli summarized many of the objections to private security when he advised his prince that mercenaries were "disunited, ambitious without discipline, unfaithful. . . . [Y]ou cannot trust them because they will always aspire to their own greatness, either by oppressing you who are their boss or by oppressing others outside of your intention."[8] Most mercenaries were inept and, Machiavelli concluded, the few competent mercenary bands potentially threatened their employers.

Nonaccountability has always stood as a major concern, since soldiers not controlled by states (and their institutions of military justice) may threaten local authorities and citizens as well as natural resources. If money determines loyalty, will a soldier's "accountability" last only until a higher bidder purchases his services? The employing state has a weak security capability—why else would it hire foreign soldiers?—and thus may not be able to control the foreigners' behavior. The countries from which the mercenaries originate may not know of their activities or be able to regulate their actions. The foreign soldiers will probably care little about the local customs and people. As a result, the commanding officers may condone brutal behavior should it further military objectives. The United Nations' Special Rapporteur on Mercenaries asks, "Who will be responsible for any repressive excesses that the security companies may commit against the civilian population? . . . Who will take responsibility for any violations of international humanitarian law and of human rights that they may commit?"[9]

Some foreign soldiers have indeed been barbaric. Many have had criminal records, and some had never seen prior combat (let alone served in a military), yet desperate regimes may still hire them without vetting their service and civilian records. Many Congolese saw the often brutal mercenaries in the country during the 1960s as "les affreux" (the frightful ones). Colonel Callan (the nom de guerre for Costa Georgiou) deliberately murdered several of his fellow mercenaries in Angola during the mid-1970s. Numerous human rights observers accused Colonel Dominic Yugo, a Serb national, of multiple abuses of international humanitarian law in the Congo in 1997. These are only a few examples of often-widespread mercenary brutality; Yugo belonged to the White Legion, many of whose soldiers apparently behaved poorly. The increasing lethality of today's weaponry raises additional concerns about foreigners operating helicopter gunships or fuel-air explosives without any accountability. A few mercenaries have switched sides in a combat, transferring military intelligence to their new employers.

Private security may be accountable only to foreign rather than local interests. Western multinational companies and countries sometimes have used private security to increase their influence within Africa—foreign policy by proxy. The British East and South African Companies operated a century ago; more recently, Union Minière of Belgium underwrote mercenaries in Congo in the 1960s. Wilfred Burchett and Derek Roebuck described mercenaries as "neo-colonialism's last card . . . a faceless . . . reserve of cannon fodder not identifiable with governments and their policies, immune to public criticism and debate."[10] Criminal organizations, especially drug cartels in Central and Latin America, have hired demobilized foreign soldiers for repressive purposes. Countries, even those that are relatively democratic, have employed private companies for covert operations. Air America, for example, provided "plausible deniability" to U.S. military operations in Southeast Asia. More recently, DynCorp, an American security company, has provided ex-U.S. special operations soldiers to the U.S.-supported drug war being waged by the Colombian government.[11]

As a result of all these factors, critics claim, private security may reduce the power of some states. Max Weber noted that the modern state arose because it "successfully upheld a claim to the monopoly of the legitimate use of physical force in the enforcement of its order."[12] Commercial security, through nonaccountable and often selfish behavior, seemingly cracks that monopoly of force and thus threatens a government's legitimacy.

Difficulties with Banning:
A Limited Justification for Private Security

If even some of the preceding arguments are true, should the world community ban private security operating abroad? The answer is that definitional difficulties, supply and demand realities, and enforcement problems will prevent any effective banning of private security. Indeed, an all-inclusive proscription could drive an already covert business farther away from public view and monitoring.

Most international organizations, including the United Nations and the Organization of African Unity, equate private security with *mercenary*.[13] But what is a mercenary? As with so much about mercenaries, what initially appears obvious becomes hazy with greater scrutiny. Defining a mercenary is not intellectual sophistry, since debate over the possible merits of private security or over whether to regulate or eliminate these soldiers requires a commonly accepted definition.

Do mercenaries serve only insurgencies, or can they also assist states? Whereas many critics assume that mercenaries are inherently destabilizing, many regimes hire these soldiers to protect the state. The Organization of African Unity does not label state-employed foreign soldiers as mercenaries, presumably because these soldiers fight to preserve stability. This definitional difficulty raises the question of whether a sovereign state has the right to provide for its self-defense, especially if that regime appears far more legitimate than the rebel force (the Sierra Leonean government versus the RUF, for example).

An allied issue is whether soldiers from another government are mercenaries. Cuban troops fought in Angola from about 1975 to 1990, and critics argue that Fidel Castro would not have supplied the soldiers without remuneration from the Angolan government or the Soviet Union. More recently, Chad supplied troops to Congo's Laurent Kabila, not because the Congo war threatened Chad but because Angola and Libya apparently offered significant cash payments.

Second, are all foreign volunteers (assuming that they receive some remuneration) to be considered mercenaries? The Americans who fought in the Abraham Lincoln Battalion during the Spanish Civil War and most of the Americans who fought for the Rhodesian government during the 1970s received compensation, yet they also believed in the cause for which they fought.

Third, does all private foreign military assistance constitute "mercenary" activity? What about experts who advise on military payroll procedures or on the merits to a military of political democratization? This is not a rhetorical question. Private security companies in America currently provide several African states both with advice and with "ground-pounding" infantry/special operations. Would a retired security official who never leaves the United States but who advises the United Nations on military matters be a mercenary?

These and other definitional questions have greatly complicated the ability of states and of the international community to define *mercenary* and then to agree on antimercenary legislation. Furthermore, several states that had previously ratified antimercenary accords have subsequently hired mercenaries when faced with significant military threat. Twelve African states have signed and/or ratified the UN's 1989 International Convention against the Recruitment, Use, Financing, and Training of Mercenaries. Yet several of these, notably Nigeria, Angola, and the Democratic Republic of Congo, have recently hired private security.

Demand and Supply

For-hire soldiers exist because regimes and insurgents want them. This reality alone will likely sink any serious attempt at proscription. Private security usually reflects more than causes existing instability. As already noted, too many African national militaries deliberately lack basic operational capabilities, and the outside world usually refuses to dispatch combat troops to nations deemed peripherally important.

Private security in this post–Cold War era can assist the state. The demobilization of Eastern European, British, American, and South African soldiers has elevated the capabilities of a business that had far too often employed clearly unprofessional individuals. Military Professional Resources Incorporated (MPRI) has employed between eight and seventeen retired U.S. generals full-time over the past six years (since 1998).[14] Tim Spicer, OBE, a retired colonel in the Royal Scots Guards along with a former commander of the U.S. Delta Force, helped head up the Sandline International security firm. Although some past mercenaries have been incompetent or disloyal, some recent private security soldiers have displayed far more capability and loyalty than the indigenous "national" militaries. A motley group of four foreigners—two South African helicopter pilots, a former British Special Air Services (SAS) officer from Fiji in his late fifties, and an Ethiopian helicopter mechanic—were critical to the defense of Freetown, Sierra Leone, mounted in 1999 by the Economic Community of West African States Military Observation Group (ECOMOG), a multinational West African intervention force in Liberia and Sierra Leone. According to the *Times* of London,

> ECOMOG officers admit that they would have lost Freetown last month without Mr. Marafuno [the ex-SAS officer] and his comrades, "Juba" Joubert and Neil Ellis, both South Africans, and their Ethiopian engineer, Sindaba. "Without these guys, we would have run out of food and ammo and fled the front. They are amazingly brave. I know they do it for money, but I wouldn't do it for anything," said a Nigerian lieutenant colonel.[15]

EO's contracts with the Angolan and Sierra Leonean governments, the service of the aforementioned soldiers in Sierra Leone, and work of International Charter Incorporated (ICI) and MPRI (discussed subsequently) point up another contrast with past mercenary operations. Established companies recently have often worked with sovereign and relatively legitimate governments against discredited insurgencies or secessionist movements. By doing so, these firms have reduced Western governments' need to become militarily involved.

Some combat or combat-support groups have gone beyond the limited peacekeeping role that the United Nations performs and in so doing perform tasks that many states want done but are unwilling to do themselves. *Harper's* magazine notes that EO "offers to do what the United Nations blue helmets cannot and will not do: take sides, deploy overwhelming force, and fire 'preemptively' on its contractually designated enemy."[16] The UN's deployment only of peacekeeping soldiers in still-contentious areas can be costly and counterproductive. The United Nations Mission in Sierra Leone cost a third of a billion dollars in 2000 but accomplished few if any of its goals. Instead, about one-tenth of the force, which had neither the mandate nor the training for counter-insurgency operations, surrendered its weaponry and vehicles to the RUF.

Foreign soldiers or advisers can be politically attractive on occasion because they do not harbor the same ethnic, regional, or religious divisions that have triggered many of Africa's coups. Their loyalty is to their paymaster, who is either the president (or his foreign supporters) or the rebel leader. Overthrowing that paymaster would kill the goose that lays the golden egg. Those for-hire soldiers (EO is one example) who avoid abusing civilians may gain local support for their employers.[17]

Private security is often cost-efficient. The Logistics Management Institute believes that private companies cost about a third the price of a national force.[18] Payment is for a time-specific contract, unlike open-ended military funding, which must be continued whether or not the force is fighting. Therefore, employers lease personnel and equipment for short periods and do not pay for upkeep when the force is not needed. Training costs are negligible, since the foreigners bring advanced skills with them. The competence of these soldiers may significantly reduce salary payments for a larger but less skilled force.[19]

Western governments encourage and often assist the work of private security companies assisting legitimate African governments. MPRI draws 75 percent of its contracts from the U.S. government and has a major U.S. government contract to provide advising and training assistance to the Nigerian military.[20] ECOMOG has relied on trucks, transport and cargo aircraft, pilots and mechanics provided by Pacific Architects and Engineering and ICI, two American companies financed by the U.S. and

British governments. DSL is "sometimes regarded in the business as Britain's officially-backed 'mercenaries,'" according to one of Africa's leading security analysts, J. 'Kayode Fayemi, director of the Centre for Democracy and Development (CDD) in Lagos, Nigeria.[21] In the 1980s, DSL furnished ex-SAS personnel to train the Mozambican military against a brutal South African–supported insurgency.

Enforcement of an all-encompassing proscription would prove difficult and often impossible. African states, citing their sovereign right to self-defense, might not cooperate with such measures. Enforcement requires knowledge, but the covert nature of the mercenary trade complicates its monitoring. Mercenaries are usually not very noticeable: a growing number of mercenaries in Africa are African, and many foreign security experts dress in civilian clothes and work in government buildings.

Enforcement also requires effective countermeasures. What international or regional organization has the desire and ability forcibly to prevent significant mercenary operations? Would the United States, China, or the United Nations deploy armed units to discourage such operations, especially those contracted by a sovereign state? These enforcement objections do not rule out legislation but do illustrate the difficulties inherent in such action.

Conclusion: Regulation as the Best–but Incomplete—Solution

Passing a law to ban all "mercenary" activity would fail because it could not void the supply of and the demand for purchasable security, because of the difficulty of even defining a mercenary, and because of the problems of enforcing such legislation. Demand for and supply of mercenaries will always exist. Proscription would prevent such companies as MPRI and ICI from aiding states against brutal insurgencies such as Sierra Leone's RUF. How to channel this physical force is the real issue.

Critics of mercenaries are correct in that failing to pass laws against private security could encourage nonaccountability and human rights abuses while weakening the nation-state system and respect for the rule of law. The foreign "affreux," Yugos, and Callans have no redeeming value and should face international opposition.

Many countries place no regulations on the export of private security, and those that do so often fail to enforce such measures. Former military officers from Russia and the Ukraine apparently operate with impunity, fearing no penalties from their governments. (Several hundred Ukrainians reportedly have assisted the RUF.) Alex Vines of Human Rights Watch argues that while the Australian government prohibits foreign causes from recruiting Australians, it does not consider citizens who fight for these causes to have broken the law.[22] The United Kingdom's Foreign Enlistment Act of 1870 "has not stopped British citizens playing important roles in mercenary-like activities," reports Vines.[23]

Some observers, including this author, have suggested the enactment of legislation to regulate rather than eliminate private security.[24] The leashing of private security would recognize two realities: (1) that state-controlled private security can assist threatened but deserving states, and (2) that nonaccountable enterprises can endanger state development and basic human rights.

Permitting security companies to establish and then promote themselves would allow greater public scrutiny of the firms and would enable companies and the governments to vet thoroughly all prospective employees. Ad hoc organizations can escape ongoing public inspection, whereas established firms that publicly bid for government contracts will necessarily attract legislative scrutiny. Established companies have proven more effective, both in fighting capability and in human rights observance, than the ad hoc, last-minute hiring by desperate regimes of unvetted and often unprofessional fighters, as has been illustrated by the contrast between EO in Angola and Sierra Leone and the White Legion in the Congo.

Strong national legislation is necessary but not sufficient to regulate commercial security. The United States offers one of the better models for authorizing private assistance to deserving states. American companies need government authorization, the conditions for which are found in the International Trafficking in Arms Regulation, the Arms Export Control Act, and the Export Administration Act. Companies hoping to operate in Africa must submit their proposals to the U.S. State Department, which sends them to its Africa Bureau and its Human Rights Office; to the Defense Department; and sometimes to the Treasury and Energy Departments. Rejection by just one of these agencies effectively halts the licensing process. Continued public and legislative scrutiny of all government contracts is also necessary.

Some supporters of private security contend that the laws of the marketplace, along with media observation and perhaps some national legislation, supply sufficient controls. Military companies saddled with a record of human rights abuses would render themselves unemployable to states and to international organizations.

But official national and informal market regulation is insufficient: international regulation is necessary. Governments may learn of misdeeds only after they occur, and the media often face difficulties when trying to report from embattled areas. Some governments may turn a blind eye to mercenary shortcomings should the overall operations serve national interests. Establishing commendable business records is irrelevant to those private companies seeking a one-shot but very rewarding contract. Some nefarious companies would establish themselves in states that have relatively weak if any private security legislation.

International regulation of companies should involve a code of conduct, registration and the determination of qualifications, specific project approval, and operational oversight, which should include observers from recognized human rights organizations. Such regulation would provide both a carrot and a stick to encourage correct behavior. Cooperation would bring lucrative contracts and international status to ex-soldiers who otherwise might rely on less accountable and often criminal employers. Failure to comply with the code could remove companies from consideration for future projects. Seizure of companies' assets or revocation of individual passports could serve as two extreme enforcement mechanisms.

While national and international regulation is necessary, it will never fully prevent abuses in the private security field. National interests will encourage some states to authorize private security actions that will assist brutal regimes or insurgencies. Such help will provide the authorizing government with foreign exchange and possible business opportunities as well as foreign employment for otherwise unemployed practitioners of violence. And, as noted earlier, the difficulty of defining private security, or mercenary, will undercut regulatory legislation.

While regulation of mercenaries is necessary, it provides only an incomplete solution. Even aboveboard security companies can only temporarily address some of the problems of a deeply troubled state. At best, foreign personnel offer a breathing space for African political and economic reform.

Indigenous political change will determine African stability and whether Africa continues to call on unregulated mercenaries. Much of Africa has been moving, however haltingly, along a democratization path, which may increase regime legitimacy and improve military professionalism. Nigeria provides an important example of how a democratically elected government, in the words of President Olusegun Obasanjo, is trying to "reprofessionalize" its armed forces. Nigeria and the United States, respectively, have provided MPRI with $4.5 million and $7 million to upgrade the military's administrative and combat capability.[25] Specific areas of attention include human rights observance, military justice, legislative relations, and payroll management. This partnership illustrates two of this chapter's major contentions: that state and private security can be complementary and that regulated commercial security can assist state development.

NOTES

1. The difficulties that international organizations face when defining *mercenary* are discussed subsequently.

2. *Equitable Securities Research*, August 27, 1997, quoted in Alex Vines, "Mercenaries, Human Rights, and Legality," in *Mercenaries: An African Security Dilemma*, ed. Abdel-Fatua Musah and J. 'Kayode Fayemi (London: Pluto, 1999), 169.

3. Richard Cheney, now U.S. vice president, served during this period as Halliburton's chief executive officer and chairman of the board ("Peacekeeping Helped Cheney Company," Associated Press, August 28, 2000).

4. This chapter focuses on Africa, which has more private security operations than any other continent.

5. Katanga (now Shaba) was a breakaway province of the Congo in the early 1960s, and the eastern region of Nigeria declared itself Biafra in the mid-1960s. Both secessionist attempts failed.

6. The Cold War hurt overall African development. Outside powers helped to stabilize numerous states but often did so by propping up authoritarian rulers with political, financial, and military assistance. Stability, in other words, worked against political and economic development. Superpower rivalry sometimes intensified local conflicts, as in Ethiopia and Angola, when non-Africans provided military hardware.

7. Robert Jackson and Carl Rosberg, "The Marginality of African States," in *African Independence: The First Twenty-Five Years*, ed. Gwendolyn Carter and Patrick O'Meara (Bloomington: Indiana University Press, 1985); Thomas Callaghy, "The State as Lame Leviathan: The Patrimonial Administrative State in Africa," in *The African State in Transition*, ed. Zaki Ergas (London: Macmillan, 1987).

8. Niccolò Machiavelli, *The Prince* (New Haven: Yale University Press, 1997), 44, 46.

9. Enrique Ballesteros, *Report on the Question of the Use of Mercenaries as a Means of Violating Human Rights and Impeding the Exercise of the Right of Peoples to*

Self-Determination, U.N. Doc. E/CN.4/1997/24 (1997), 93, www.un.org/documents/ga/res/44/a44r081.htm.

10. Wilfred Burchett and Derek Roebuck, *Whores of War: Mercenaries Today* (Harmondsworth: Penguin, 1977), 17. The authors are referring specifically to mercenaries serving the white Rhodesian government.

11. "Secrecy in Colombia," http://www.janes.com/regional_news/americas/news/fr/fro10329_1_n.shtml.

12. Max Weber, *The Theory of Social and Economic Organization* (New York: Free Press, 1964), 154.

13. The United Nations International Convention against the Recruitment, Use, Financing, and Training of Mercenaries (1989; www.icrc.org/ihl/nsf/0/6478) and the Organization of African Unity's Convention for the Elimination of Mercenarianism, reprinted in *Documents of the Organization of African Unity* (New York: Mansell, 1992), 58.

14. According to the MPRI Website, www.mpri.com/channels/home.

15. "Mercenaries' Rage Kindled by Atrocities," *Times of London*, January 24, 1999. The single-day accomplishments against the RUF by Will Scully, an ex-SAS officer, show the force multiplier capability of one individual (Will Scully, *Once a Pilgrim* [London: Headline, 1998]).

16. Elizabeth Rubin, "An Army of Their Own," *Harper's*, February 1997, 45.

17. See "Executive Outcomes and Private Security," in Herbert Howe, *Ambiguous Order: Military Forces in African States* (Boulder: Lynne Rienner, 2001), 203–4.

18. "War and Piecework, *The Economist*, July 10–16, 1999, 67.

19. Several recent examples of cost savings include the following: In the mid-1990s, the Angolan government acknowledged a defense budget of about $500 million for the Angolan Armed Forces, which could not contain Jonas Savimbi's UNITA. The government's stated payment to EO, which did contain UNITA, was $40 million. Similarly, EO probably cost the Sierra Leonean government far less than what it paid for its larger and less capable national military. U.S. defense officials agree with ICI claims that the company completed its logistics task for ECOMOG in Liberia and Sierra Leone for a third of what the U.S. military would have charged.

20. www.mpri.com/channels/home.

21. Quoted in Musah and Fayemi, eds., *Mercenaries*, 18.

22. Vines, "Mercenaries," 170.

23. Ibid., 171.

24. This section borrows from Herb Howe, "Global Order and Security Privatization," *Fletcher Forum* 22 (summer 1998): 2; and Howe, *Ambiguous Order*.

25. Interview, MPRI official, January 2004.

6

The Costs of Legalized Gambling

An Economic Approach

John Warren Kindt

Introduction

The United States entered the twenty-first century in a positive economic mood, notwithstanding the significant market correction that followed. Along with a record bull market and economic optimism, state legislatures and Native American tribal governments propelled a gambling boom during the 1980s and 1990s. This boom has been built largely on two myths. First, gambling invigorates an economy. Second, gambling, remarketed by the industry as "gaming," is a benign form of family entertainment like theme parks, sports, and the movies.

Behind these myths lies the reality that commercial gambling produces several negative externalities. Like the more commonly cited examples of industrial pollution and exhaustion of scarce resources, the effects of gambling on communities extend far beyond the immediate impacts. This extended impact often obfuscates the origin of the problem, leaving cleanup costs to the public sector.

Myth #1. "Gambling invigorates an economy." Widespread decriminalization during the 1980s and 1990s resulted in a $10.4 billion industry in 1982 expanding to a $50 billion industry in 1997.[1] As evidence of economic invigoration, a 1996 Arthur Andersen report financed by the gambling industry's lobbying organization claimed that legalized gambling was accounting for 300,000 direct and 400,000 "indirect" jobs as well as stimulating new economic development.[2] However, an explosion of gambling can have an economic value far less real than gross dollar amounts imply. While the cash explosion of any newly unleashed cash enterprise creates the illusion of development, the sanctioned boom in gambling does not change its basic economic principles. As Nobel laureate Paul Samuelson indicates, gambling activities are simply "sterile transfers of wealth."[3] When analyzed on a regional/strategic basis, gambling produces no net gain in real economic activity despite the impressive sums of money that change hands.

Myth #2. "Gambling is a benign form of family entertainment." Unlike traditional family diversions, such as movies and tourism, legalized gambling depends on the creation of new gamblers (who may become addicted) and fosters bankruptcies and crime. Contrary to the illusion of painless prosperity, a gambling boom is not an engine of real growth for the host economy. Rather, it is a parasite. Furthermore, there is reason to believe that increased legalization[4] and access[5] to gambling not only increase growth in the legal market, but result in the growth of illegal gambling as a "shadow market," because illegal gambling acts as a competitor by providing: (1) better odds, (2) better credit, (3) better service, and (4) a heightened sensation factor.[6] In fact, there are no authoritative studies indicating that legal gambling activities draw gamblers away from the illegal gambling market. Legalization of gambling simply makes it easier to pass taxpayers the bill for gambling's socioeconomic fallout.

Gambling has been cyclically recriminalized throughout modern history in recognition of the economic realities rather than in response to temperance crusades. Turkey, for example, legalized casinos in 1983 and experienced widespread addictions, bankruptcies, crime, and corruption, which resulted in the recriminalization of casinos in 1998.[7] In another example, India recognized that its lotteries were making poor people poorer, with social negatives paralleling the experiences in Turkey. Therefore, India recriminalized the lottery in 1998 despite intense lobbying by U.S. gambling interests.[8] In the United States, economic history indicates that the costs of legalized gambling are so great that they have not been fully or even reasonably internalized to the gambling industry. As a result, gambling has been criminalized at the conclusion of each gambling wave. According to this cyclical perspective, the current boom of American gambling is likely to end with recriminalization.[9]

A "wave" or "cycle" of gambling refers to the pattern of decriminalization, realization of costs, and eventual recriminalization. The country's first wave came in the aftermath of the American Revolutionary War. The second cycle paralleled the Civil War. The limited records surviving from both eras show a dramatic upswing in the societal ills and a dramatic reduction in such ills following the recriminalization phase of each wave. The negative social and economic effects associated with legal and illegal gambling were so apparent that the Ohio State Constitution of 1851, for example, prohibited "absolutely" all gambling. By the beginning of the twentieth century, there was very little legal gambling in the United States. In 1910, when New York and Nevada outlawed gambling and casinos, virtually no legalized gambling existed in the nation. Isolated states slowly began to decriminalize gambling. For example, Nevada legalized gambling again in 1931, and the gambling industry there became well established by 1946. In 1964, almost a century after the last state lotteries had been abolished, New Hampshire reopened its state-run lottery. By 1974, eleven states had lotteries, and in 1977 legal casino gambling was introduced in Atlantic City, New Jersey. In the 1980s and 1990s, legalized gambling spread throughout the United States, ushering in the country's third wave of legalized gambling. By 2001, gambling in some form had taken hold in every state except Hawaii and Utah.[10]

The complexity of this third wave exceeds that of the first two in several aspects: the range and diversity of modes of gambling; gambling's image makeover from vice to social and leisure pastime; its interactions with host economies and communities; and its impact on local, regional and national economies. By the twenty-first century, citizens and the government alike began to recognize gambling's downside. The complexity that distinguishes this wave from earlier ones is evidenced by the range of participants in the debate. In considering the third wave of gambling in the United States, this chapter will discuss the legitimization of gambling, the definition of gambling and its related aspects, and negative externalities associated with gambling. The chapter will conclude with policy implications.

The Legitimization of Gambling

The majority of Americans consider gambling to be a legitimate form of entertainment. Most adults have participated in some form of gambling, and only 10 percent believe that gambling is not acceptable for anyone.[11] The public's overall attitude toward gambling tends to influence the types of regulations that public policy officials will impose on the industry. Lobbyists must convince state officials that gambling is a profitable investment for their state, and these officials must sell this concept to the public.[12]

Lobbyists

The American Gaming Association is a political lobbying group located in Washington, D.C., that has consistently argued that gambling stimulates the economy and raises revenue for community projects.[13] Furthermore, gambling is advertised by the industry as a way for state governments to generate significant revenue without raising taxes.[14] However, antigambling activists claim that the social and economic costs of gambling clearly outweigh the supposed benefits. This argument has entered the political arena, but the gambling industry has remained quite successful at achieving its goals.[15]

The gambling industry is represented in Washington, D.C., by some of the most powerful individuals in both political parties, and the relationship between legislators and gambling institutions has grown quite comfortable. The industry lobbies tirelessly and makes enormous political contributions.[16] While lawmakers are receiving campaign contributions from gaming interests, efforts to curb the expansion of gambling practices continue to fail. By the end of the twentieth century, gambling interests were legally influencing politicians by contributing large amounts of soft money to key state legislators' campaigns in the hopes of casino-friendly legislation. According to a study by the Center for Responsive Politics, the gaming industry ranked thirty-seventh among ninety-two industry and special interest groups in 1998 election contributions.[17] In Florida, for example, the industry spent more than $16.5 million in 1994 to campaign for pro-casino legislation, exceeding the cost of both gubernatorial campaigns combined.

The Role of Government

The state has played a key role in legitimizing and expanding the gambling industry. Legislators have argued for the introduction of legal gambling on the basis of politically acceptable "higher purposes," including economic stimulation, job creation, tax benefits, and revitalization of tourist destinations.[18] Governments have also introduced gambling as a way of dealing with fiscal crises. Claims on gambling profits alone are a powerful incentive for states to encourage people to participate in all legal games. The state government keeps approximately 7.5 cents of every dollar bet at the racetrack and 40–45 cents of every dollar spent on the state lottery.[19] Therefore, the development and expansion of gambling activities reflects the state's revenue needs rather than ethical or constitutional considerations.[20]

The gambling laws passed during the 1930s and 1970s were clearly financial measures enacted in times of economic crises. Legalization of casino gambling in Nevada in 1931 exemplifies the use of gambling to meet the state's financial needs. When the Nevada Territory was created, commercial gambling was declared a felony, and betting was considered a misdemeanor. As a result, gambling prospered illicitly, and the operators of illegal gambling activities received money that had once supported the legal markets. The onset of the Great Depression increased Nevada's critical need for funds, and the state eventually decriminalized commercial gambling.[21] Yet it is notable that Franklin Roosevelt's administration did not decriminalize gambling on a strategic level, as an anathema to U.S. economic recovery overall. After the decriminalization of gambling in Nevada, New Hampshire voters approved the state lottery in 1964, and in 1976 New Jersey became the second state to legalize Las Vegas–style casino gambling.[22] Gambling is now considered one of the fastest growing sectors of the national economy.

Over the past several decades, shifts in government policies have contributed to the general acceptance of legal gambling.[23] States that operate lotteries have helped transform a previously illegal and hidden activity into one that has sponsorship, active encouragement, and the blessing of the state.[24] Politicians and legislators who opposed gambling during the 1970s and 1980s began to view it as a new source of revenue without new taxes. It has thus been argued that state governments have contributed to the breakdown of moral opposition to gambling by becoming lottery operators.[25] The public's demand for gambling surges when gambling's status shifts from illegal to legal.[26]

Finally, advertisement plays a large role in the legitimization of gambling activities, particularly when endorsed by the state. Today, lotteries are the most profitable public enterprise owned by the state, ranking second behind higher education as the most important product sold to the public.[27] States advertise gambling to increase the number of lottery players and the amount of money they spend.[28] Indeed, lottery and gambling advertisements can be found in almost every mass-marketing venue, including television, radio, Internet, newspapers, billboards, and buses.

Defining the Problem

As the debate on the merits and problems of gambling intensifies, there is little consensus on the fundamental question of what constitutes gambling. Because a standard definition of it would better serve the cause of reform, it is not surprising that such a definition is absent from most of the industry-sponsored inquiries into gambling's ills. For example, the recent *Final Report* of the National Gambling Impact Study Commission (NGISC) offers no definition of its subject.[29] (As discussed later in this chapter, the commission was initially stacked in favor of the industry.)

When definitions of gambling are offered, they merely demonstrate the difficulties involved. Journalist Timothy O'Brien encapsulates "the classic legal definition" of gambling as "any activity that involves three things: consideration (i.e., a cash bet), chance, and a prize."[30] Though this definition is exemplary for being both general and succinct, it includes activities that most of the public would not readily identify as gambling, such as charity raffles and derivatives. Moreover, it allows some forms of gambling to slip through the criteria. For example, a sports gambler stakes a consideration on athletes' relative abilities, not on mere chance. The annual U.S. national gambling ritual of pools on the Academy Awards operates not on chance but on the revelation of a mystery.

In another attempt to define gambling, Ronald M. Pavalko describes rather than defines the activity, stressing two ideas that are useful in working toward a definition—risk and convention. Risk may involve chance, skill, or a combination of these and other determining forces. A computer poker game programmed to pay off at a certain ratio is not operating on chance, for example. Because risk is an element of much economic activity, however, Pavalko concedes that it is not peculiar to gambling. Whether the risking of a given consideration against the prospect of a prize constitutes gambling, Pavalko argues, is a question decided by convention.[31]

This paraphrase of the "we know it when we see it" mentality brings the discussion back to the initial query regarding the definition of gambling. However, to identify gambling as a subset of risk-driven ventures that convention calls gambling does more than beg the question. It infers that gambling is a part of U.S. culture that takes many forms and is difficult to isolate in any one set of activities, distinct from other activities in the range of human entertainment, transactions, investments, and acts of irrationality.

Provisional acceptance of a non-definition or the convention-based definition offers theoretical benefits for understanding gambling. First, the admission that gambling has several dimensions implies that an effort to address gambling activities as a class must also consider the various forms of gambling activities. In considering any one form, analysts must look at its specifics: which elements produce what effects. Analysts must consider its inherent odds. The analysis should include not just the likelihood of a monetary loss versus a payoff but also the chance of real benefits versus detriment to the immediate community, the resulting social enhancement versus social deterioration and the self-serving financial actions of those who sponsor it. Second, using a conventional definition of gambling indirectly points out that many ordinary activities could reasonably be called gambling. The difficulty of isolating gambling from other activities that involve a "gamble" speaks to the public's great ingenuity at inventing new ways to put assets at risk (for example, derivative investments). Whatever definition of gambling one uses, it reveals the widespread urge to engage in activities involving chance, consideration, and a reward, which indicates an inclination toward gambling that is rooted in human nature.

Problem and Pathological Gamblers

Next arises the need to define the two categories of gamblers with which society is concerned: problem and pathological gamblers. The American Psychiatric Association's *Diagnostic and Statistical Manual of Mental Disorders* lists the criteria by which to diagnose these disorders.[32] These criteria focus on three areas: "damage or disruption, loss of control, and dependence."[33] It is generally accepted that a patient who satisfies five or more of the ten criteria constitutes a pathological gambler, while a patient satisfying fewer than five criteria would be classified as a "problem" gambler. A more widely accepted set of criteria is the South Oaks Gambling Screen developed by Professor Henry Lesieur, which has been the academic standard for most studies in the 1980s and 1990s. The National Research Council Review on Pathological Gambling noted that in 1999 the American Psychiatric Association used *abuse* or *dependence* rather than *addic-*

tion. However, the majority of academic literature tended to delimit pathological gambling as an "addiction" until the 1990s, when the gambling industry began funding studies that obfuscated the issues and tried to recategorize pathological gambling as a "compulsion." In any event, it was still universally accepted that pathological gamblers are largely defined by the destructive behaviors in which they engage. They often commit crimes, run up large debts, damage relationships with family and friends, and/or commit suicide.[34]

Research and the Gambling Industry

A review of the literature highlights other issues as academics seek to understand gambling's impact on individuals and society. First, the research and researchers seem to be biased in favor of the gambling industry. Second, the gambling industry attempts to influence the relevant research. Third, research fails to address some of the critical issues of gambling.

A clearinghouse for answers about the spread of pathological gambling was envisioned by Congress when enacting the NGISC in 1996. While there was some balance between commissioners predisposed toward gambling and those critical of it, a breakdown of the nine Commission members reveals that the progambling faction also represented the casino industry. Three commissioners had career-long ties with the Nevada-based industry, and a fourth commissioner represented Indian tribal governments dependent on casinos.

Unsurprisingly, the NGISC failed to obtain basic and essential information that would highlight the casinos' exploitation of problem and pathological gamblers. The NGISC was urged—to no effect—to solicit the missing analyses from industry-financed data collections, such as the Harvard Addictions Meta-Analysis (discussed later in this chapter), and to request and be prepared to subpoena the high-rollers list from every U.S. casino. The Commission's *Final Report* shows a clear bias in favor of the casino gambling industry as scrutiny is consistently diverted away from casino gambling and focused on the casinos' competitors, including pari-mutuel operations, "convenience" and Internet gambling, and lotteries.

The gambling industry also influences research on the impact of gambling by funding academic studies, thereby affecting the nature of the gambling that researchers consider. In fact, studies financed by the gambling industry have admitted that they were "benefit-benefit" studies rather than cost-benefit studies. For example, the 1998 Missouri study financed by Civic Progress chose not to analyze or even consider socioeconomic

costs.[35] In addition, the 1996 Arthur Andersen study of preselected industry positives[36] specifically stated that it made "no attempt to analyze the
socioeconomic effects of . . . gaming."[37]

Another example of how the gambling industry influences research of
important issues relevant to gambling is the first commissioned report of
the National Center for Responsible Gaming, a $140,000 project financed
by the gambling industry and generally known as the Harvard Addictions
Meta-Analysis. This analysis omits the summary totals for the pathological gamblers and problem gamblers reported by the 120 to 152 studies analyzed. In 1998 the NGISC was urged to prod the authors of the Harvard
Addictions Meta-Analysis to present the number of pathological and
problem gamblers reported in the analyzed studies, a process that would
have been relatively simple. NGISC, with several members that represent
the gambling industry, did not even request this basic background research
from the Harvard authors. The net effect was the suppression of research
information potentially embarrassing to the gambling industry.

The industry's studies for internal use customarily focus on how quickly
and efficiently money can be extracted from the public. Research also considers techniques to accomplish these goals, such as faster gambling technology and more sophisticated marketing ploys. In addition, large amounts
of funding go to research to market gambling, with the goal of attracting
new gamblers.

The Negative Socioeconomic Consequences of Legal Gambling

Despite the gambling industry's attempt to dominate the research on gambling and thereby obfuscate its more negative effects, research on the topic
does reveal the consequences of gambling for society. This impact comes
in many social and economic forms, including increases in the number of
gambling addicts, in bankruptcies, in crime, and in the social and economic costs thereof. Furthermore, the impact of gambling extends beyond
the United States and has negative consequences for the economic stability of other nations.

Addiction

The industry's intense commitment to the expansion of gambling is man-
ifest in the figures for gambling's growth in the last quarter of the twentieth century as well as its recent about-face embrace of Internet gambling.

(Even MGM-Mirage chairman J. Terrence Lanni described his shift as a "180-degree turn.")[38] The relationship between the excessive gamblers and profits is arguably a motivating force for increased expansion. Furthermore, the virtual inevitability of some gamblers going bust argues for a reliable supply of new gamblers.

The gambling industry has used two methods to expand the supply of new gamblers. First, certain models of gambling specifically appear to encourage excessive gamblers. In 1997, for example, Colorado began to use a "Mindsort" model for the lottery system. Research on the model has indicated that consistent gamblers exposed to various techniques to encourage gambling were "lower on [marketing] trial, but once hooked, hooked."[39] Second, an extensive media campaign has also increased the pool of potential gamblers by shaping the public attitude toward gambling. In 1997, the *Chicago Sun-Times* conducted an in-depth survey that indicated that lower-class individuals viewed instant games as a source of income. In another survey that targeted gamblers, respondents revealed that they were gambling to win money rather than for entertainment.[40] Without those gamblers, casinos would not only be unable to finance their lavish shows, constant expansion, and famously lavish decor but arguably would go broke. Behind the sequins and neon and free day care, a sophisticated machine cranks away. As *Time* reported in 1997,

> By purchasing lists from credit-card companies, the casinos know what you buy, and then they can track census data to approximate your home value and income. Then there are the direct-mail lists. One such list from the early 1990s was baldly called the "Compulsive Gamblers Special" and promised to deliver, 200,000 names of people with "unquenchable appetites for all forms of gambling." Another list features "some 250,000 hard-core gamblers." Yet another purveys the names of 80,000 people who responded to a vacation-sweepstakes-telemarketing pitch.[41]

Gambling interests have argued that the marketing and advertising are aimed at maintaining already active gamblers. Figures on the rising rates of new gamblers suggest otherwise. For example, during a time of rapid gambling expansion between 1994 and 1997, the number of pathological gamblers in the United States increased 50 percent to 1.5 million and the number of problem gamblers increased to 3.5 million.[42]

Addiction creates both economic and social costs. First, gambling addicts often face economic hardship as a result of their addictions. For example, in one night they can lose not only their paychecks but also their entire assets, including all of their retirement savings (particularly with self-directed retirement accounts). This scenario is only exacerbated by gambling on the Internet,[43] which has the potential to place gambling at every workstation, in every home, and even in schools. Another economic cost of gambling addiction occurs in the business and public sectors. Pathological and problem gambling are estimated to cost insurance companies $6.6 billion in insurance fraud per year and $13.2 billion in surrendered policies per year.[44] Finally, it is estimated that new pathological and problem gamblers created between 1994 and 1997 have cost the taxpayers between $24 billion and $88 billion in taxes during that three-year period (with gambling industry–financed estimates at the lower range).[45]

One social cost of gambling addiction is the risk it presents in the military environment. By definition, pathological gamblers are not only addicted but are compromised by their addiction, which is quite problematic when the addicts are military personnel. For example, in 1995, the U.S. Air Force commander, General John M. Loh, provided the military's general perspective on this problem: "I am generally opposed to riverboat [casino] gambling near our bases because of the problems it creates for our people and the communities in which they live."[46] Business groups near military bases provide a similar perspective, stating, "We have talked to almost all of the base commanders in Tidewater [Virginia] and found *none* who favor Riverboat Gambling. . . . Riverboat gaming will drive our military [bases] away."[47] In one case involving illegal off-base slot machines, air force personnel lost between 13 and 19 percent of the entire base's monthly payroll. In addition, two lieutenants who were pathological gamblers committed suicide.[48] By 1997 the 1,257 illegal slot machines involved in this 1951 scenario had been replaced by 11,624 off-base legal video slot machines.[49] By 1999 it was public knowledge that in this same area, during one three-month period, there were five gambling-related suicides by military personnel. An additional economic cost of gambling for this particular military base came in the form of instituted "gambling awareness" classes for military personnel.[50]

Bankruptcy

Increases in the bankruptcy rate since the mid-1990s coupled with the rapid expansion of the gaming industry have prompted critics of gambling to raise questions about a possible connection between the two. According to industry representatives, there exists no possible link.[51] However, studies for the American banking industry vehemently refute the findings of the gambling lobbyists and suggest that gambling is the fastest-growing cause of personal bankruptcy to date.[52]

In favor of gambling critics is research that compares the rates of bankruptcy in regions with legalized gambling against the rates in regions that prohibit it. A 1997 study conducted by the SMR Research Corporation reported that bankruptcy rates were 18 percent higher in counties with a gambling facility (than in non-gambling countries) and 35 percent higher in counties with five or more gambling facilities. Additionally, the bankruptcy rate in Nevada was 50 percent higher than the national average, and the bankruptcy rate in Atlantic City was 71 percent higher than that of any other county in New Jersey.[53]

Furthermore, research indicates that the 1998 annual U.S. bankruptcy cost as a result of legalized gambling was at least $3 billion, with 105,000 new bankruptcy filings.[54] Specifically, problem gamblers accounted for at least $1 billion, with 30,000 new bankruptcy filings. These 1998 numbers were projected to increase by 50 percent by 2004 as more of the new pathological (addicted) gamblers finally bottom out.

Gambling, Crime, and Its Costs

Gambling also has a criminogenic effect with an associated economic cost. Virtually all pathological gamblers commit crimes, with a tendency toward committing multiple property crimes, including white-collar crimes. In fact, 42 percent of pathological gamblers admit stealing from their employers.[55] For example, one pathological gambler in Iowa embezzled $4.5 million,[56] and a banker in the same state embezzled $10.2 million.[57] As a result of criminal activity, experts and studies prior to 1999 reported that between 12.5 percent and 15 percent of pathological gamblers would become incarcerated. Even the 1999 NGISC *Final Report* indicated that 23 percent of pathological gamblers and 13 percent of problem gamblers would eventually be incarcerated.[58]

The massive increase in crime and concomitant incarceration adds significantly to society's gambling bill. Based on an incarceration rate of 12.5 to 15 percent of new pathological gamblers, taxpayers paid at least $2 billion between 1994 and 1997 for incarceration associated with gambling-related crimes. This estimate may be conservative, however, in light of NGISC's 1999 reported rates of incarceration—23 percent for pathological gamblers and 13 percent for problem gamblers.[59] The true cost and extent of crime motivated by a gambling addiction remains hidden, however, since the crimes are often committed against family and friends who choose not to report the incidents.

Destabilizing Foreign Economies

A final economic concern is the impact which the U.S. gambling industry has on the stability of financial systems in foreign countries. As the United States influences gambling standards for the world, the spread of U.S. legalized gambling during the 1980s and 1990s precipitated and then catalyzed the acceptance of legalized gambling in other countries. In addition, the gambling industry has been active in exporting U.S. gambling technologies and philosophies to other countries. It is also important to note that as the U.S. public backlash against gambling gained momentum during the 1990s, U.S. gambling interests intensified their efforts to expand in other countries.

Less-developed countries such as Mexico, Taiwan, Namibia, and nations in the Pacific Rim region in the mid-1990s began to view casinos as valid strategies for economic development. For example, in 1986 and 1987, Mexico was a recipient of billions of dollars in loans from the United States and the World Bank, who loaned the money with the intent to support a country suffering from economic and financial instabilities. Upon receipt of these funds, Mexico announced that part of its economic salvation would involve bringing U.S. casinos to Mexico City.

Bringing in casinos has not proven to be an economic salvation for some countries. During the 1997 economic crisis in the Pacific Rim region, Taiwan and other countries had been flirting with developing their own gambling industries. This move toward gambling was backed by gambling technology exported from the United States. The spread of legal gambling contributed to economic instability in a region which already lacked political stability, infrastructure, and the cultural norms essential to regulate gambling in any country.

Calculating the Costs of Gambling

With the increase in gambling across the country, it is important for governmental decision makers to know how to calculate some of the socio-

economic costs of increased gambling activity. With an understanding of
the extent of the costs, steps can be taken to slow the trends and eventually reverse gambling's impact on an area. Therefore, the three steps to calculating the strategic socioeconomic costs of pathological and problem
gambling will be reviewed.

Step One: Calculate the Relevant Population Base

On a regional/local level, the population base should be totaled to correspond as closely as possible with the "feeder market" populations; in gambling industry studies, these are usually defined geographically, as the
thirty-five-mile radius and the one-hundred-mile radius around the proposed gambling facilities.[60]

Step Two: Calculate the Relevant Percentages of
Pathological Gamblers and Problem Gamblers

With a population of 5.5 million, Missouri serves as a state example. The
baseline of .77 percent pathological gamblers[61] and 2.33 percent problem
gamblers[62] before legalized gambling in Missouri increased to 0.84 percent
for pathological gamblers[63] and approximately 2.93 percent for problem
gamblers by 1994.[64] By 1997 another 0.5 percent of Missouri's population
had become pathological gamblers, and another 2 percent had become
problem gamblers.[65]

Once the relevant population base is established, the same percentages
can be generally applied to a number of groups within the state. Therefore,
the increased percentages in the base rate[66] would generally transpose to
the state's businesses, such as banks, insurance companies, financial institutions, credit agencies, manufacturing companies, and service companies.
Between 1994 and 1997, for example, an average company with one thou-

TABLE I.

	1976[a]	1994[b]		1997[c]
Pathological Gamblers	.77%	.84%	(.5% Increase) →	1.29%
Problem Gamblers	2.33%	2.93%	(2% Increase) →	4.88%

[a]U.S. Commission, *Gambling in America*, 73.
[b]Harvard Addictions Meta-Analysis, 43, tables 13, 16.
[c]Ibid.

sand employees would have experienced a .5 percent increase in pathological gamblers in its workforce and a 2 percent increase in problem gamblers.

Studies have targeted specific populations of interest. For example, as a
general rule, the percentages of pathological and problem adolescent gamblers are double those of the adult population.[67] While adolescents do not
have the asset base of adults, resulting in lower calculations of the socioeconomic costs of adolescent addiction, it is relevant to consider that this
is the first U.S. generation since the 1890s raised to believe that gambling
is an acceptable activity and provides career opportunities.

Furthermore, in a 1991 study, the U.S. military established a baseline of
2 percent pathological gamblers and 5.1 percent problem gamblers. Using
the general population increases from 1994 to 1997 reported in the Harvard Addictions Meta-Analysis, by 1997 the anticipated increases among
military personnel were 50,250 new pathological gamblers (a 66 percent
increase) and 162,000 new problem gamblers (a 108 percent increase), for
new respective costs of $2 billion and $1.6 billion per year.[68] This raises
serious questions about national security issues of military readiness.

*Step 3: Multiply the Numbers (and Increases) by the
Socioeconomic Costs of One Pathological Gambler
and/or One Problem Gambler*

According to experts, each pathological gambler creates socioeconomic
costs of between $10,000 (partial listing of costs)[69] and $80,000[70] per year.
A conservative range of $30,000–50,000 per year is quite reasonable.
Applying these figures to the earlier example of Missouri, from 1994 to
1997, the socioeconomic costs to the state's taxpayers increased $830 mil-
lion plus $1.1 billion, for a total of nearly $2 billion.[71] Until the market is
saturated (e.g., Las Vegas has a reported 8 percent pathological gamblers
and 8 percent problem gamblers),[72] the number of pathological gamblers
in Missouri will probably increase at a rate of 0.15 per year, while the
state's rate of problem gamblers will increase at a rate of 0.7 percent per
year, resulting in a cost increase to taxpayers of $633 million per year. The
same rates would apply to Michigan after Detroit initiated downtown
casino gambling and would result in increased socioeconomic costs of at
least $45 million per year for pathological gamblers and $70 million per
year for problem gamblers.

Conclusion/Policy Implications

One option to reduce the negative externalities associated with gambling is recriminalization. Some observers have considered this option for U.S. gambling and lotteries except in Nevada, Atlantic City, and some Native American locations. Because of the economic impacts of eliminating Indian gambling establishments, they could be phased out over a five-year period, with gambling revenues going into a federal trust fund to benefit Native Americans as well as to transition the gambling buildings and other resources into long-term education establishments. Proponents of this policy suggest that money diverted from gambling would be pumped back into the consumer market,[73] crime costs associated with new problem gamblers would be reduced, and trends in socioeconomic costs would be reversed. Criminalization advocates also cite research suggesting that fewer opportunities to gamble lead to fewer addictions.[74]

Recriminalization, however, is not the only option. The fight against the tobacco and alcohol industries illustrates two methods of reducing negative externalities. First, the tobacco industry came under fire from the public and the government when the media publicly exposed the industry's manipulation of addiction statistics and its purposeful attempts to encourage problematic smoking. Similarly, the government and the media should seek to expose the gambling industry's marketing techniques designed to attract and expand the pool of potential pathological and problem gamblers.

Second, both the tobacco and the alcohol industries have suffered economic attacks through litigation. The tobacco industry has made substantial payments for smoking-related health costs. The alcohol industry also received a wake-up call in the form of liability for the destructive actions of drunk patrons. Arguably, the gambling industry should be held responsible for the destructive actions of the gamblers whom it cultivates and exploits. Legislation should recognize the right to litigation for those entities harmed by resulting bankruptcies, including banks, credit card companies, public treasuries, and even spouses and children. Such a right-of-action approach would cut into gambling revenues significantly enough to force the industry to reform and rethink its approach.

Research on gambling also suggests ways to reduce negative externalities without recriminalizing gambling. Eighteen- to twenty-five year-olds have been found to be the age segment that suffers from the highest rate of gambling addiction.[75] Raising the minimum gambling age to twenty-five could help decrease the number of pathological gamblers since those most prone to addiction would be prevented from participating in legal gambling. In fact, even the NGISC has recommended that gambling remain restricted for anyone under twenty-one.[76]

Another recommendation is to change the current structure of lotteries and casinos. First, states should consider privatizing the lottery system. States have supported lotteries under the guise of earmarking its revenues for state expenses, most commonly education. However, lotteries have not proven to be the financial salvation proponents envisioned. Therefore, some researchers have suggested that governments exit the lottery business, allowing nonprofit organizations and other gaming operations to take over. State governments could continue to make money off the industry by taxing the licenses to sell lottery tickets and lottery winnings.

States should also consider changing the regulatory schema for casinos, which could have a variety of results. Regulators commonly limit the number of casino licenses in each state, thereby ensuring that initial casinos have economic success and that job opportunities remain stable. According to Richard McGowan, this stability is costly.[77] Allowing casinos to compete with each other would give customers more choices and higher payback. Casinos, like any other industry, should have to prove their ability to operate successfully.

Furthermore, some predict that competition is the most apparent threat to the gaming industry.[78] Industry representatives complain that there are too many casinos and not enough players. This market saturation will ultimately provoke fierce competition among the states and the gaming industries. In the past few years, several casinos and casino operators in Las Vegas and Atlantic City have gone bankrupt.

Finally, the NGISC has suggested a number of areas for further study.[79] Existing federal, state, local, and Native American tribal government policies and practices should be reviewed with respect to the legalization or prohibition of gambling, including the costs of such policies and practices. The relationship between gambling and levels of crime should be assessed, as well as existing enforcement and regulatory practices intended to address any such relationship. Further assessments should also be performed of pathological and problem gambling, including the impacts on individuals, families, businesses, social institutions, and the economy generally, including the role of advertising in promoting gambling and the impact of gambling in depressed economic areas. Studies are also necessary to analyze the extent that gambling provides revenues to state, local, and

Native American tribal governments, as well as what possible alternative revenue sources may exist for such governments. The interstate and international effects of gambling by electronic means, including interactive technologies and the Internet, need particular scrutiny and should be banned to maintain economic stability of expectations.[80]

ABBREVIATED BIBLIOGRAPHY

In addition to the *Final Report* of the NGISC, from the overall U.S./strategic perspective, the most relevant authoritative reports remained as follows:

a. *Addictions*
Alcohol and Drug Abuse Administration, Maryland Department of Health and Mental Hygiene. *Task Force on Gambling Addiction in Maryland* (Dr. Valerie C. Lorenz and Dr. Robert M. Politzer, cochairs). Baltimore: State of Maryland, 1990 (esp. 58–61).

b. *Bankruptcies*
SMR Research Corporation (George R. Yacik, vice president). *The Personal Bankruptcy Crisis*. Hackettstown, NJ: SMR Research, 1997 (esp. 116–30). Summarized in "New National Study Shows Correlation between Gambling Growth and the Significant Rise in Personal Bankruptcies." *Business Wire*, June 26, 1997.

c. *Crime*
Dr. Subhasis Das, ed. *Casinos in Florida: An Analysis of the Economic and Social Impacts*. Tallahassee: Office of Planning and Budgeting, Florida Office of the Governor, 1994 (esp. executive summary and 66–76).

The authoritative *Casinos in Florida* was paralleled by the classic overview in

Better Government Association of Chicago (Terrence Brunner, executive director). *Staff White Paper: Casino Gambling in Chicago*. Chicago: Better Government Association, 1992.

To visualize the strategic/regional impact of gambling, a short report was

California Governor's Office of Planning and Research. *California and Nevada: Subsidy, Monopoly, and Competitive Effects of Legalized Gambling*. Sacramento: State of California, December 1992.

NOTES

The analysis in this paper has been updated and modified from the statement and testimony of Professor John Warren Kindt before the hearing of the National Gambling Impact Study Commission, Chicago, May 21, 1998.

1. *National Gambling Impact Study Commission, Executive Summary* (Washington, DC: Government Printing Office, June 1999), 3. See also John W. Kindt, testimony and tables presented before the National Gambling Impact Study Commission, Chicago, May 21, 1998.

2. Arthur Andersen, *Economic Impacts of Casino Gaming in the United States: Macro Study* (Las Vegas: Arthur Andersen, December 1996), 3, 7 (commissioned by American Gaming Association). See *National Gambling Impact Study Commission, Executive Summary*, 4 (reporting only the claimed total as "700,000 direct and indirect jobs"). Arthur Andersen, Enron's auditing firm, no longer exists.

3. See Paul A. Samuelson, *Economics*, 10th ed. (New York: McGraw-Hill, 1976), 425. Samuelson won the 1970 Nobel Prize in economics.

4. The "acceptability factor" means that the more types and forms of gambling become acceptable by being legalized, the more increases there will be in the numbers of pathological and problem gamblers.

5. The "accessibility factor" means that the more accessible various forms of gambling are to the public, the more increases will occur in the numbers of pathological and problem gamblers.

6. See generally, National Gambling Impact and Policy Commission Act: Hearing on H.R. 497 before the House Committee on the Judiciary, 104th Cong., 1st sess. (1995), 60–89. See also Peter Reuter, "Police Regulation of Illegal Gambling: Frustrations of Symbolic Enforcement," *Annals of the American Academy of Political and Social Sciences* 474 (1984): 36.

7. See, e.g., Daren Butler (Reuters News Service), "Casino Industry Nears Final Days in Turkey," *St. Louis Post-Dispatch*, February 4, 1998, p. A8; Associated Press, "Edict in Turkey Closes Casinos in Anti-Crime Move," *Chicago Tribune*, February 12, 1998, sec. 1, p. 16.

8. See "India Plans Lottery Ban," *USA Today*, July 5, 1998, p. A26; Neelesh Misra (Associated Press), July 4, 1998. For increasing trends in the numbers of pathological and problem gamblers, see Howard J. Shaffer, Matthew N. Hall, and Joni Vander Bilt, Division on Addictions, Harvard Medical School, "Estimating the Prevalence of Disordered Gambling Behavior in the United States and Canada: A Meta-Analysis," (Division on Addictions, Harvard Medical School, December 15, 1997), appendix 2 [hereinafter Harvard Addictions Meta-Analysis]; "Harvard Medical School Researchers Map Prevalence of Gambling Disorders in North America" (press release), December 4, 1997 (from .84 percent in 1993, "the prevalence rate for 1994–1997 grew to 1.29 percent of the adult population").

9. John W. Kindt, "U.S. National Security and the Strategic Economic Base: The Business/Economic Impacts of the Legalization of Gambling Activities," *St. Louis University Law Journal* 39 (1995): 567–84.

10. John W. Kindt, "The Business-Economic Impacts of Licensed Casino Gambling in West Virginia: Short-Term Gain but Long-Term Pain," *West Virginia University Public Affairs Reporter* 13 (1996): 22–25; Ronald J. Rychiak, "The Introduction of Casino Gambling: Public Policy and the Law," *Mississippi Law Journal* 64 (1995): 291–362.

11. Ronald M. Pavalko, *Risky Business: America's Fascination with Gambling*

(Belmont, CA: Wadsworth, 2000); Meir Gross, "Legal Gambling as a Strategy for Economic Development," *Economic Development Quarterly* 12 (1998): 203–12.

12. Robert Goodman, *The Luck Business* (New York: Simon and Schuster, 1995), 1–14.

13. John W. Kindt, "Follow the Money: Gambling, Ethics, and Subpoenas," *Annals of the American Academy of Political and Social Science* 556 (1998): 85–97.

14. Jennifer Vogel, *Crapped Out* (Monroe, ME: Common Courage Press, 1997), 28–48.

15. Ibid., 4, 6–7, 49.

16. Ibid., 4, 6, 11–40, 49.

17. American Gaming Association, Fact Sheets, 1999, http://www.aga.com.

18. Goodman, *Luck Business*, 1–14.

19. See Vogel, *Crapped Out*, 47–66; Gross, "Legal Gambling," 208–10.

20. See Tyler Bridges, *Bad Bet on the Bayou* (New York: Farrar, Straus, and Giroux, 2001), 149–69, 371–75.

21. See Goodman, *Luck Business*, 15–19, 130.

22. Gross, "Legal Gambling," 208–10.

23. Bill Kearney, *Comped* (Philadelphia: Ian-Scott Press, 2000), 79–89.

24. Gross, "Legal Gambling," 204–7.

25. See John W. Kindt, "Legalized Gambling as Subsidized by Taxpayers," *Arkansas Law Review* 48 (1995): 889–931.

26. John M. Eades, *Gambling Addiction* (Winchester, TN: John M. Eades, 1999), 16–17; see Henry R. Lesieur, *The Chase*, 2d ed. (Rochester, VT: Schenkman Books, 1984), xiii–xxvii.

27. Vogel, *Crapped Out*, 59–78.

28. Ibid., 137–60.

29. *National Gambling Impact Study Commission, Final Report* (Washington, DC: Government Printing Office, June 1999) [hereinafter *NGISC Final Report*].

30. Timothy L. O'Brien, *Bad Bet: The Inside Story of the Glamour, Glitz, and Danger of America's Gambling Industry* (New York: Random House, 1998), 12.

31. Pavalko, *Risky Business*.

32. American Psychiatric Association, *Diagnostic and Statistical Manual of Mental Disorders*, 4th ed. (Washington, DC: APA, 1994), 617–18, section 312.31.

33. *NGISC Final Report*, 4-1.

34. National Research Council, "Pathological Gambling: A Critical Review" (Washington, DC: National Research Council, April 1, 1999), p. Exec-2.

35. Charles Levin, Don Phares, and Claude Louishomme, "The Economic Impact of Gaming in Missouri," April 1998 (commissioned by Civic Progress Group, St. Louis, MO), 73.

36. See, e.g., statements of Professor William Eadington, University of Nevada—Reno, Panel Discussion, Tenth International Conference on Gambling and Risk Taking, Montreal, Canada, May 31–June 4, 1997. (The communities selected for the Arthur Andersen study would be expected to yield positive local impacts, but the casinos in the Kansas City economy are probably draining a net $40 million per year from the area, and the Kansas City economy is so large that these economic losses go unnoticed.)

37. Arthur Andersen, *Economic Impacts*, 1.

38. *New York Times*, May 17, 2001 [Web edition].

39. Mindsort (Denver: Colorado Lottery Commission, 1996), 15 (emphasis added). See Joanne Conte, "Case Study of Colorado Advertising and Marketing," paper presented at the Marketing and Public Policy Conference, American Marketing Association, Arlington, Virginia, June 5–6, 1998 (discussing the Colorado Lottery's Mindsort marketing and other advertising concerns involving gambling).

40. Tim Novak and Jon Schmid, "Lottery Picks Split by Race, Income," *Chicago Sun-Times*, June 22, 1997, pp. 1, 24–25. See also Mississippi State University Gambling Group, Social Science Research Center, *National Gambling Survey* (1995). Summarized in Division on Addictions, Harvard Medical School, *The Wager*, March 17, 1998.

41. S. C. Gwynne, "How Casinos Hook You: The Gambling Industry Is Creating High-Tech Databases to Reel in Compulsive Players," *Time*, November 17, 1997, 68, 69.

42. See, e.g., Harvard Addictions Meta-Analysis, 43, tables 13, 16.

43. Gambling on the Internet is illegal under the Wire Act, 18 U.S.C., sec. 1084, but to tighten controls U.S. Senator Jon Kyl sponsored new legislation. See S.474, The Internet Gambling Prohibition Act of 1997: Hearing before the Subcommittee on Technology, Terrorism, and Government Information, Senate Committee on the Judiciary, 105th Cong., 1st sess., July 28, 1997. This bill became the model for subsequent legislation, which came close to passing during subsequent congressional sessions and was reintroduced in 2004.

44. Henry R. Lesieur and Kenneth Puig, "Insurance Problems and Pathological Gambling," *Journal of Gambling Behavior* 3 (1987): 123 (adjusted to 1997 dollars).

45. John W. Kindt, "The Costs of Addicted Gamblers: Should the States Initiate Mega-Lawsuits Similar to the Tobacco Cases?" *Managerial and Decision Economics* 22 (2001): 44, table A3.

46. Letter from U.S. Air Force Commander General John M. Loh to U.S. Representative Herbert H. Bateman, February 10, 1995 (citing specific negative impacts of recently opened riverboat casino on Barksdale Air Force Base, Louisiana).

47. Know Casinos (business group, William Kincaid, cochair), memorandum to Virginia cities, September 1, 1995 (opposing proposal for Virginia casinos).

48. Hearing on "Illegal Gambling Activities Near Keesler Air Force Base," Preparedness Subcommittee, U.S. Senate Committee on the Armed Services, Biloxi, Mississippi (1951).

49. Ben C. Toledano, "Gambling 'Carpetbaggers' Make Mississippi a Lesson to Other States," *Omaha (Nebraska) World Herald*, April 13, 1997, B13 (abbreviated reprint of April 7 *National Review* article).

50. John W. Kindt, "Gambling with Terrorism and U.S. Military Readiness: Time to Ban Video Gambling Devices on U.S. Military Bases and Facilities?" *Northern Illinois Law Review* 24 (2003): 1–39.

51. American Gaming Association, Fact Sheets.

52. "When the Wheels Won't Stop: Statistics Show That Compulsive Gam-

bling Is Becoming a Problem for a Growing Number of Americans," *The Economist*, December 13, 1997, 22.

53. SMR Research Corporation, "The Personal Bankruptcy Crisis" (commissioned by the American Banking Industry) (Hackettstown, NJ: SMR Research, 1997).

54. Kindt, "Costs," tables A4, A5, and accompanying footnotes.

55. Kindt, "Costs," 47, table A8, and accompanying footnotes.

56. Debra Illingworth Greene, "Gambling: Wins and Losses," *The Lutheran*, December 1997, 46, 47.

57. Henry R. Lesieur, "Pathological Gambling, Work, and Employee Assistance," *Journal of Employee Assistance Research* 1 (1992): 32.

58. NGISC Final Report, 7–14.

59. Ibid.

60. For the United States: http://www.census.gov/population/estimates/nation/intfile2–1.txt; for Canada: http://www.statcan.ca/english/Pgdb/People/Population/demo10a.htm.

61. U.S. Commission on the Review of the National Policy toward Gambling, *Gambling in America* (Washington, DC: U.S. Government Printing Office, 1976), 73.

62. Ibid.

63. Harvard Addictions Meta-Analysis, 43, tables 13, 16.

64. Ibid.

65. Ibid.

66. Ibid. See also Kindt, "Costs," 44, tables A1–A2 and accompanying footnotes.

67. See Kindt, "Costs," 48, table A10 and accompanying footnotes; Harvard Addictions Meta-Analysis, 51, table 16; John W. Kindt, "The Economic Impacts of Legalized Gambling Activities," *Drake Law Review* 43 (1994): 51, 66, nn. 117–18.

68. See Kindt, "Costs," 48, table A11.

69. Ibid., 44, table A3 and accompanying footnotes.

70. Alcohol and Drug Abuse Administration, Maryland Department of Health and Mental Hygiene. *Task Force on Gambling Addiction in Maryland* (Dr. Valerie C. Lorenz and Dr. Robert M. Politzer, Cochairs) (Baltimore: State of Maryland, 1990), 59–61.

71. *The National Impact of Casino Gambling Proliferation: Hearing before the House Committee on Small Business*, 103d Cong., 2d sess.(1994), 77, 80. See also generally, Kindt, "Economic Impacts," 90–91, table 3.

72. Professor Frederick W. Preston, University of Nevada—Las Vegas, paper presented at the National Conference on Gambling Behavior, National Council on Problem Gambling, Chicago, Sept. 3–5, 1996. See also Frederick W. Preston, Ricardo Gazel, and Bo Bernhard, "Gambling in Las Vegas: Survey of a Gaming Supportive Community," at sec. 4.1–4.2 (reporting lower rates of 5.3 percent pathological gamblers and 2.6 percent problem gamblers). It is significant that pathological gamblers in Las Vegas outnumber problem gamblers by a ratio of two

to one. In most studies, the problem gamblers greatly outnumber the pathological numbers.

73. See Kindt, "U.S. National Security," 567; National Gambling Impact and Policy Commission Act: Hearing on H.R. 497 before the House Committee on the Judiciary, 104th Cong., 1st sess. (1995), 519–45 (statement and article of Professor John W. Kindt).

74. Robert D. Carr, Jerome E. Buchkoski, Lial Kofoed, and Timothy J. Morgan, "Video Lottery and Treatment for Pathological Gambling," *South Dakota Journal of Medicine* 49 (1996): 30.

75. See, e.g., Kindt, "Economic Impacts," 66.

76. *NGISC Final Report*, 3–17, rec. 3.2.

77. McGowan, A. Richard. *Government and the Transformation of the Gaming Industry* (Northampton, 2001).

78. John W. Kindt, "Legalized Gambling Activities: The Issues Involving Market Saturation," *Northern Illinois Law Review* 15 (1995): 271–306.

79. *NGISC Final Report*, 8-2, 8-3, 8-4, 8-5, recs. 8.1–8.20.

80. Ibid.

7

The Licit and Illicit Trade in Antiquities

Patty Gerstenblith

Introduction

The international market in antiquities is both big business and booming business. While the fortunes of the art market fluctuate with the global economy in general and the stock market, in particular, the consistent pattern over the past twenty-five years has been one of considerable growth in the numbers of objects offered for sale both privately and through public auction and in the prices that these objects bring. The art market is most often viewed by and portrayed to the public in its benign functions. A dealer may foster and promote new artists, bringing them to the attention of potential patrons who will purchase their works, thereby allowing the artist to work and eventually win fame and recognition. Dealers and auction houses may also cultivate collectors, who buy objects and artworks offered for sale. Collectors may care for these works for a number of years, eventually donating them to museums, where they become available to the general public for education and enjoyment and to academics and scientists for research. Those who engage directly in the art market and who benefit pecuniarily from it—primarily dealers and auction houses—have associated themselves in the American mind and in the minds of legislators with public institutions, such as museums, and thus taken on an altruistic and educational facade. Yet all is not as benign as it may appear. The art market imposes significant negative externalities on both the public and the specialized audience through its methods of operation and through its intentional or unintentional ignorance of the background of many of the works that pass through the market. This chapter will illustrate these externalities and demonstrate the extent to which the legal and illegal aspects of the international market for antiquities are so tightly connected that it is difficult for outside observers, and even specialists, to separate the two.[1] This permits the market to transfer what seems to be a large proportion of illegally acquired objects with the result that archaeological sites and cultural monuments are being looted and dismembered throughout the world, with a concomitant loss of scientific, historical, and cultural information that would significantly inform our understanding of the past.

This situation is fostered by a number of quirks in both the national and international legal regimes. For example, the fact that foreign nations do not enforce other nations' export controls and that there are significant differences between the common law and civil law systems allow for the "laundering" of antiquities through European civil-law countries. Some professional organizations, such as the International Council of Museums, have passed codes of ethics and professional conduct that attempt to go further than what the law requires. However, these codes lack any enforcement mechanisms, and professional organizations are reluctant to expel or discipline members. The art market has successfully tapped into the strong U.S. emphasis on free markets and the fact that we have very few import or export controls. However, an unfettered trade in undocumented antiquities does not bring the same public benefits, such as an improved economy and more jobs, as does free trade in ordinary commercial goods.

The challenge confronting the law is to devise a system in which the distinction between the legal and illegal incorporates the public policy concern for preservation and in which the negative effects on preservation through the unregulated activities of the art market are eliminated. This requires imposing financial and legal consequences on the participants in the market in undocumented antiquities, holding these participants accountable for the negative effects of their activities. In addition, public perceptions must be changed so that it becomes a stigma to acquire looted cultural objects, and our major cultural institutions must incorporate this change into their practices. Finally, our public institutions must take their educational role more seriously and adopt practices that reflect not merely the minimum that the law requires but the highest standards established through codes of ethical conduct.

Description of the Industry

The struggle over cultural artifacts—objects of great artistic, historic, or religious significance—is not new. Even in ancient Mesopotamia, military victors plundered conquered cities for artistic and cultural trophies. Although the Romans made it a routine practice to carry off cultural monuments as a prize of war and symbol of victory, what was perhaps the first prosecution for theft of cultural objects occurred in the time of the Roman republic. The looting of cultural objects revived during the Renaissance but took on its modern form only in the early nineteenth century. The use of ancient historic and artistic objects as symbols of modern national identity and political legitimacy received a new incarnation in the Napoleonic dream of re-creating Paris as the "new Rome." In pursuit of that dream, Napoleon moved to Paris numerous Italian and Roman artworks, including the Apollo Belvedere, the Laocoon, and the Discobolus from the Vatican and Capitoline museums. In fact, Napoleon took artworks from much of Europe, including Belgium, the Netherlands, Austria, Russia, and Germany as well as Italy (in addition to the antiquities carried off from Egypt). Immediately after Napoleon's defeat, the victors demanded restitution in the 1815 Treaty of Vienna, although many of these artworks never found their way home.

The justification for this movement was presented to Napoleon in a 1796 petition, signed by many of the great French artists of the day, that stated,

> The Romans, once an uncultivated people, became civilized by transplanting to Rome the works of conquered Greece. . . . Thus . . . the French people . . . naturally endowed with exquisite sensitivity will . . . by seeing the models from antiquity, train its feeling and its critical sense. The French Republic, by its strength and superiority of its enlightenment and its artists, is the only country in the world which can give a safe home to these masterpieces. All other Nations must come to borrow from our art, as they once imitated our frivolity.[2]

Since that time, the justifications for the looting of cultural objects have changed little. Proponents first focus on the benefits that will accrue to the individual or nation by taking possession of the cultural objects and, second, assert a right to the object based on a moral or intellectual superiority. The third element of this justification is an expression of altruism—because the possessor has a greater ability to care for the object, the possessor is, in fact, not acting primarily for its own benefit but rather for the benefit of everyone else (all humanity), including the original owner.

Napoleon's attempt to re-create the new Rome in Paris was answered by the British desire to re-create London as the new Athens. Thus, Lord Elgin's taking of the Parthenon sculptures to London and their later acquisition by Parliament for the British Museum fit into the political reality of the military rivalry between France and Britain in the early nineteenth century. Recent revelations concerning doubts about the legality of Elgin's original transactions, about Elgin's allegedly altruistic motives, and about the British Museum's care of the Marbles, particularly during the 1930s, have not changed the official British attitude toward the Marbles, and their presence in London endures as the preeminent symbol of cultural heritage dispossession.[3] This continues despite Greek requests to have the Marbles returned for the 2004 Olympics to be held in Athens and the construction of a new museum near the Acropolis where all the Parthenon sculptures would be reunited.

In the second half of the nineteenth century and the first half of the twentieth, military codes of conduct began to recognize that artistic works should not serve as plunder or war booty. The Lieber Code, formulated during the U.S. Civil War, and the early Hague Conventions of 1899 and 1907 gradually incorporated this principle. However, not until World War II, with its massive destruction and movement of cultural objects and monuments, did the international community think it necessary to craft a legal regime specifically for the protection of cultural heritage. The Hague Convention on Protection of Cultural Property in the Event of Armed Conflict, formulated in 1954, was the first international convention devoted exclusively to this issue.

While threats to cultural heritage caused by war and military conflict have not ceased—as illustrated by recent situations in the former Yugoslavia, Afghanistan, and Iraq—another threat appeared in the years following World War II. With the postwar expansion of wealth and economic power (particularly of the United States, Western Europe, and Japan), the international art market has grown and flourished. In the movement of cultural objects the art market often works in tandem with war and other misfortunes, as attested by the appearance on the international stage of Iraqi objects for sale, beginning with the looting of regional museums and the economic boycott following the 1991 Gulf War and recently renewed with the 2003 looting of the Iraqi National Museum and archaeological sites during the spring 2003 U.S.-led attack on the country.

Another characteristic of the market is that it has expanded beyond the traditional artistic or aesthetically pleasing objects to include a range of utilitarian antiquities as well as ethnographic objects representative of the various indigenous cultures. The increasing role of the market in the movement of cultural objects provided the impetus for a second international convention: the 1970 United Nations Educational, Scientific, and Cultural Organization (UNESCO) Convention on the Means of Prohibiting and Preventing the Illicit Import, Export, and Transfer of Ownership of Cultural Property.

Much of the current debate focuses on the operation of the international art market and in particular on the extent to which this market combines legal and illegal trade. While relatively few people might consciously choose to enter an illegal market, many people do so unwittingly. Conversely, some buyers backed by considerable wealth and prestige are willing to do so to attain rare, perhaps unique, "museum-quality" pieces.

Objects are looted from archaeological sites, including ancient habitation areas and burials, and even buildings and monuments are dismembered so that sections of architecture, wall carvings, mosaics, and paintings can be removed. These objects then move through the market from the looter to the smuggler, to auction houses and dealerships, and finally to private collectors and museums in major cities in Western Europe, North America, and Japan. This movement was first chronicled by Clemency Coggins, who wrote in 1969 of the dismemberment of monumental sculptures in Central America and their subsequent smuggling into the United States, where they were sold. A few years later, Karl Meyer documented the looting of sites in both Central America and the Mediterranean in his book, *The Plundered Past*.[4]

Since then, market-driven looting has spread throughout much of the world. Some of this phenomenon has been documented in occasional published court cases, while much more of it has been documented in newspaper articles and scholarly journals. Although relatively few disputes go through litigation with results that become publicly known, even this small sample reveals some interesting data. Claims for recovery of cultural objects or prosecutions for theft have involved the nations of Guatemala (monumental wall reliefs and pre-Columbian artifacts),[5] Mexico (pre-Columbian artifacts),[6] Cyprus (Byzantine church wall mosaics),[7] Peru (Inca artifacts),[8] and the Central European nations of Hungary and Croatia (the Sevso Treasure, a hoard of silver and other objects dating from the

Roman empire that Sotheby's brought to New York for auction).[9]
Another case that was ultimately settled out of court involved a collection
of Mycenaean jewelry and artifacts in the possession of dealer Michael
Ward. The collection, reportedly purchased for $150,000 but priced by the
gallery at $1.5 million, was ultimately returned to Greece, and Ward
received a charitable tax deduction in return.[10]

Three claims in the late 1980s and 1990s involved the Republic of
Turkey. The first of these sought the return of the Lydian Hoard, held for
more than twenty-five years in New York's Metropolitan Museum of
Art.[11] The hoard of more than 360 objects included fragments of wall
paintings; marble sphinxes; vessels such as pitchers; bowls and incense
burners made of gold, silver, and bronze; and gold, silver, and glass jewelry.
The Lydian Hoard began its long journey in the mid-1960s, when tumuli
in the Uşak region of west-central Anatolia, reputed to contain treasures
dating from the time of King Croesus of Lydia, were broken into and
looted. Although police recovered some objects, many of the finest were
smuggled out of Turkey and ended up in the hands of antiquities dealers in
New York. Between 1966 and 1970, the objects were acquired by the
Met's Department of Greek and Roman Art.

Rumors of the Met's acquisitions began to circulate during the early
1970s. Although the Met's documents reveal that the museum recognized
the objects as among its greatest acquisitions, the purchase of this collection received relatively little publicity.[12] Finally, when a few objects were
placed on display in 1984, the Republic of Turkey identified the treasure
and sued to recover it. After six years of expensive and time-consuming litigation, when discovery was finally ordered, the Metropolitan agreed to
settle the case and return the treasure to Turkey.

At about the same time, it was alleged that half of a statue known as the
Weary Herakles, jointly owned by the Boston Museum of Fine Arts and
private collectors Shelby White and Leon Levy, had been looted from
Turkey. The other half of the statue was found in southwestern Turkey.
Turkey's claim has never been resolved, but it was established through
comparison of plaster casts that the two halves join and that the break is
fresh, indicating that the breakage and theft are recent. Part of the statue
is now on display in the local museum at Antalya, while the other fragment remains in Boston.[13] A third claim brought by Turkey was for return
of a hoard of approximately seventeen hundred rare and valuable ancient
coins, including several Athenian decadrachms minted in 465 B.C. and in

very good condition. These coins were looted directly from the ground, like the Lydian Hoard, and after several years of litigation, U.S. businessman William Koch agreed to return the coins to Turkey.[14]

A more recent case is particularly illuminating because the facts of the case published in the court's opinion shed considerable light on how an antiquity of considerable monetary value and historical interest moved from where it was found through the market and ultimately to the home of a wealthy New York collector, Michael Steinhardt.[15] This case involved a gold phiale of Sicilian origin, which, based on the Greek Doric inscription on its rim could be dated to the late fourth or early third century B.C. In 1980, a Sicilian antiquities collector traded the phiale to a Sicilian coin dealer, Vincenzo Cammarata, for artworks valued at about $20,000. Cammarata later indicated that the bowl had been found during work to install electric light poles in a state-protected archaeological area in Caltavuturo, near Palermo. The phiale was subsequently acquired by a Swiss art dealer, William Veres, in exchange for objects valued at approximately $90,000. Robert Haber, a New York art dealer, then arranged to purchase the phiale on behalf of his client, Steinhardt, who had agreed to pay approximately $1.2 million (including Haber's 15 percent commission).

Steinhardt asked no questions about the dealer's claim to ownership and agreed to pay for the phiale in two installments, pending the outcome of analysis as to its authenticity by experts at the Metropolitan Museum of Art, which has in its collection a near-twin of the phiale. A one-page document entitled "Terms of Sale" was executed and signed by Veres. It provided for compensation to Steinhardt in the event that the object was confiscated by Customs or a claim was made by any country or governmental agency. The document further provided that a "letter is to be written by Dr. Manganaro which is an unconditional guarantee of the authenticity and Swiss origins of the object." Haber manually crossed out the words following *Manganaro* and rewrote the sentence to provide that a "letter is to be written by Dr. Manganaro that he saw the object 15 years ago in Switz." Manganaro never agreed to write a letter asserting the Swiss origins of the object and never provided such a letter.

In December 1991, Haber flew to Switzerland to take possession of the phiale in Lugano, a town near the Swiss-Italian border that is known as a transhipment point for antiquities smuggled out of Italy. Haber then went to Geneva and from there returned with the phiale to New York. The customs forms listed Switzerland as the phiale's country of origin and stated its value at $250,000. The steep increase in the value of the bowl between

Sicily and New York and the bowl's transfer through Switzerland, a country that has no cultural patrimony laws, show how the market operates. Another interesting addendum is that in December 1998, Italy arrested most of the Italians involved in this transaction, including Cammarata and Manganaro. Antiquities valued at approximately $35 million were found hidden in Cammarata's home. The government authorities concluded that the group's activities demonstrated clear links to the Mafia.[16]

Continuing with the example of Italy, other documentation exists for the extent of the trade in illegal antiquities and, in particular, for the use of Switzerland as a point through which antiquities are transferred so that they can be "laundered" and then appear on the international market with clean backgrounds. It has been documented that looting affects nearly 50 percent of recorded sites and archaeological areas under the supervision of the Italian regional archaeological superintendencies. Between January 1991 and April 1993, Italian law enforcement officials recovered more than sixty-eight hundred illicitly excavated artifacts in the southern Italian province of Taranto alone.[17] In January 1997 Swiss authorities seized the contents of warehouses at the Geneva airport's free transit zone, which included ten thousand Italian antiquities worth $42.5 million.[18] The antiquities, some of which were destined for auction at Sotheby's in London, had been illicitly excavated from sites all over Italy. In fact, revelations regarding the Sotheby's London office dealings in illegal antiquities eventually led to the closing of its antiquities department after publication of Peter Watson's book, *Sotheby's: The Inside Story*.

The most significant recent legal decision, which also shed considerable light on the operation of the antiquities market, is the conviction of the prominent New York dealer Frederick Schultz.[19] Until shortly before his indictment in 2001, Schultz was the president of the National Association of Dealers in Ancient, Oriental and Primitive Art. Schultz was charged with conspiring to deal in antiquities stolen from Egypt in violation of the National Stolen Property Act (NSPA). In 1983, Egypt enacted a law vesting ownership of all antiquities that had not yet been unearthed in the nation. Excavation and removal of such antiquities without permission of the Egyptian government constitutes theft, and such objects, when brought to the United States, are still characterized as stolen property. The NSPA criminalizes the knowing import of stolen property that is worth more than $5,000.

Schultz defended the charge on numerous bases including the notion that such antiquities are not truly stolen property. He also claimed that prosecution should be limited to the handling of cultural objects stolen from the documented inventory of a museum or other public collection, as the Cultural Property Implementation Act (which will be discussed later) has a special provision for the forfeiture and return of such objects. Both the trial court and the appellate court rejected Schultz's legal theories. He was convicted in February 2002 on the single conspiracy count and has been sentenced to serve thirty-three months in jail.

The Schultz prosecution was considerably assisted by the testimony of Schultz's coconspirator, the British restorer Jonathan Tokeley-Parry. Tokeley-Parry had previously been convicted and served a prison sentence in Britain for handling stolen property. Tokeley-Parry would paint over newly discovered antiquities to make them look like cheap tourist souvenirs so that he could smuggle them out of Egypt. Once the objects were in London, he would remove the paint and restore them. Among the objects he and Schultz handled was a head of the Egyptian Eighteenth Dynasty pharaoh Amenhotep III, which Schultz sold for $1.2 million. Of the greatest interest were Tokeley-Parry's records that revealed that he and Schultz fabricated a false "old collection," which they dubbed the Thomas Alcock collection. They claimed that these objects came from this old collection, supposedly formed in the 1920s. They soaked labels in tea and microwaved them to make them seem old. This evidence substantiates the notion that dealers fabricate old collections to create a false provenance, both to evade law enforcement and to induce purchasers to acquire recently looted antiquities. The decision is also significant because it clearly establishes that the federal court with jurisdiction for the New York area recognizes that antiquities taken in violation of a national ownership law are stolen property. This may have an impact on the methods by which dealers and auction houses do business in relation to archaeological objects and on both museum and private collecting.[20]

Asia has gained new attention in recent years. For years architectural sculptures have been removed from Cambodia, including from the World Heritage site of the fabled temples at Angkor Wat.[21] These works are smuggled across the border to Thailand and from there to the market in different parts of the world. Also the subject of controversy are antiquities looted from China. In March 2000, a tenth-century marble sculpture was about to be sold at auction by Christie's in New York when it was seized by U.S. Customs officials. Chinese officials had recognized the sculpture from the auction catalog as one of ten that had been taken by raiders who "blasted their way into the Five Dynasties tomb of Wang Chuzhi in Hebei

Province, in northeastern China, in 1994." At the request of the Chinese government, U.S. Customs filed a civil forfeiture suit to take possession of the sculpture, estimated to be worth $500,000. The complaint filed by the U.S. government says that "the sculpture's stone, carving style, pigments and decoration match those of other artifacts in the tomb. . . . [T]he size of the sculpture precisely fits an empty space in the tomb."[22] The relief panel was returned to China in May 2001.[23]

Watson also documented that participants in the art trade commonly do not inquire too closely into the background of objects being sold. In this sense, the art market differs from most other industries based on the sale of goods.[24] In *Porter v. Wertz*, the New York State Supreme Court commented that the dealer's

> claim that the failure to look into [the seller's] authority to sell the painting was consistent with the practice of the trade does not excuse such conduct. This claim merely confirms the observation of the trial court that "in an industry whose transactions cry out for verification of . . . title . . . it is deemed poor practice to probe." Indeed, commercial indifference to ownership or the right to sell facilitates traffic in stolen works of art. Commercial indifference diminishes the integrity and increases the culpability of the apathetic merchant.[25]

In summary, Manus Brinkman, secretary-general of the International Council of Museums, stated, "Everybody knows certain things are stolen, or should know it, and yet these things still appear on the market. . . . This involves famous dealers and art houses, not just shady operators. . . . And it's not only from China. . . . It's Cambodia and Thailand, Peru and Bolivia, Nigeria and Eastern Europe."[26]

Negative Effects of the Trade

The trade in artworks has two negative effects. First, the trade often involves artworks that are simply stolen from public or private collections. This aspect of the market has received considerable attention in the past few years because of the information that has come to light concerning the artworks stolen by the Nazis during World War II. To this extent, stolen artworks are not necessarily different from other types of stolen personal property, except in the fact that, as mentioned earlier, it has been the art trade's common practice not to inquire too closely into the background of objects sold. What has caught the attention of the public and the media concerning the artworks looted during the Holocaust is not just the wide-scale theft and expropriation of artworks during the war but also the fact that many of these artworks are still offered casually for sale today, despite a few well-publicized court cases and voluntary restitution.[27] It has taken considerable political pressure for the art market and for museums to respond to the fact that they are at least complicit in the aftereffects of these thefts.

The second and more significant negative externality applies specifically to the trade in antiquities and goes well beyond the original owner's loss of his property, significantly affecting the development of scientific and historical knowledge about the past. The illicit art market is valued at $2–6 billion annually, and it draws from archaeological sites throughout the world—from the United States, Latin America, Europe, Africa, the Middle East, and Asia. Interpol now lists the illicit art trade as ranking second or third among international crimes, in company with the trade in illegal weapons and the trade in illegal drugs. Lynne Chaffinch, program manager for the Art Theft Program of the Federal Bureau of Investigation, and Angela Meadows, former cultural property program manager at INTERPOL—U.S. National Central Bureau, stated in an interview that "internationally cultural property theft transcends into every other criminal enterprise. This has also included violent crimes, such as murder, assault and kidnapping."[28] Since the 1970s, illicit traffic in antiquities has increased dramatically, in part as a result of the inflation of the art market and the marketing of antiquities as investment opportunities. The trade in antiquities has also become one of the easiest ways to launder money internationally. The consequences for archaeological sites, monuments, and local collections have been dire.

Preservation of the archaeological and historical context in which an object is found is a matter of utmost importance to modern society. In the past, collections were often built by simply taking works of art and antiquities from ancient sites. These collectors' actions were perhaps not terribly different from what early archaeologists did, and until at least the mid–nineteenth century it was not easy to tell the looters from the archaeologists. Even though their methods might today be criticized, early archaeologists such as Heinrich Schliemann working at Troy, Sir Arthur Evans at Knossos on Crete, Sir Flinders Petrie in Egypt and southern Palestine, and later Dame Kathleen Kenyon in Jericho and Jerusalem gradually developed the scientific understanding of stratigraphy of sites and the need to excavate a site layer by layer, with each layer representing a time period and all objects and architectural features within a layer bearing a chronological relation that has significance for the understanding of the ancient world's history, social organization, and cultural life.

Preservation of an object in situ often allows it to be placed in its correct chronological sequence and to be used to date other objects, architectural features, and even entire stratigraphic levels. This preservation also allows those studying past cultures to reconstruct the functions of such objects and to learn more about diet, technology, trade, living patterns, religion, and literature—in short, about every aspect of a past society. Once the object is ripped out of that context, this knowledge is lost forever. Most archaeologists believe that it is better to leave an object or a site unexcavated, temporarily undiscovered, than to risk the loss of such irretrievable information.

Concern for the preservation of this type of knowledge led much of the archaeological and scientific community to adopt codes of ethics and academic conduct. This concern has also led to attempts to restrict the market in objects of undocumented origin (provenance). If the demand for looted objects could be eliminated, the looting of sites would be discouraged and the archaeological context preserved for future study. The imposition of legal consequences on purchasers is intended to reduce demand.

Several scholars working with material cultural remains from different parts of the world have tried to quantify the extent of this looting and its effect on the ability of modern historians and scientists to reconstruct the past. Studying eight published collections of pre-Columbian antiquities containing 2,300 objects, Professor Ricardo Elia of Boston University found that not a single object had been obtained from a legal excavation.[29] Furthermore, of the total known corpus of 341 terra-cotta figures from Mali, 91 percent have no documented source.[30] For these objects, it is not possible to determine where they were found, their authenticity, or the significance of unique types. Similarly, Dr. David Gill and Dr. Christopher Chippindale conducted an extensive study of Cycladic figurines of the third millennium B.C. and determined that 90 percent of the known figurines do not have a provenance, which means that nothing is known about their archaeological contexts.[31] These figurines have been highly prized by collectors for their eerie resemblance to modern sculptures, and a large number of them flooded the market during the 1960s, '70s, and '80s. Demand for these figurines produced such a large, undocumented supply that it is now thought that many are likely fakes. It has become virtually impossible to tell the genuine from the fake figures. At the same time, an estimated 85 percent of Cycladic burial sites have been destroyed by looting.

A second quantitative study conducted by Gill and Chippindale is a comparison of seven contemporary classical collections, all of which were exhibited and published in catalogs during the 1990s.[32] The study categorized objects by the information concerning provenance—that is, the degree of certainty and specificity with which the object's find spot was reported—and the length of time during which the object was known. This study revealed that 74 percent of the objects in these catalogs have no indication of archaeological origin aside from what can be deduced from stylistic features, only 9 percent of the objects have a history documented before 1945 or can be traced back to the ground, 74 percent surfaced after 1973, and 38 percent made their first appearance at the time of the exhibition in the 1990s.

Yet another study, by Emily Salter, focused on catalogs published since World War II by the various major London auction houses.[33] Once again, approximately 95 percent of the objects auctioned had no indication of where they were found, while just under 90 percent of the objects had no information regarding previous owners. The author commented on these statistics, "Silence is always the rule, surprising since it is so much a rule of collecting that objects with provenance [are] worth more than those without, and those with a provenance considered good—either in archaeological terms (findspot) or historical (previous owners)—are worth even more."

Professor Ricardo Elia has studied Apulian red-figured vases, utilizing a similar quantitative methodology.[34] The category of Apulian red-figured vases is stylistically distinct and comes exclusively from sites in southern Italy. In addition, all known vases in both public and private collections were cataloged and published between 1978 and 1993.[35] Again, some of the statistics that emerged from this study are particularly striking. For example, an average of nine tombs must be excavated to find one Apulian vase (the exact numbers vary depending on the relative wealth of the individuals buried), and one tomb will contain perhaps forty to fifty other types of objects. Thus, for each looted Apulian vase, as many as four hundred other objects are also looted and their contexts destroyed. Thousands of tombs must have been looted to produce the known corpus of Apulian vases. Elia's study also compiled data on the current locations of Apulian vases (both by type of collection and by country). While 9,347 vases were known as of 1980 (representing approximately two hundred years of collecting activity), some 4,284 new vases appeared in just the next twelve years. Of the total corpus of known Apulian vases, only 5.5 percent have been recovered archaeologically, 1.4 percent have precisely known find spots but were not recovered archaeologically (mostly in nineteenth-century removals of large tombs), and the rest have no contextual information. Finally, a study of auction catalogs revealed that between 1980 and 1993, Sotheby's auctioned 30 percent of the Apulian market. None of the vases auctioned by Sotheby's listed an archaeological find spot, 85 percent had no provenance information at all, and the remaining 15 percent had information relating only to previous owners or sellers.

Elizabeth Gilgan has used a similar methodology to analyze the state of cultural heritage in Belize and, more particularly, the market for Belizean antiquities in the United States.[36] Gilgan studied auction catalogs from the 1970s through the 1990s to identify and track the appearance of pre-Columbian materials on the market. In particular, she compared the volume of materials sold to the policies of the United States toward import of archaeological materials following implementation of the UNESCO Convention and requests from various countries for the imposition of import restrictions. Maya cultural remains are found in five modern countries—Mexico, Guatemala, Belize, Honduras, and El Salvador. As Guatemala and El Salvador requested and later received recognition from the United States of their export restrictions, the effect of these agreements may be seen. Gilgan was able to discern a change in the descriptions of Maya artifacts used in the auction catalogs during the 1990s. During the preceding decade, Sotheby's catalogs routinely described Maya artifacts as having originated from Guatemala's Petén region. But after 1991, when the United States imposed import restrictions on undocumented material from Guatemala, the catalog descriptions changed dramatically, using the term *lowlands*, a more vague geographic area that could apply to any of the five countries in which Maya culture flourished. This generic description, of course, makes it difficult to determine the sources of these objects and points out the need for a regional approach to the implementation of the UNESCO Convention so that the use of such terminology to obfuscate the origin of antiquities will no longer subvert internationally accepted import restrictions.

These quantitative studies are a growth area of research for scholars concerned with the preservation of cultural heritage. Such works document both the looting of sites and the correlations with the appearance of particular categories of objects on the market in the past three decades. The studies are particularly useful because they provide the hard data that legislators and policymakers often demand before changing the legal structure to confront specific social problems.

Another way to analyze the negative effects of the trade in antiquities is to examine the justifications offered by those involved in the trade and to compare them to the actual effects of the trade, thereby enabling us to discern many of the problems fostered by the trade in looted antiquities.

First, the market is said to find the collectors, both public and private, best suited to care for cultural objects. Promoters of the art market often suggest that placing a high monetary value on cultural objects is the best means of ensuring their physical protection. Yet we should recognize that the market does not always succeed even at what it purports to do best—protecting the integrity of individual objects. For example, tomb robbers and site looters often inadvertently or intentionally destroy objects, either to make them transportable or simply out of ignorance. Placing monetary value on antiquities in fact encourages theft and destruction, as looters, well aware of objects' market value, seek out the most lucrative objects. Even in remote Chinese provinces, looters have been caught with Sotheby's catalogs in hand.

Particularly for objects that end up in private collections, there are no guarantees of appropriate conservation, and objects are sometimes recut or altered in other ways to suit their owners' tastes. In a case involving the Kanakariá Church in northern Cyprus, pre-Iconoclastic Byzantine mosaics had been stolen from the curved wall of the church apse.[37] Not only were the mosaics injured while being removed, but the Indianapolis dealer who purchased them had a conservator reset the tiles, thinking that the mosaics would be more saleable if flattened. The restorer caused extensive damage to the individual tesserae and then reset them with Elmer's glue. In the process, many of the tiles were broken, and much of their depth and perspective was lost. Even after the mosaics were returned to Cyprus, the now-flattened surfaces could not be replaced in their original locations.

Second, the market is said to move objects throughout the world, thereby making them accessible to larger numbers of people. This argument always seems to assume a one-way flow—from areas of the world that are rich in cultural heritage to collections in a few major cities, primarily New York, London, Paris, Zurich, and Tokyo. Yet the numbers of people to whom these collections are actually accessible remain small. Because of nineteenth-century colonialism and the twentieth-century market, some parts of the world are today almost entirely devoid of their cultural heritage, and their people are not in a position to travel to the centers of the modern art world to see these objects. Furthermore, in this age of technology, it seems decidedly old-fashioned to suggest that the only way objects can be appreciated over distances is through their physical movement—especially if this comes at the expense of their loss of context.

Third, the market is said to serve an educational function and to inspire members of the public through appreciation of objects. Yet the market's appreciation for decontextualized objects remains mired in a one-dimensional view of the value of objects as exclusively aesthetic. While the scientific study of archaeology does not impede this aesthetic value, the unregulated market certainly impedes scientific study. I have previously given several examples of the complete or near-complete destruction of an entire corpus of knowledge as a result of the looting of sites. In the cases of the Cycladic figurines from Greece, because the majority of the examples are known first from their appearance on the market and do not come from excavated contexts, it is not possible to determine which are genuine and which are fake, nor do we have a very clear idea of their original meaning beyond the aesthetic criteria that modern scholars have imposed to make up for the lack of context. While some claim that authenticity can be determined from aesthetic evaluation or connoisseurship, the truth is that it is almost impossible to come to any definitive determination of authenticity through these methods. Even for more recent and better-documented artworks, disagreements among experts often continue for decades and never reach any conclusion. In addition, those who replicate ancient objects become more and more skilled at fooling even the scientific methods of analysis. So, for example, a modern pot made from pottery fired in antiquity can trick the analysis of thermoluminescence dating. Thus, the appearance of undocumented antiquities has severe consequences for both the aesthetic and intellectual understanding of the past, which becomes distorted beyond any recognition through the pillage of sites and sale of looted objects on the market.[38]

Fourth, source nations are said to have an excess of cultural objects and to be incapable of caring for those they have. However, the museums of North America and Western Europe are also filled with artworks and antiquities, which are often in storage, displayed occasionally, sometimes uncataloged, and not necessarily accessible either to the general public or for scholarly research.[39] This may well be part of good museum practice or the result of necessity, but museums in archaeologically rich nations also have reasons for what is displayed or not and for keeping excavated material in the region, and they should not be singled out for practices that are normal in the United States. Nor should they be subject to demands to sell off similar objects, a practice that no reputable museum professional in this country would countenance on a large scale for his or her collection.[40] Furthermore, disagreement with a country's policies or laws concerning the desirability of selling off cultural objects scarcely justifies looting and theft. Rather, such disagreement justifies increased efforts at cooperation that will enhance efforts at preservation both at home and abroad.

Even if one were to posit a world in which countries rich in cultural resources might decide to enter into a legal market, what little evidence there is indicates that such a legal trade would not stop the looting. In those countries that have permitted legal trade to be conducted, sites were still looted. Local officials believe that the existence of a legal market encourages looting and makes it easier for smugglers to trade in stolen antiquities.[41] According to a study by Dr. Patrick O'Keefe, lawyer and consultant to UNESCO, an influx of objects on the market is as likely to stimulate additional demand as to satisfy the current demand.[42] In addition, individuals and institutions with considerable wealth and prestige to back them will not be content with anything less than unique, museum-quality pieces, which are not likely to be sold off. Many tombs are looted and many cultural objects with less aesthetic appeal are destroyed in the search for pieces that will satisfy high-end collectors.

The Legal Response

National Legal Approaches

The biggest problem with defining the illicit market is determining what is illegal. Three elements can contribute to or make illegal particular types of conduct involved in the international art market: theft, smuggling (illegal import and export), and illegal excavation. The most obvious form of theft is the taking of an object that is in the possession of an individual or institution with recognized legal title to the object. In countries that follow common law (primarily the United States, Great Britain, and other countries influenced by British law), a thief cannot transfer good title to a stolen object. This may be contrasted with the situation in many civil law nations, where under certain conditions, a thief can pass title to a good-faith purchaser. However, even in the United States, an original owner's claim to recover stolen property may be barred by the statute of limitations, which restricts the length of time after an injury has occurred during which an individual can bring a claim relating to that injury. Statutes of limitations apply to most types of legal claims and have the goal of preventing the bringing of claims after evidence and witnesses are no longer available.

In most of the United States, the statute of limitations for the recovery of personal property ranges between three and six years. Most art thefts, however, involve considerably longer periods of time because it is easy to conceal artworks and it usually takes the owner many years to locate the stolen work. Thus, in theory, many of these claims should be barred. However, the statutes do not define the beginning of the time period for the statute of limitations. Should it be when the object is stolen? Or when the original owner learns the location of the object? Or when the owner asks the possessor to return it and the possessor refuses? Because artworks are easily hidden for long periods of time and owners may have difficulty learning where and whom to sue for the objects' return, several jurisdictions that are deeply involved in the art market have evolved particular rules that delay the expiration of the statute of limitations out of concern for fairness to original owners.

In New York, the courts apply a "demand and refusal" rule that provides that the statute of limitations does not begin to run until the owner has demanded that the possessor return the stolen property and the possessor refuses. This rule was used in a decision in the late 1960s involving a Chagall painting stolen during World War II and later bought by a New York collector, allowing the original owner to sue many years after the original theft.[43] The New York approach was reaffirmed as recently as 1991 in a case involving a painting stolen from the Guggenheim Foundation.[44] However, in that case, the New York court added another element in that a defendant could use a different defense, known as the equitable defense of laches, to bar the owner's claim if an unreasonable delay by the owner in some way prejudiced the current possessor.[45]

Several other jurisdictions have adopted a "discovery" rule that permits original owners a reasonable amount of time to institute recovery action after they learn or should have learned, with due diligence, the location of the artwork. This rule originated in a New Jersey Supreme Court opinion,

O'Keeffe v. Snyder,[46] involving two paintings allegedly stolen from the artist Georgia O'Keeffe and has subsequently been adopted in other jurisdictions as well.

This approach is perhaps best illustrated by the decision previously discussed involving the theft of several Byzantine mosaics from a Greek Orthodox Church located in northern Cyprus.[47] After the war in 1974, when Cyprus's northern Turkish section was separated from the southern Greek section, many of the Byzantine churches in the northern section were vandalized. These mosaics from the Kanakariá Church, which were very unusual in that they were pre-Iconoclastic in date, were chiseled off the walls of the apse, taken to Germany, and sold by a Dutch dealer to an Indianapolis dealer specializing in Impressionist and modern European paintings. The Indianapolis dealer completed the transaction in a matter of days after viewing the mosaics only in the Geneva Free Transit zone and making a few phone calls to various embassies and subsequently tried to sell the mosaics in the United States. Although she had paid about $1 million for them, she tried to resell them a short time later for $20 million.

Fortunately, photographs of these mosaics in situ had been published during the 1950s. The Indianapolis dealer contacted Marion True, curator of the Getty Museum, who recognized the mosaics as having been stolen from the Kanakariá Church and notified the Cypriot government. Approximately ten years had elapsed between the time the mosaics were removed from the church and the time when the church brought its claim, so the court had to determine whether the church's claim would be barred by the statute of limitations. The court adopted the discovery approach and decided that the church had done everything reasonable within its power to learn the location of the mosaics. While coming out with the right result in this case, this approach may be criticized for focusing attention on the diligence of the original owner, who does not generally know where to look for the property, rather than on the reasonableness of the actions of the purchaser in deciding whether to purchase the stolen artwork. A purchaser can decide whether to enter the market and which objects to buy. The victim of a theft does not have this choice. The law should therefore place the risk of loss, if an object turns out to have been stolen, on the purchaser, who is in the best position to influence the market.

Another complication for the recovery of stolen artworks lies in the fact that the civil law nations, which include most of continental Europe and Japan, permit thieves to pass title to stolen objects when purchasers are acting in good faith. This approach opens the possibility that antiquities may be laundered by selling them in continental European nations to bona fide purchasers who would thus get good title, which would then be recognized by courts in common law jurisdictions. It seems likely that this was what the Indianapolis dealer was trying to do by buying the mosaics in Switzerland, and the court did in fact consider whether she had acquired good title under Swiss law.[48] Fortunately, the court also concluded that she was not acting in good faith. Nevertheless, the international art market's definitions of *good faith* and *due diligence* remain unclear.

Theft also occurs when archaeological objects are removed without permission from the ground when a nation has declared ownership of antiquities. Many archaeologically rich nations have passed laws vesting ownership of certain categories of antiquities in the national government. Any taking of such objects without government permission is therefore theft. Some American legal scholars, particularly those involved in the antiquities trade, argue that the United States should not recognize this form of ownership based only on constructive possession of unexcavated objects. This argument is ironic because the U.S. federal government, Native American tribes, and every state government declare themselves to be the owners of all cultural property found on publicly owned land.[49] Yet this inconsistency is often ignored by those who argue that the United States should not recognize foreign national ownership laws based on constructive possession.

Foreign countries that have attempted to recover stolen antiquities based on national ownership laws have had varying amounts of success. Many of the court cases previously discussed recognized the claims to ownership of antiquities brought by such countries as Guatemala, Mexico, Turkey, Egypt, and Italy. In a few cases, such as those involving the Inca objects claimed by Peru and the Sevso Treasure claimed by Hungary and Croatia, the nations failed to establish that the objects had come from within the modern borders of the claimant country or that the national laws clearly vested ownership in the national government. In affirming the recent conviction of prominent New York dealer Frederick Schultz, the federal appellate court for the Second Circuit, which includes New York, has now clarified that this legal doctrine is the applicable law for the heart of the United States art market.[50] Given the number of jurisdictions that have now accepted this doctrine, there can no longer be any doubt that antiquities illegally removed in violation of a foreign nation's national ownership law are stolen property. Such objects may be seized and forfeited by the U.S. government, and anyone who knowingly or intentionally deals in such objects is subject to criminal prosecution.

The second element in the international art market is the question of smuggling—that is, the illegal export or import of antiquities without a permit. Many art-rich nations have enacted strict export controls for their cultural property—either prohibiting entirely such exports or requiring a permit. These restrictive export policies may also be utilized to curb looting of sites. Art-importing nations, including the United States, allow the free import of cultural property and generally disregard the question of illegal export from the country of origin in the absence of a specific agreement to recognize these export controls.

The case involving the Sicilian phiale presented a less typical version of smuggling in that the phiale was brought into the United States illegally:[51] the importer had listed Switzerland rather than Italy as the country of origin and the value as $250,000 instead of the approximately $1.2 million the collector paid. The U.S. government alleged that the phiale had been imported illegally into the United States due to these materially false statements on the Customs forms and that the phiale had been taken from Italy in violation of that country's 1939 Law on Protection of Objects of Artistic and Historic Interest; therefore, the object constituted stolen property.

In 1997, the federal district court decided in the government's favor on both issues, concluding that a declaration of Italy as the country of origin would have alerted the Customs Service that the bowl was being exported from a country with strict cultural patrimony laws. Of interest is the court's clear statement that Italy is in fact the phiale's country of origin. The requirement that Italy be listed as the country of origin will have some effect on the art market, which has for years passed works through countries such as Switzerland to launder the objects and give them respectable backgrounds. The Second Circuit Court of Appeals affirmed the district court's holding on this basis.

The third element of the illicit market involves illegal excavation. Almost everyone at least purports to agree that this is the heart of the matter. Yet mere illegal excavation does not produce "tainted" objects unless one of the previously discussed forms of illegality is also involved. It is relatively easy today to document whether a cultural artifact originated from a permitted excavation and to presume that undocumented artifacts did not come from such a source. The truth is, however, that many people involved in the international market simply ignore this point.

International Cooperation

A broad and significant attempt at international agreement to reduce the illegal trade in cultural materials was achieved in the 1970 UNESCO Convention on the Means of Prohibiting and Preventing the Illicit Import, Export, and Transfer of Ownership of Cultural Property.[52] The UNESCO Convention recognizes the significance of the common cultural heritage and attempts to encourage international exchanges and sharing of cultural objects and information while making serious efforts to restrict the illegal trade in antiquities and ethnographic objects and to encourage respect for national laws that regulate and protect cultural property. At first, relatively few art-importing nations ratified it. Although the United States signed the UNESCO Convention in 1972, implementing legislation was required and was not passed until 1983, having been held hostage throughout the 1970s by the strong lobbying efforts of the auction houses and dealers, largely through their influence on New York Senator Daniel Patrick Moynihan.[53]

The implementing legislation, the Convention on Cultural Property Implementation Act (CPIA),[54] effectively enacted only two of the UNESCO Convention's provisions. The first allows for the recovery of stolen cultural property that had been documented in the inventory of a museum, religious institution, or other public institution. This added little to existing U.S. law because any individual, institution, or national government could already bring suit to recover stolen cultural property in U.S. courts. However, it did provide a more effective mechanism for recovery by allowing the U.S. government to seize stolen objects through forfeiture proceedings and without need for the government to establish knowledge or intent on the part of the importer or another individual.

The second provision of the CPIA allows the president, upon a request by a foreign country and with the advice of the Cultural Property Advisory Committee, to enter into a bilateral agreement with another State Party to the UNESCO Convention or to impose import restrictions unilaterally in the case of an emergency situation. Through either mechanism, the United States can impose import restrictions on cultural property that is not accompanied by the appropriate documentation from the country of origin. Although as of October 2003 there were 101 States Parties to the convention,[55] the United States at the same time had bilateral agreements with only nine nations (Guatemala, El Salvador, Nicaragua, Peru, Bolivia, Mali, Cyprus, Italy, and Cambodia). The United States also imposed emergency import restrictions for Byzantine and ecclesiastical materials from Cyprus.[56] The agreement with Canada, which expired in April 2002, was particularly interesting in that it specifically provided reciprocal protections for cultural property illegally taken from the United States.

The failure of most art-importing nations to adopt the convention in its early years led UNESCO officials to ask Unidroit, an international body that promulgates uniform international laws, to draft a new international agreement. As of January 2004, twenty-one nations are party to the 1995 Unidroit Convention on Stolen and Illegally Exported Cultural Property.[57] Several of the most significant changes introduced by the Unidroit Convention were designed to encourage civil law nations to join.[58]

First, Unidroit requires the country of origin to pay compensation to a good-faith purchaser who returns stolen or illegally exported cultural property. This is an attempt to satisfy the concerns of civil law countries because they recognize the passage of title to good-faith purchasers. Unidroit does not, however, clearly spell out what is meant by *good faith* other than requiring that the possessor "neither knew nor ought reasonably to have known that the object was stolen and can prove that it exercised due diligence when acquiring the object." The requirement of compensation would put the original owner in a less advantageous position than under current U.S. law and would not necessarily be adopted in any potential U.S. implementing legislation.

The second feature is the adoption of an absolute statute of limitations for recovery of both stolen and illegally exported objects. In both cases, a claim must be brought within three years from the time when the claimant knew the location of the cultural object and the identity of its possessor and in any case within fifty years from the time of the theft or illegal export, even if the claimant was unable to locate the property within that time period. If, however, the cultural object forms "an integral part of an identified monument or archaeological site" or belongs to a public collection, then the only limitations period is the three years from time of discovery. Again, this absolute time limit has been proposed to attract Western European nations but is not likely to be adopted into U.S. law, particularly as the Unidroit Convention does permit the continuation of prior national legislation that is more favorable to the restitution of cultural property.

Third, and most controversial, is the equation of illegal excavation with theft when this is consistent with local law. This would be a significant expansion of protection, which gets to the crux of the matter (that is, the problem of looting of sites and the loss of context) and which has elicited the most objection within the United States from the art market community, collectors, and museums.[59] These groups object that the United States will become the international police for the enforcement of the domestic laws of other nations, thereby introducing significant uncertainty into the art market's operation. These groups also assert that this provision is not in the best interests of the United States. On the other side is the argument that this is, indeed, of primary concern to U.S. interests because we currently have extensive laws regulating excavation of archaeological sites and our cultural property is now subject to illegal sale and export. In particular, we need to recognize that the United States is now in the position of being both an art-importing and art-source nation, and we need to acquire some protection for our cultural property on the international market. The perhaps ironic result of the promulgation of the Unidroit Convention, which was primarily intended to bring Western European nations and Japan within an international treaty regime, is that it has stimulated interest in ratification of the UNESCO Convention. In 1997, France ratified the UNESCO Convention. In 2002 and 2003, several significant art-importing nations ratified or joined the convention, including the United Kingdom, Japan, Denmark, and Switzerland. In 1993, the European Union also enacted a directive and regulation to restrict the trade in undocumented antiquities; this may signal a new approach through regional agreements to complement the global international agreements.

Solutions

Public Opinion.   The role of public opinion in shaping policies and in influencing the conduct of the market and our leading public institutions cannot be underestimated. Many archaeological organizations, the National Trust, the federal government's National Park Service, and many state governments have undertaken efforts to educate the public about the significance of historic preservation. Articles about archaeological and historic preservation appear remarkably frequently in the public media, although these pieces do not always draw the full connection between the looting of sites and the acquisition of undocumented antiquities by museums and private collectors.

In early 2000, a coalition of archaeological and preservation organizations commissioned Harris Interactive to conduct a survey to measure public opinion.[60] This survey explored public attitudes concerning several aspects of archaeology, including the public's awareness of archaeology, its perceived value, and its role in education. Of particular interest was the public's attitudes about conservation, laws, and the management of archaeological sites. For example, 96 percent of respondents felt that there should be laws to protect historical and prehistoric archaeological sites; 85 percent of this group thought that there should be laws to prevent the general public from constructing houses or businesses on sites of prehistoric Indian villages, while 73 percent thought laws should prevent such construction on the sites of former Revolutionary or Civil War battles and 67 percent thought that laws should prevent the general public from digging up arrowheads or pottery on their own property. About the same number (69 percent) thought that laws should prevent the general public from selling artifacts found on their property, and 82 percent thought that laws should prevent the general public from selling artifacts found on someone else's private property.

When asked to indicate what value archaeological sites hold for them, 99 percent of respondents said that the value of sites is educational and scientific; 94 percent said aesthetic or artistic; 93 percent indicated personal heritage; and 88 percent chose spiritual. Conversely, 73 percent of respondents felt that sites had monetary value, presumably reflecting their awareness that objects removed from sites are sold on the market. Finally, 59 percent believed that sites had political value. While all of these values are relatively high, it is clear that nonmonetary values hold far greater significance than monetary values.

In turning to issues that directly affect the functioning of the market, the responses were even more illuminating. Ninety percent of respondents thought that laws should prevent the general public from importing artifacts from countries that do not want those artifacts exported. It is important to reiterate that this response concerns export laws rather than national ownership laws, so the respondents were not considering the implications of theft. In a similar vein, 92 percent of respondents disagreed (with 28 percent strongly disagreeing) with the statement, "Museums and individuals should be able to buy archaeological objects from abroad even if they were taken out of the country of origin without the country's permission."

What is interesting and ironic is the respondents' awareness—or, more accurately, lack of awareness—of the current legal system, in contrast to the respondents' opinions regarding what the law should provide. Only 22 percent of respondents knew of any laws protecting shipwrecks; 24 percent knew of laws protecting unmarked human burial sites; 23 percent knew of laws concerning the buying and selling of artifacts; and 28 percent knew of laws protecting archaeological sites. Overall, despite what seems to be general ignorance of the law, much of the public seems to support the regulation and protection of archaeological sites for which the law in fact provides.

In April 2003, as the Saddam Hussein regime in Iraq fell, the extensive looting of the Iraq National Museum in Baghdad was widely reported. While it turned out that the original numbers were incorrect, nonetheless it is believed that approximately fifteen thousand objects were, in fact, stolen. In the weeks that followed, the world media also reported the looting of many archaeological sites, particularly in southern Iraq. The story had considerable staying power. Numerous stories ran during the next two months, and even eight months later, the world media continue to follow the story. This public attention presents an opportunity that may be rescued from the otherwise sad story of the cultural losses visited upon Iraq during the second Gulf War. Certainly the press and the general public seem to be displaying a much better understanding of the significance of the looting of sites and cultural monuments. Whether this will translate into public policy and legislative action still remains to be seen.

Perhaps the most significant issue concerning public opinion, however, is that legislators must be convinced to act accordingly. Many legislators are overly swayed by the lobbying efforts and political influence of art market professionals and private collectors, which represent the narrow interests of dealers and auction houses motivated by financial self-interest. If legislators would instead respond to broad-based public opinion, the laws of this country could be fashioned to deal more effectively with the problems caused by the unfettered market in undocumented antiquities.

Legal Solutions.   Three changes in the legal system would help greatly in reducing or eliminating the trade in undocumented antiquities. The first change, which is to some extent already entering the U.S. legal system is to require that the current possessor of an antiquity act in affirmative good faith before the statute of limitations expires or the equitable defense of laches will operate in the possessor's favor to bar a claim for recovery by the true owner. In this context, good faith should be defined as requiring demonstration of due diligence and an affirmative search on the part of the purchaser for an object's provenance and background. The more valuable and rare a particular object, the greater the effort that a purchaser should be expected to make in researching its background. Any doubts regarding background should be resolved against the legitimacy of the transaction, and the purchaser should continue to bear the risk of loss of the object. By shifting this burden in this way, the purchaser will have the incentive to demand complete documentation. If purchasers avoid transacting in undocumented antiquities, then the motive of middlemen, looters, and smugglers to obtain undocumented antiquities will be eliminated and the looting of sites will be discouraged. Additional incentives for purchasers to require documentation would also help to break down the veils of secrecy that surround most art market transactions. Legitimacy and legality can be achieved only when transparency replaces the secrecy that is now the accepted norm for art market professionals.

The second change in the law would involve uniform recognition of the export laws of countries of origin of antiquities. In theory, the United States is already obligated under the UNESCO Convention to grant reciprocity for the export controls of all nations that are party to the convention. However, the convention's implementation by the United States through the CPIA is slow and cumbersome, posing heavy burdens on parties to the convention to seek recognition through bilateral agreements or emergency provisions. In addition, all agreements automatically expire after a maximum of five years, thus requiring the foreign nation to repeat the process of requesting a renewal of the agreement. The U.S. response needs more permanency to achieve the CPIA's goals.[61] Finally, to seriously stem the flow of undocumented antiquities into the country through the market, the United States needs to fully implement the remaining portions of the UNESCO Convention.

The third change would focus on the income tax deduction currently available to those who donate art objects to public charitable organizations. The close relationship between museums and donors will be discussed in the next section. However, here it is suggested that donors should receive deductions only when they can provide the museum with documentation showing the legitimate sources of art and cultural objects. While some may suggest that this would present overly complex issues for the Internal Revenue Service to resolve, donated art objects above a certain value now require an independent appraisal of their value. An independent board could determine whether the documentation met an acceptable standard of due diligence and clear background. At the least, the presence or lack of such documentation and its quality should be a factor in the determination of the value of the antiquity and thus of the extent of the charitable deduction.[62]

Another area of concern is the art market lobby's political influence, particularly in Congress. It would be facile to suggest, however, that limitations on campaign contributions would solve the problem of this influence. The source of the influence seems much deeper and more subtle because it extends to the sophisticated nature of the legal representation that art market professionals can afford to hire, the influence of wealthy private collectors who may move in the same social circles as high government officials,[63] and the ability of art market professionals to hire former government officials to assist in lobbying efforts.

Other solutions that have been suggested also seem to offer little promise. While settlement of lawsuits is always a desirable outcome because of the savings in litigation costs and time, such settlements should not come with significant payments to the current possessor, as in the restitution of the Quedlinburg treasures,[64] or with substantial tax benefits to the possessor (a form of compensation), as in the case of the Michael Ward Gallery's return of Mycenean jewelry to Greece. If the reason to impose legal duties on the purchaser is to provide a disincentive to trade in looted antiquities, compensation will negate that disincentive.

Another proposal of limited efficacy in the case of looted antiquities is an international registry. Some registries or computerized databases are in use for the recovery of artworks, including antiquities, when they have been stolen from known and cataloged collections. Such databases are useful in encouraging both original owners to register thefts and purchasers to search to see if artworks are stolen before purchasing them. Databases are, however, ineffective in the case of antiquities looted directly from the ground, which are generally unknown in their countries of origin before appearing on the market.

Museums and Other Public Institutions.   Museums and other public educational institutions have a particular role and responsibility to play in
eliminating the pillage of sites. As was previously explained, the scientific
excavation of sites is primarily of educational value. What can be learned
from decontextualized objects is of relatively little value. Museums must
take seriously their role as educational institutions and as standard-bearers
for the highest ethical conduct in society. To accomplish this goal, museums must do more than follow the minimum that the law requires, at least
until the law changes in the ways previously suggested.

One of the biggest problems is the gap between what U.S. law requires
and the violation of other nations' laws. As has been previously outlined,
these foreign laws are often designed to reduce the incentives to pillage
and destroy archaeological sites. Yet laws that prohibit unauthorized excavation or illegal export are not automatically enforceable within the
United States. This lacuna is often filled by ethical codes of conduct,
which have no legal force.

The Code of Ethics of the International Council of Museums (ICOM)
attempts to fill this gap by stating,

> The illicit trade in objects and specimens encourages the destruction of
> historic sites, ethnic cultures and biological habitats and promotes theft
> at local, national and international levels. It places at risk endangered
> species of flora and fauna, violates the UN Convention on Biological
> Diversity (1992) and contravenes the spirit of national and interna-
> tional patrimony. Museums should recognise the destruction of human
> and natural environments and loss of knowledge that results from the
> illicit servicing of the market place. The museum professional must war-
> rant that it is highly unethical for a museum to support the illicit market
> in any way, directly or indirectly.
>
> A museum should not acquire any object or specimen by purchase,
> gift, loan, bequest or exchange unless the governing body and respon-
> sible officer are satisfied that a valid title to it can be obtained. Every
> effort must be made to ensure that it has not been illegally acquired in,
> or exported from, its country of origin or any intermediate country in
> which it may have been owned legally (including the museum's own
> country). Due diligence in this regard should establish the full history of
> the item from discovery or production, before acquisition is considered.
>
> In addition to the safeguards set out above, a museum should not
> acquire objects by any means where the governing body or responsible
> officer has reasonable cause to believe that their recovery involved the

unauthorised, unscientific or intentional destruction or damage of ancient monuments, archaeological or geological sites, or natural habitats, or involved a failure to disclose the finds to the owner or occupier of the land, or to the proper legal or governmental authorities. Nor should a museum acquire, directly or indirectly, biological or geological material that has been collected, sold or otherwise transferred in contravention of any local, national, regional or international wildlife protection or natural history conservation law, or treaty, of the museum's own country or any other country.

A professional conflict can exist when an acquisition, highly desired by a museum, lacks provenance. However, the ability to establish legal title to the item must be an overriding factor when considering acquisition. In very rare cases an item without provenance may have an inherently outstanding contribution to knowledge that it would be in the public interest to preserve. Such discovery is likely to be of international significance and should be the subject of a decision by specialists in the discipline concerned. The basis of the decision should be without national or institutional prejudice, based on the best interests of the subject discipline and be clearly stated.[65]

Museums in the United States should adhere to these ethical requirements. Instead, the two leading museum organizations in the United States, the American Association of Museums (AAM) and the Association of Art Museum Directors (AAMD), largely sidestep the issue in their codes. The AAMD Professional Practices in Art Museums states only, "The Director must not knowingly acquire or allow to be recommended for acquisition any object that has been stolen, removed in contravention of treaties and international conventions to which the United States is a signatory, or illegally imported into the United States." The AAMD Code thus ignores the issue of illegal excavation and illegal export from the country of origin, relying solely on the minimum required by U.S. law. The code also seems to permit museum directors to act out of willful ignorance, forbidding only those actions the director knows to be illegal. The AAM Code of Ethics is even more vague, stating that "the museum ensures that: . . . acquisition, disposal, and loan activities are conducted in a manner that respects the protection and preservation of natural and cultural resources and discourages illicit trade in such materials." It establishes no specific standards of conduct and requires no due diligence or effective search on the part of the museum in acquiring objects. In addition, the recent record of some of the leading museums in the United States and of the AAM in particular on this subject has been abysmal.

In earlier years, the dealers' organizations had stood alone—for example, in the amicus curiae brief submitted by the American Association of Dealers in Ancient, Oriental, and Primitive Art in the case of U.S. v. McClain, which focused on whether the United States should regard as stolen property antiquities taken from a country with national ownership laws.[66] During the 1980s, when attempts were made to undo the McClain decision through amendments to the National Stolen Property Act, the museum organizations, particularly the AAM, opposed these amendments and favored preservation of the McClain doctrine. By 1995, a shift in attitude of the museum organizations was apparent when the AAM, AAMD, some additional museum organizations, and a few major museums in the United States joined with the dealers' trade organizations and Christie's and Sotheby's in preparing a statement opposing the Unidroit Convention.[67] In 1998, however, the museum community, led by the AAM, went it alone, without even the encouragement or support of the dealers or auction houses, in submitting an amicus curiae brief in support of the collector in U.S. v. An Antique Platter of Gold.[68] While it is not illegal to argue various points of the law or to argue for changes in the law, these legal positions contradict the ethical provisions of the ICOM Code. It is puzzling that museums have chosen to invest so much time, energy, and money in opposing legal positions intended to preserve the scientific and educational value of archaeological sites, and these actions lead to questions about whether such strategies enable museums to fulfill their educational and charitable missions and their tax-exempt purposes under the Internal Revenue Code.

Museums and private collectors acquire cultural objects through the market. Museums acquire objects not only directly through purchase but also through donations from private collectors and through loans and temporary exhibitions. Unlike private collectors, museums are public charitable organizations with the purpose of furthering educational and scientific values. As such, museums and their boards of trustees have a fiduciary duty to the public. Museums that ignore the educational and scientific value of cultural objects are committing a breach of these obligations.

Despite differences, there is a close symbiotic relationship between museums and private collectors. This relationship often benefits both in

that individuals may donate collections to museums as well as funds
with which museums can acquire additional artworks, while donors
receive tax breaks, psychological benefits, and public recognition of
their actions. Sometimes, however, the relationship becomes too close
and it becomes too easy for museums to evade the law or ethical codes
by defining donations out of their policies for acquisitions. Donors may
purchase artworks that museums have brought to the donors' attention,
recommended, researched, and validated, as happened with a Degas
monotype purchased by Daniel Searle on the advice of Art Institute of
Chicago curators in the hope that he would later donate it.[69] Collector
Michael Steinhardt purchased the gold phiale stolen from Italy and then
had the object authenticated by the Metropolitan Museum of Art,
which possesses a near-twin of the phiale. A collector may purchase an
antiquity under a much lower standard of care or concern for the legal
issues and then donate it to a museum, receiving the advantage of a tax
deduction.

This leads us finally to the necessity of fostering a new culture of collecting that focuses on the full story that cultural objects can tell. The
world's major museums have previously built their collections primarily
through the art market either as direct purchasers or as recipients of
donated objects and artworks. A major step in altering this culture of collecting would be to place a moratorium on the acquisition of antiquities.[70]
Such a moratorium would provide the time, space, and funds for museums
to examine their collections and to develop cooperative arrangements
with both foreign museums and smaller museums in the United States. It
would likely also create a deterrent to private collecting, if collectors could
no longer be assured of a sizable charitable tax deduction and the prestige
that accompanies such donations.

In the future, museums should seek an alternative based on loans and
exhibitions, which are grounded in interinstitutional cooperation. The
U.S.-Italy bilateral agreement under the CPIA presents an example of this
type of cooperation in that it encourages Italy to make long-term loans of
the types of cultural objects whose import is restricted under the agreement. Such loans are to be made to American museums for purposes of
scholarship, education, and conservation concerning the loan objects.[71]
Although ownership of objects may have seemed to provide permanence
to collections, this is questionable. Rather, an approach based on a spirit of
cooperation brings several advantages. First, it ensures that the world's

artistic and cultural heritage really does circulate throughout the world rather than remaining in a few well-endowed institutions and private collections. Second, it allows these institutions to move away from reliance on the market, which has often furnished aesthetically pleasing, costly, but unprovenanced objects whose story is muted for lack of scientific and historical context. Third, it permits the museums of Western Europe and North America to enter into mutually beneficial partnerships with the institutions and governments of other nations rather than perpetuating an antagonistic stalemate. Exchange of objects allows sections of the same objects or several objects that originally formed a single corpus to be reunited. It also allows objects to be viewed through new eyes. Not only have advances in conservation techniques resulted, but new discoveries have been made when objects are placed on loan with different institutions.

Professor Willard Boyd, former president of the Field Museum of Natural History in Chicago, has described this needed transformation:

> Traditionally, museums have stressed the benefits of the "movement" of objects without adequate regard for the detrimental aspects of movement from the point of view of others. Certainly, the cross-cultural transfer of the human ideas surrounding objects is regarded positively in an age of communication. However, the movement of objects that results in cultural and environmental loss, destruction, and desecration cannot be justified. Museums must realign their acquisition and retention policies to promote cultural understanding and respect for the objects and ideas of others. An ethical attitude requires that we do so.[72]

Examples of this contextual, collaborative perspective include international loans for exhibition purposes, longer-term international loans for those museums that agree to abide by national and international laws as well as ethical standards, and international collaborations ranging from excavation to conservation and site preservation and interpretive projects. When this perspective is adopted, it will become possible to increase the free exchange of cultural materials, in turn enhancing the acquisition of knowledge as well as the appreciation of aesthetic values. Although this approach omits the market perspective and auction houses and dealers may suffer financially from such a change in policies, museums and their public beneficiaries will benefit from an increase in educational and scientific understanding.

NOTES

1. This chapter does not address revelations concerning antitrust practices at the two largest auction houses, Sotheby's and Christie's, as well as many of the smaller art dealerships. See Carol Vogel, "Christie's Says It Is Cooperating with Antitrust Inquiry in Art World," *New York Times,* January 29, 2000, p. B4. Sotheby's and Christie's have each agreed to pay $256 million to settle the class-action suit. Sotheby's has pleaded guilty and agreed to pay another $45 million to settle the criminal case. Diana Brooks, former president and chief executive officer of Sotheby's, has pleaded guilty to conspiracy to violate antitrust laws in collusion with Christie's and faces a possible three-year federal prison sentence and large fine. Brooks also testified against her former boss, A. Alfred Taubman, who was subsequently convicted and sentenced to one year in jail (Ralph Blumenthal and Carol Vogel, "Former Sotheby's Chief Is Said to Be Planning to Plead Guilty," *New York Times,* October 5, 2000, p. A1; Ralph Blumenthal and Carole Vogel, "Ex-Chief of Sotheby's Gets Probation and Fine," *New York Times,* April 30, 2002, p. B3). Despite these legal problems, Sotheby's, the firm that appears to be in greater legal trouble, turned in very successful modern and Impressionist art sales during the spring of 2000 (Carol Vogel, "Despite Legal Troubles, Sotheby's Makes a Strong Showing at Art Auction," *New York Times,* May 11, 2000, p. B6).

2. Quoted in John Henry Merryman and Albert E. Elsen, *Law, Ethics, and the Visual Arts,* 3d ed. (London: Kluwer, 1999), 5.

3. The literature on the Marbles is extensive and includes William St. Clair, *Lord Elgin and the Marbles: The Controversial History of the Parthenon Sculptures* (New York: Oxford University Press, 1998); William St. Clair, "The Elgin Marbles: Questions of Stewardship and Accountability," *International Journal of Cultural Property* 8 (1999): 397–521; David Rudenstine, "The Legality of Elgin's Taking: A Review Essay of Four Books on the Parthenon Marbles," *International Journal of Cultural Property* 8 (1999): 356–76; John Boardman, "The Elgin Marbles: Matters of Fact and Opinion," *International Journal of Cultural Property* 9 (2000): 233.

4. Clemency C. Coggins, "Illicit Traffic of Pre-Columbian Antiquities," *Art Journal* 29 (1969): 94–98. Karl E. Meyer, *The Plundered Past* (New York: Atheneum, 1977). For a more recent chronicling of the looting of archaeological sites throughout the world, see Neil Brodie, Jennifer Doole, and Colin Renfrew, eds., *Trade in Illicit Antiquities: The Destruction of the World's Archaeological Heritage* (Cambridge, Eng.: McDonald Institute for Archaeological Research, 2001).

5. *United States v. Hollinshead,* 495 F.2d 1154 (9th Cir. 1974); *United States v. Pre-Columbian Artifacts and the Republic of Guatemala,* 845 F. Supp. 544 (N.D. Ill. 1993).

6. *United States v. McClain,* 545 F.2d 988 (5th Cir. 1977), 593 F.2d 658 (5th Cir.), *cert. denied,* 444 U.S. 918 (1979).

7. *Autocephalous Greek-Orthodox Church of Cyprus v. Goldberg & Feldman Fine Arts, Inc.,* 717 F. Supp. 1374 (S.D. Ind. 1989), *aff'd,* 917 F.2d 278 (7th Cir. 1990).

8. *Peru v. Johnson*, 720 F. Supp. 810 (C.D. Cal. 1989), *aff'd sub nom. Peru v. Wendt*, 933 F.2d 1013 (9th Cir. 1991).

9. *The Republic of Croatia v. The Trustee of the Marquess of Northampton 1987 Settlement*, 610 N.Y.S.2d 263 (Sup. Ct., App. Div. 1994), *lv. to appeal denied*, 84 N.E.2d 325 (N.Y. 1994). In this case and in *Peru v. Johnson*, the claimants failed because they were unable to prove that the archaeological objects were found within the modern borders of the claimant nation.

10. Emily C. Ehl, "The Settlement of *Greece v. Ward*: Who Loses?" *Boston University Law Review* 78 (1998): 661.

11. *Republic of Turkey v. The Metropolitan Museum*, 762 F. Supp. 44 (S.D.N.Y. 1990); Lawrence M. Kaye and Carla T. Main, "The Saga of the Lydian Hoard: From Uşak to New York and Back Again," in *Antiquities: Trade or Betrayed? Legal, Ethical, and Conservation Issues*, ed. Kathryn W. Tubb (London: Archetype, 1995), 150–61.

12. The Met's acquisition of the Lydian Hoard was described by Thomas Hoving in his book, *Making the Mummies Dance* (New York: Touchstone, 1993), 217: the junior curator at the museum had gone to the tomb, where he saw parts of objects purchased by the museum. Hoving quotes himself as having said, "We all believe the stuff was illegally dug up. . . . We took our chances when we bought the material."

13. Grace Glueck, "Statue in Met Show Said to Be Stolen," *New York Times*, November 22, 1990, p. C15. Cornelius C. Vermeule III, curator of the Classical Art Department at the Boston Museum of Fine Arts at the time of the sculpture's acquisition, stated years later, "It's now clearly recognized that the 'Weary Herakles' fits together to form a complete statue." In 1992, the Turkish government sent a cast of the fragment in Turkey, and the two pieces were admitted to join. Nevertheless, the museum and the collectors refuse to return the piece, claiming that its acquisition was legal (Anne E. Kornblut, "Getting to the Bottom of Split Statue," *Boston Globe*, December 27, 1998, p. A30).

14. *Republic of Turkey v. OKS Partners*, 1994 U.S. Dist. LEXIS 17032 (D. Mass. 1994). Anne E. Kornblut, "In Settlement, Koch to Return Coins to Turkey," *Boston Globe*, March 5, 1999, p. A1; Barry Meier, "The Case of the Contested Coins: A Modern-Day Battle over Ancient Objects," *New York Times*, September 24, 1998, p. C1.

15. *U.S. v. An Antique Platter of Gold*, 991 F. Supp. 222 (S.D.N.Y. 1997), *aff'd*, 184 F.3d 131 (2d Cir. 1999), *cert. denied*, 2000 U.S. LEXIS 835 (2000).

16. Mike Toner, "The Past in Peril: Buying, Selling, Stealing History," *Atlanta Journal and Constitution*, September 19, 1999, p. 1H.

17. D. Graepeler and M. Mazzei, *Provenienza: Sconosciuta! Tombaroli, Mercanti e Collezionisti: L'Italia Archeologica allo Sbaraglio* [Provenience: Unknown! Tomb Robbers, Dealers, and Collectors: Archaeological Italy at Risk] (Bari: Edipuglia, 1996), 47.

18. Peter Watson, *Sotheby's: The Inside Story* (New York: Random House, 1997), 290–93.

19. *United States v. Schultz*, 178 F. Supp. 2d 445 (S.D.N.Y. 2002), *aff'd*, 333 F.3d 393 (2d Cir. 2003).

20. See, e.g., Nathan Vardi, "The Return of the Mummy: How to Get Your Hands on Artifacts—Without Going to Jail," *Forbes*, December 22, 2003, pp. 156–68.

21. Bonnie Burnham, "Architectural Heritage: The Paradox of Its Current State of Risk," *International Journal of Cultural Property* 7 (1998): 149–50, 162. Angkor Wat was listed as World Heritage in Danger by UNESCO in 1992, the same year in which the site was placed on the World Heritage list. In 1996, Angkor Wat was included in the first World Monuments Watch List of 100 Most Endangered Sites, published by the World Monuments Fund. The World Heritage List in Danger may be found at http://whc.unesco.org/danglist.htm#debut. The World Monuments Fund's List of 100 Most Endangered Sites may be found at http://www.wmf.org/html/programs/watchlist2004.html. More recent discussion of the problems of looting of archaeological sites and cultural monuments in Asia may be found in Hannah Beech, "Stealing Beauty," *Time*, October 27, 2003, pp. 58–66.

22. Julian E. Barnes, "Alleging Theft, U.S. Demands Rare Sculpture Go Back to China," *New York Times*, March 30, 2000, p. B3. Watson, *Sotheby's*, 246–75, has also documented the looting of antiquities from India.

23. Lawrence Van Gelder, "Restoration Project," *New York Times*, May 24, 2001, p. E1.

24. Hoving, *Making*, 307–40, vividly describes the cavalier attitude of the Metropolitan Museum and its staff in acquiring the notorious Euphronios vase in 1972.

25. *Porter v. Wertz*, 416 N.Y.S.2d 254, 259 (Sup. Ct., App. Div. 1979).

26. Erik Eckholm with Calvin Sims, "Stolen Chinese Relic A Showpiece in Japan? Archaeologists See an Epidemic of Theft," *New York Times*, April 20, 2000, p. E1.

27. Recent voluntary restitutions of artworks stolen during the Holocaust, although generally accompanied by initial litigation, include the Degas monotype in the collection of Daniel Searle: Ron Grossman, "Tracing Histories: How a Family's Degas Traveled from Their Estate to the Center of Controversy," *Chicago Tribune*, January 28, 2001, p. C1; Howard J. Trienens, *Landscape with Smokestacks: The Case of the Allegedly Plundered Degas* (Evanston: Northwestern University Press, 2000); and Matisse's *Odalisque* in the Seattle Art Museum: *Rosenberg v. Seattle Art Museum*, 124 F. Supp. 2d 1207 (W.D. Wash. 2000); Sheila Farr, "Seattle Art Museum, Gallery Agree to Settle Dispute with Cash," *Seattle Times*, October 21, 2000, p. A1. On the other hand, several other cases involving artworks stolen during the Holocaust are still in litigation. See, e.g., *Altmann v. Austria*, 317 F.3d 954 (9th Cir. 2002), *cert. granted*, 124 S. Ct. 46 (2003); *United States v. Portrait of Wally*, 2002 U.S. Dist. LEXIS 6445 (S.D.N.Y. 2002); and a controversy concerning a Picasso painting currently in the collection of Chicago collector Marilyn Alsdorf (Howard Reich, "Whose Picasso Is It?" *Chicago Tribune*, January 19, 2003, p. C1).

28. Transcript of the online discussion may be found at http://www.discuss .washingtonpost.com/wp-srv/zforum/00/fbio810.htm.

29. Ricardo J. Elia, "Chopping Away Culture; Museums Routinely Accept

Artifacts Stripped of Context by Looters," *Boston Globe*, December 21, 1997, p. D1.

30. Ibid.

31. David J. Gill and Christopher Chippindale, "Material and Intellectual Consequences of Esteem for Cycladic Figures," *American Journal of Archaeology* 97 (1993): 601–60.

32. Christopher Chippindale and David J. Gill, "Material Consequences of Contemporary Classical Collecting," *American Journal of Archaeology* 104 (2000): 463.

33. Christopher Chippindale, David Gill, Emily Salter, and Christian Hamilton, "Collecting the Classical World: First Steps in a Quantitative History," *International Journal of Cultural Property* 10 (2001): 1, 18–20.

34. Ricardo J. Elia, "Analysis of the Looting, Selling, and Collecting of Apulian Red-Figure Vases: A Quantitative Approach," in *Trade in Illicit Antiquities: The Destruction of the World's Archaeological Heritage*, ed. Neil Brodie, Jennifer Doole, and Colin Renfrew (Cambridge, Eng.: McDonald Institute for Archaeological Research, 2001), 145–53.

35. A. D. Trendall and Alexander Cambitoglou, *The Red-Figured Vases of Apulia*, vols. 1–3 (Oxford: Oxford University Press, 1978, 1982), and supplements (London: University of London, Institute of Classical Studies, 1983, 1991, 1992, 1993).

36. Elizabeth Gilgan, "Looting and the Market for Maya Objects: A Belizean Perspective," in *Illicit Antiquities: The Destruction of the World's Archaeological Heritage*, ed. Neil Brodie, Jennifer Doole, and Colin Renfrew (Cambridge, Eng.: McDonald Institute for Archaeological Research, 2001), 73–87.

37. *Autocephalous Greek-Orthodox Church of Cyprus v. Goldberg & Feldman Fine Arts, Inc.*, 717 F. Supp. 1374 (S.D. Ind. 1989), aff'd, 917 F.2d 278 (7th Cir. 1990). For a detailed analysis of the work by the restorer and the damage to the mosaics, see Catherine Sease and Danaë Thimme, "The Kanakariá Mosaics: The Conservators' View," in *Antiquities*, ed. Tubb, 122–30.

38. See Chippindale and Gill, "Material Consequences," and Oscar W. Muscarella, *The Lie Made Great: The Forgery of Ancient Near Eastern Cultures* (Groningen: Styx Publications, 2002).

39. In explaining why U.S. museums have had so much difficulty in determining which art objects in their collections may have been looted during the Holocaust, James Wood, director of the Art Institute of Chicago, noted during congressional hearings that barely 20 percent of the museum's European paintings had been fully cataloged (Walter V. Robinson, "Museums' Stance on Nazi Loot Belies Their Role in Key Case," *Boston Globe*, February 13, 1998, p. A1).

40. For example, the AAM Code states that "disposal of collections through sale, trade, or research activities is solely for the advancement of the museum's mission." The AAMD statement provides, "Disposal of works of art from a museum's collection by sale, exchange, or otherwise, requires particularly rigorous examination and should be pursued with great caution." The AAM Code of Ethics may be found at http://www.aam-us.org/aamcoe.cfm. This excerpt from the AAMD's state-

ment on Professional Practices may be found at http://www.aamd .org/documents/deaccess.html.

41. "Israelis Seize Looted Artifacts," Associated Press, August 15, 2000.

42. Patrick J. O'Keefe, *Trade in Antiquities: Reducing Destruction and Theft* (London: Archetype, 1997).

43. *Menzel v. List*, 253 N.Y.S.2d 43 (1964) and 267 N.Y.S.2d 804 (Sup. Ct. 1966), *modified on other grounds*, 279 N.Y.S.2d 608 (1967), *modification rev'd*, 246 N.E.2d 742 (N.Y. 1969).

44. *Solomon R. Guggenheim Foundation v. Lubell*, 550 N.Y.S.2d 618 (1990), *aff'd*, 569 N.E.2d 426 (N.Y. 1991).

45. *Greek Orthodox Patriarchate of Jerusalem v. Christie's*, 1999 US. Dist. LEXIS 13257 (S.D.N.Y. 1999).

46. *O'Keeffe v. Snyder*, 405 A.2d 840 (1979), *rev'd and remanded*, 416 A.2d 862 (N.J. 1980).

47. *Autocephalous Greek-Orthodox Church of Cyprus v. Goldberg & Feldman Fine Arts, Inc.*, 717 F. Supp. 1374 (S.D. Ind. 1989), *aff'd*, 917 F.2d 278 (7th Cir. 1990).

48. A new Swiss law, the Cultural Property Transfer Act, is scheduled to go into effect in late 2004 or early 2005. Article 16 of this law offers a more restrictive definition of good faith in the purchase of cultural objects: "In the art trade and auctioning business, cultural property may only be transferred when the person transferring the property may assume, under the circumstances, that the cultural property: a. was not stolen, not lost against the will of the owner, and not illegally excavated; b. not illicitly imported." The text of the law is available at www.kultur-schweiz.admin.ch/arkgt/files/kgtg2_e.pdf.

49. See, e.g., Archaeological Resources Protection Act, 16 U.S.C. secs. 470ee–470mm (2000). Such laws in the United States generally apply only to antiquities found on publicly owned land, not privately owned land, while many foreign countries' laws apply to all antiquities, regardless of where they are found. Even in the United States, approximately 40 percent of the land is owned or controlled by a government entity, so a large proportion of the archaeological sites are, in fact, protected in this way.

50. *United States v. Schultz*, 333 F.3d 393 (2d Cir. 2003).

51. *U.S. v. An Antique Platter of Gold*, 991 F. Supp. 222 (S.D.N.Y. 1997), *aff'd*, 184 F.3d 131 (2d Cir. 1999), *cert. denied*, 2000 U.S. LEXIS 835 (2000).

52. 823 U.N.T.S. 231, 10 I.L.M. 289 (1971).

53. The influence of Senator Moynihan can again be seen in the proposed amendments to the CPIA, which he introduced in the Senate in October 1999 (S.1696).

54. 19 U.S.C. section 2601 *et seq.* (2000).

55. The current list of States Parties may be found at http://www.unesco.org/culture/laws/1970/html_eng/page3.shtml.

56. Current information concerning the status of such import restrictions can be obtained at the Web site maintained by the Cultural Property Advisory Committee: http://e.usia.gov/education/culprop.

57. The current list of States Parties may be found at http://www.unidroit.org/ english/implement/i-95.htm.

58. For complete discussion of the Unidroit Convention, see Lyndel V. Prott, *Commentary on the Unidroit Convention on Stolen and Illegally Exported Cultural Objects 1995* (London: Institute of Art and Law, 1997). Some archaeologically rich nations have been reluctant to join the Unidroit Convention because they are satisfied with the UNESCO Convention and because they do not want to have to buy back their cultural objects as a result of the compensation requirement (discussed later in the chapter).

59. Perhaps the first time that the leading museums and museum organizations in the United States joined with the market in legal action was the submission of a "Statement of Position of Concerned Members of the American Cultural Community Regarding the Unidroit Convention on the International Return of Stolen or Illegally Exported Cultural Objects" (May 31, 1995). The brief was submitted by, among others, the AAM, the AAMD, ten individual museums (including the Metropolitan Museum of Art, the Museum of Modern Art, the Art Institute of Chicago, and the Museum of Fine Arts, Boston), Christie's, Sotheby's, the Art Dealers Association of America, and the National Association of Dealers in Ancient, Oriental, and Primitive Art.

60. "Exploring Public Perceptions and Attitudes about Archaeology," Harris Interactive, February 2000, www.saa.org. The coalition included the Society for American Archaeology, the Archaeological Institute of America, the Archaeological Conservancy, the National Park Service, the Society for Historical Archaeology, the Bureau of Land Management, the Fish and Wildlife Service, and the Forest Service. There was a margin of error of +/–3 percent at the 95 percent level of confidence.

61. Following reports of the looting of the Iraq National Museum in Baghdad in April 2003, legislation was introduced in the House of Representatives (H.R. 2009) to impose a ban on the import of cultural materials illegally removed from Iraq. This bill, if enacted, would also amend the CPIA, among other things, to allow import restrictions imposed under the CPIA to last for up to ten years, rather than the five years allowed under current law.

62. A similar suggestion has been made by O'Keefe, *Trade*, 64–65.

63. For example, the close relationship between New York Senator Moynihan and collectors Leon Levy and Shelby White was documented in Ward Harkavy, "Statues of Limitations," *Village Voice*, August 29, 2000, p. 23.

64. William H. Honan, "Deal on Stolen German Art Meets with Mixed Reaction," *New York Times*, January 9, 1991, p. C13.

65. ICOM Code of Professional Ethics, sec. 3.2, available at http://icom .museum/ethics_rev_engl.html#3.

66. *United States v. McClain*, 545 F.2d 988 (5th Cir. 1977).

67. "Statement of Position of Concerned Members of the American Cultural Community."

68. The AAM brief was answered by one submitted by the Archaeological Institute of America and several other scientific and preservationist organizations, which I helped to prepare. The AAM has taken an additional step by entering the

litigation concerning an Egon Schiele painting, *Portrait of Wally*, seized by the U.S. Customs on the grounds that it is stolen property. The painting, which was stolen from its owners during the Holocaust, was on loan to the Museum of Modern Art when it was originally subpoenaed in January 1998 in state court litigation. The federal litigation is still ongoing. However, neither the museum organizations nor any individual museums joined any of the amicus curiae briefs submitted on behalf of the dealer Frederick Schultz in *United States v. Schultz*. Perhaps this was the result of criticism of the roles of the AAM and AAMD in the Steinhardt phiale case. Most recently, however, particularly the AAMD has worked with the National Association of Dealers in Ancient, Oriental and Primitive Art to oppose passage of H.R. 2009, the bill that would ban the import of illegally removed Iraqi cultural materials and amend the CPIA.

69. Walter V. Robinson, "Holocaust Victims' Heirs Given Share of a Degas," *Boston Globe*, August 14, 1998, p. A1.

70. For a similar suggestion, see Clemency C. Coggins, "A Proposal for Museum Acquisition Policies in the Future," *International Journal of Cultural Property* 7 (1998): 434–37.

71. The U.S.-Italy agreement and information concerning the long-term loan program may be found at http://exchanges.state.gov/culprop/itfact.html.

72. Willard L. Boyd, "Museums as Centers of Controversy," *Daedalus* 128 (3) (1999): 198.

8

The High Price of Cheap Food

Mark Ritchie

Advertising and the mass media portray the U.S. food supply as an almost magical system delivering the safest and cheapest food in the world, thanks to space-age technology and the world's most efficient agribusiness industry. The evening television news acts as a promotional film for the U.S. food industry, with both the news anchors and advertisements dramatizing the wonders of the system. We see images of farm families walking the land, talking about the importance of agriculture—followed by a marvelously clever tag line from one of the dozen or so giant agribusiness corporations that sponsor these misleading image campaigns on television and in print media. In the United States, where many of us are only a generation or two away from the farm and where we have been raised in the rich historical context of independent, entrepreneurial, and pioneering farming, we want to believe what they tell us.

Unfortunately, a closer look reveals a food and agriculture system that puts products on the shelves of supermarkets at blinding speed but poisons land and water and damages the health and happiness of farmers and food workers. This current system is disastrous for many and deadly for some.

The current industrial agriculture approach is to replace smaller family farms with large-scale factory farms, all in the name of efficiency. Proponents of industrial agriculture in the Clinton administration and elsewhere argued that it takes fewer people to raise crops and livestock in an industrial-style system. However, like many seemingly efficient systems, factory farm agriculture externalizes significant environmental, social, and political costs. Agribusiness pushes the costs of air and water pollution, disease resulting from toxic exposure, and social dislocation onto individuals, the public sector, and future generations. The savings thereby gained by the industry are rarely passed on to consumers. Almost all economic gains show up as higher returns for the management and shareholders of food industry companies.

The effort to replace family farms with factory farms is not new.[1] However, the speed and scale of this assault is increasingly powerful, thanks in large part to many federal, state, and local government agencies as well as universities that use tax dollars to actively promote the growth and expansion of this factory farm system. The use of tax breaks and exemptions from basic social welfare laws to promote the destruction of family farms by agribusiness is certainly legal, but is it right? Can we as a society continue to tolerate a practice that impoverishes rural communities, pollutes our rivers, depletes our soils, destroys our wilderness, extinguishes wildlife species, mistreats animals, and sickens and kills people? Should we sit idle while this incredibly destructive food system profits a few through the suffering of so many?

A few local and state governments have passed laws or taken legal action to support family farmers in their struggle against corporate giants, but these have been the exceptions that often prove the rule. The federal government and the World Trade Organization (WTO) have overruled a number of local and state laws that were pro–family farm, such as tax breaks for small producers.[2] Although there have been few successes thus far in the legal challenges to the factory farm takeover, the courtroom testimony from these cases provides some of the most graphic and gruesome details of how our current corporate food system negatively affects the lives of millions of people, especially in the areas of food safety, health, and the environment.[3]

Arguments for the Current Food System and Policies

Supporters of the current food system have developed a series of powerful arguments to convince policymakers, opinion leaders, and the general public that the current system should not be seriously challenged or reformed. Furthermore, laws have been passed that make even the criticism of certain food system practices illegal[4] and that make it very difficult to produce and distribute food in ways that are not under the control of the current agribusiness system.

Three broad categories of arguments are used to defend the current food system:

- It is simply the best system, and any problems will be fixed by technological advances.
- Industrial agriculture is necessary to feed the world.
- The system is inevitable, both because of corporate power and because it is a natural outcome of "progress."

Perhaps the most famous promoter of the view that the industrial system is the best way to organize the food system is the Hudson Institute's Dennis Avery. His book, *Saving the Planet through Pesticides and Plastics*,[5] argues that factory farms dominate the food system because they are the most efficient way to deliver large quantities of cheap food with the least negative environmental or social cost. Unfortunately, this argument does not hold up well to close examination.

We should know: we all have some experience with the food system as consumers. Millions of us have spent some portion of our work life at a job in the food system—on a farm, in a restaurant, or somewhere else along the chain from field to fork. Most of us read or watch the news. We have heard about or been the subjects of stories like the following:

1. Five thousand people die each year from food poisoning, 76 million become ill, and 300,000 are hospitalized as a result of illnesses caused by contaminated food.[6]
2. Financially strapped farmers commit suicide at a higher percentage than do members of any other profession.[7]
3. Farm workers die each year from pesticide poisoning and accidents.
4. Between 100 and 150 children die each year in farm-related accidents, and another 32,000 are injured.[8]
5. The number of deaths from infections that can no longer be treated with antibiotics is increasing because bacteria have become resistant to antibiotics used to stimulate growth in livestock.[9]

In reaction to consumers' legitimate concerns, sophisticated promoters of the industrial system eventually acknowledge some of the dangers. They take the position that these problems are unfortunate but unavoidable side effects of feeding the world. Agribusiness proponents might even concede that organic agriculture is preferable but would argue that we could never feed the world without using lots of pesticides and artificial fertilizers.

This line of argument has been around for a long time—since long before Malthus. It is built on the idea that there is not enough food (or will not be enough food at some unknown but certain point in the future) and that to avoid famine, we must produce more, no matter the short-, medium-, or long-term costs. Fortunately, this argument is wrong. Even the shrillest proponents of the idea that industrial farming is necessary to feed the masses admit that we currently produce more than enough food for an adequate diet for every person on the planet. According to the Food and Agriculture Organization, we produce three thousand calories per day per person. An adequate diet is about twenty-five hundred calories.[10] Scientific evidence also shows that we can produce an adequate diet for up to 5 billion more people in the global population.[11]

Meanwhile, farmers all over the world are demonstrating the incredible productivity of organic and other sustainable agriculture approaches. Permaculture, integrated pest management, holistic range management, nutrient balancing, rotational grazing, and a whole host of other nonindustrial approaches to farming are turning out to be much more productive than factory farming—just as gardening is often much more productive (as well as less expensive) than large-scale agriculture.

Given that some organic, sustainable, and nonbiotech production techniques match and sometimes exceed chemical-intensive methods in yields and productivity, industrial agriculture supporters are forced to claim that the rush to globalization, corporatization, and monopolization is simply inevitable. Their critics may be right, they say, but the criticism is futile and wasted. Proponents of sustainable agriculture should just stop complaining about the dangers and inefficiencies of the industrial model and get used to it. This argument ends with a plea for more safety nets for social victims and technological fixes for pollution, but there is not a word of acknowledgment that the deadly but legal current food system can (or should) be changed.

One need only recall the fate of industrial-style farming in the former Soviet Union to question the "inevitability" of globalization. Old clichés like "You can't fight city hall" and "Big business always wins" may still be powerful arguments, but the Internet has turned this kind of conventional thinking upside-down. Perhaps the most compelling responses lie in U.S. history, where the plantations of the early 1800s and the bonanza farms of the late 1800s both peaked and declined to near extinction because they were of a size and scale that could not be supported. Both were once considered inevitable and permanent, and both were smashed by economic and political realities. The events surrounding the WTO meetings in Seattle in the fall of 1999 indicate that serious damage has been done to the belief that globalization of the industrial agriculture model is inevitable.

Corporate Hogs—A Case Study

The prototype of the industrial agriculture system is the corporate hog factory. The rapidly emerging system of gigantic factory hog farms demands aggressive political action as well as public debate, and a growing movement in the countryside is responding. Let us take a closer look at the impacts of "big pig," as these industrial hog corporations are sometimes called, and the exciting political movements that are working to change the future of agriculture.

The impact of industrial hog operations spreads like ripples in a pond, with those working on the farms facing the most immediate risks, followed by neighbors and consumers. Workers in hog factories are at high risk. A single giant hog operation can produce as much fecal waste as a city of 360,000 people. This waste is most often stored in open pits, called lagoons, where the manure decomposes into nearly four hundred volatile chemicals, primarily methane, hydrogen sulfide, ammonia, and carbon dioxide.[12] More than 500,000 people work on these corporate hog farms and are exposed to these chemicals every day.[13] There are literally hundreds of terrifying stories of farm workers and farmers dying from asphyxiation from these hog lagoons, many documented in *The Price We Pay for Corporate Hogs*, sponsored by the Funding Group on Confined Animal Feed Operations.[14] In one 1989 incident in Michigan, five family members died, one after another, as each tried to save the others from the deadly fumes.[15] Minnesota alone had more than a dozen fatalities in hog lagoons during the 1990s.[16]

Many farmers and farm workers have also suffered extreme respiratory damage from breathing toxic fumes in overcrowded hog houses, where hogs are confined throughout their lives. In addition to manure gases, the inside air contains dust with dander, dried fecal matter, feed, broken hairs, inflammatory spores, bacteria, ammonia, pollen grains, bacterial toxins, fungal spores, and insect parts. The health impacts on workers from all of this toxic and allergic dust can include a loss of lung capacity, occupational asthma, chronic bronchitis, airway obstruction, and organic toxic dust syndrome.[17]

Finally, antibiotic-resistant diseases from intensively raised cattle, poultry, and hogs are spreading to the farmers and farm workers who handle these animals each day. The *New England Journal of Medicine* reported on the case of a twelve-year-old Nebraska boy who contracted an antibiotic-resistant strain of salmonella from the animals for which he was caring on his family's farm.[18] The explosion in intensive animal production could lead to more frequent transmission of deadly diseases from animals to humans, as happened in Southeast Asia among hog farmers in 1999. An early-twentieth-century avian flu epidemic spread to people, killing millions worldwide.

People who live close to hog factories are also at risk. The same gases and toxic pollutants that affect farmers and farm workers are poisoning their neighbors, especially those located downwind from the largest facilities. The list of toxins, carcinogens, and mutagens released into the environment by these giant hog farms includes benzene, phosphate, sulfides, disulfides, organic acids, alcohols, aldehydes, amines, nitrogen heterocycles, mercaptans, carbonyls, and esters.[19] Numerous scientific and medical studies of psychological and physiological impacts are summarized in *The Price We Pay for Corporate Hogs*.[20] These studies generally agreed with epidemiologist Steven Wing's finding that residents living near hog factories had higher occurrences of headaches, runny noses, sore throats, excessive coughing, diarrhea, and burning eyes than did the control group.[21]

To make matters worse, many state and local environment and health departments ignore the concerns of hog factory neighbors, regularly siding with the giant hog farms in disputes over negative impacts. In a case that eventually won national attention, after suffering years of constant nausea and vomiting, one Minnesota family finally convinced the state's Pollution Control Agency to test the air coming from a giant hog factory located within a mile of their farm. The tests found that the family was being exposed to dangerous levels of toxic gases hundreds of times each year.[22]

Many of these factory farms have also leaked nitrates and pesticides into drinking water sources, resulting in serious health consequences and the need to replace wells or buy water. Nitrate-contaminated water has been linked to a wide range of very serious health problems, including blue baby disease (methemoglobinaemia) and other developmental diseases in infants and children. Nitrate pollution is one of the fastest-growing and most dangerous environmental problems that we face today. The negative impacts of the smells and toxins coming from factory livestock farms have been so severe in some places that local tax assessors have reduced by 10 percent or more the property values of neighboring homes. In DeWitt County, Illinois, all property values within a couple of miles of a corporate hog farm were driven down by the stench.[23]

Beyond the health impacts on farmers, farm workers, and neighbors, these factory farms are harming the health of millions of people who live far from the corporate farms by damaging the environment and our food supply and by accelerating the spread of disease and infection. One of the most significant threats to those of us far away is the pollution of the air and the water. Many giant hog farms have inadequate wastewater treatment facilities, which means that much of the waste flows into lakes or rivers or filters into underground water basins or aquifers. In addition to nitrates and other nutrient pollutants, this waste can contain disinfectants, insecticides, and other pharmaceuticals and can be a pathway for spreading pathogens throughout the environment.[24] Sometimes the impacts can be as dramatic as the huge dead zone off the coast of New Orleans, where the runoff of manure and artificial fertilizer from farms throughout the entire Mississippi River basin has created a hypoxic (oxygen-depleted) zone of as much as five thousand square miles.

The huge open lagoons where factory hog farms store their waste are also a source of dangerous emission into the air. As much as 70–80 percent of the nitrogen in an open manure storage lagoon changes from liquid to gas and goes into the atmosphere. Some returns to earth as acid rain and some as nutrients that can cause waterway-choking algae growth. Methane, which is a significant greenhouse gas, is also emitted in large quantities from these lagoons.

Our food supply is also threatened through the sale of pork products that contain dangerous bacteria, toxins, and contaminants. A good example is the crisis caused by the reckless use of antibiotics by these giant pig factories. Factory hog, poultry, and cattle farms use these crucial medicines not to treat disease but to artificially stimulate growth. Factory livestock and fish establishments have recently used nearly 45 percent of all antibiotics produced in the United States, with 80 percent used to increase growth and only 20 percent to treat diseases.[25] The National Academy of Sciences has called the use of antibiotics to stimulate artificial growth "sub-therapeutic use," defining the term as "the use of an antibiotic as a feed additive at less than 200 grams per ton of feed . . . doses below those required to treat established infections."[26] Eleven of the major antibiotics used to promote food animal growth are the same or are closely related to antibiotics used or formerly used to treat human infections, including penicillin, the class of antibiotics known as tetracyclines, and a few of the most important human "treatments of last resort," such as vancomycin.[27] Bacterial infections that were once easily controlled with common and inexpensive antibiotics are now killing people because these antibiotics have been rendered ineffective through overuse.

Resistant bacteria infect people through meat consumption, inhalation, drinking infected water, and direct transmission. Farmers and workers in slaughterhouses can become contaminated and pass diseases along to family members. As more and more antibiotics are rendered ineffective, new drugs have to be developed at very high cost, and they are often less effective as well as more dangerous. For people on fixed or limited incomes, this can be especially harmful. The cost of one of the older antibiotics, amoxicillin, is around five dollars for a full treatment, but its new generation replacement, cephalosporin, costs around eighty dollars. For some, including children, the elderly, and those with impaired immune systems, such as HIV-infected individuals, there may no viable alternative methods of treatment. Many illnesses and deaths each year are now attributed to these untreatable infections.[28]

The controversy over this sub-therapeutic use goes back fifty years and includes major reports published in the United Kingdom and in the United States. As far back as 1977, the U.S. Government Accounting Office called for the Food and Drug Administration to strictly regulate the use of antibiotics in feed.[29] In response, the administration proposed regulations on the use of penicillin and tetracyclines, but the animal feed and drug industries intervened and killed the proposal. Later studies by the National Science Council and the Centers for Disease Control and Prevention confirmed the seriousness of the problem but were unable to overcome the political power of those pushing sub-therapeutic antibiotic use to promote factory farms. Organizations such as the Natural Resources Defense Council petitioned the government to act. Although a few members of Congress have introduced legislation to control this deadly but legal practice, there is little hope of its becoming law.[30]

Moreover, factory farms produce another type of externality: they wipe out small farming communities. As of 1999, the one hundred biggest hog factories controlled 40 percent of all U.S. hog production, with the largest four firms accounting for 20 percent of the total.[31] Factory farms are responsible for creating major economic dislocations by destroying many economically and ecologically sustainable family farms. Between 1990 and

2000, nearly 90 percent of family-scale farmers were driven out by giant operations. When we replace thousands of family farms with a handful of corporate farms, we are losing a generation of farmers who know how to care for their land and animals and substituting corporate management, often thousands of miles away, that does not know the land, the animals, the surrounding community, or the region's ecological conditions.

It's Not Just Hogs: The Whole Industrial Food System Is Hazardous

Gigantic corporate hog farms are simply one aspect of the industrial food system. The powerful confluence of fast food restaurants, biotechnology companies, food fabricators, and supermarkets is creating a modern diet that is not only tasteless but often hazardous to our health. Chemical and pharmaceutical residues outside and inside fruits and vegetables, high fat and cholesterol content in processed and fast foods, and the presence of untested genetically engineered foods threaten the food supply. Many of the so-called Green Revolution's miracle crops are being found to be dangerous as well, as the ecological costs of their production are documented along with their loss of nutrients. Studies published in the United Kingdom have indicated that the loss of micronutrients in many of the new Green Revolution varieties of crops can hurt brain development in children. Up to 1 billion Third World children are thought to be at risk from these crops.[32]

The public debate over genetic engineering of our food supply has been elevated to an issue of human rights. Some experts argue that the promotion by the U.S. government and food corporations of genetically engineered foods without adequate testing to determine potential impacts on human health is a violation of international human rights laws that prohibit medical experimentation on people without their permission.[33]

Big Pig, Big Lobby: Factory Farms and Agribusiness Drive Public Policy

The growth in the industrial food system has generated significant resistance and public criticism. Factory farm promoters have reacted with extreme measures to quell unrest and silence criticism. We are familiar with the violence used by employers against farm workers and meatpacking plant workers who have attempted to organize to protect their health and well-being. But with the growth in consumer criticism has come a new generation of corporate activism in search of help from the government in three major ways. First, agribusiness has persuaded legislatures to pass laws that ban public criticism of factory farming. Second, the industry has found ways to get factory farming exempted from basic environmental and social regulations. Third, the industry has supported the passage of laws and treaty provisions that make it difficult to produce food in nonindustrial ways.

Agribusiness corporations have pushed many state legislatures to pass laws to make it illegal to criticize giant factory farms. In the most celebrated prosecution under these "veggie libel laws," the state of Texas sought on behalf of its largest factory farm operator to silence Oprah Winfrey. The popular television talk show host had questioned cattle factories' common practice of feeding ground-up dead animals to live cattle.

Agribusiness has also convinced policymakers to exempt the industry from most social and labor rights laws. For example, farm workers are generally excluded from protection under many U.S. labor and occupational health and safety laws. The Clean Water Act was written in such a way that it excluded from enforcement "nonpoint sources" of pollution—primarily the chemical, nutrient, and soil runoff from factory farms and other agricultural lands. The Occupational Safety and Health Administration has set no standards for factory hog farms, although many workers and unions have for years called for such standards.[34] Many of the most powerful companies in the food industry, especially supermarkets and fast food companies, are fighting hard to get Congress and state legislatures to further weaken various child labor, minimum wage, and environmental laws.

Beyond these efforts to silence critics and avoid social responsibility, agribusiness companies have worked for the passage of laws and the implementation of international treaties that make it nearly impossible and, in some cases, practically illegal for farmers to choose nonindustrial approaches such as organic or other sustainable agriculture methods. For example, agribusiness corporations pushed hard to ensure that recent regional and global free trade deals, such as the North American Free Trade Agreement and other agreements promoted by the WTO, put highly restrictive conditions on the use of consumer labeling to promote organic and sustainable agriculture. At the same time, the U.S. Department of Agriculture (USDA) has shifted the focus on research funding away from ecologically sound integrated pest management research to research on how to put pesticides inside our food through biotechnology. This aggressive reduction in research on ways to control pests without dangerous chemicals, pesticides, and genetic manipulations makes it harder for farmers to farm organically and sustainably.

One of the new technologies being promoted by the USDA is the use of genetic engineering to put Bacillus thuringiensis (Bt), a bacterium that emits an insect toxin, inside corn, potatoes, and other crops. Bt has long been one of the few natural pesticides approved for use by organic and sustainable farmers under the strict rules for organic certification and labeling. As with antibiotics, when Bt is overused, the bugs that once could be controlled by careful, low-dosage applications of this relatively safe pesticide become resistant. Many organic farmers now find that they cannot control pest losses because Bt no longer works, leading to significant financial losses that in a few cases have included the loss of the farm itself. Furthermore, these genetically engineered Bt crops seem to be responsible for the reduction of such beneficial pollinating insects as bees and butterflies,[35] leading to lower yields in many crops that require insect-assisted pollination.

The push to hand over control of our food supply to the biotechnology companies is the most recent and perhaps most dangerous of the USDA's activities, creating extraordinary risks for present and future generations. For example, the USDA has developed and given to private companies a number of biotechnology products—for example, the "terminator gene," which can be used to render all plants sterile.[36] Another example is the move by USDA and other government agencies to allow private companies to patent life forms such as plants, animals, and even parts of the human body. This puts farmers and ultimately consumers into a position of near-total dependence on a handful of seed monopolies.

The Ultimate Threat

The ultimate irony of the debate about food system industrialization is that it leads some people to lump family farmers together with the industrial farms of agribusiness. As a result, all food becomes suspect when some is tainted and unsafe, and consumers blame all farmers for the pollution of a few giant corporate farms. Consumers cannot easily distinguish the food produced by careful stewards of the land from that produced by ecologically destructive agribusiness. Even something as minor as allowing farmers who choose not to use artificial growth hormones in milk to label their products as hormone free was prohibited in several states and is still discouraged by the federal government.

As family farms are being wiped out, they are being replaced by global monopoly corporations attempting to control the food chain from pitchfork to fork. The weakness of U.S. antitrust laws and the lack of enforcement of those that do exist[37] means that these monopolies will continue to expand their control. Unless we find ways to pay farmers enough for their crops and livestock to support them to farm the right way and to stay on the land, deadly policies and practices will become the norm.

Fortunately, it is not too late to reverse this trend. There are still 2 million family farms in the United States, but nearly all are struggling to survive. In addition, tens of thousands—and perhaps many more—of young people and new immigrants are looking for ways to farm. Many of these potential future family farmers are experimenting with new structures, like community-supported agriculture, in which urban and suburban consumers contract in advance to buy harvests. Other family farmers are marketing over the Internet. A new Web site (www.eatwellguide.org) helps connect consumers with meat and poultry farmers that raise these animals sustainably, without hormones and non-therapeutic antibiotics. It is up to us to decide if we want a food system that gives life to both the consumers of the food and to the Earth. And it is up to us to decide if we will allow our political democracy, including cherished rights of freedom of speech and freedom from discrimination, to be subverted by a mad rush to a factory-farm system of food production. As with many other critical ecological and social problems, the longer we wait to decide and act, the more difficult the solution will be.

What Is to Be Done?

While the forces pushing the industrial food model are powerful, they can be and are being effectively challenged and, in some cases, defeated or redirected by organized political efforts. For example, an international consumer boycott forced the Nestle Corporation to change its dangerous baby formula marketing practices.

Farmers are banding together to form cooperatives to help undermine marketplace monopolies, while consumers are seeking out alternative paths to the kinds of foods they want—fresh, free from chemicals, and locally grown. Some of the most important efforts organized at the national and international levels are campaigns to end the sub-therapeutic use of antibiotics in animal agriculture, to force biotech companies to withdraw untested genetically engineered foods from the market, to label all genetically engineered foods that reach the market, and to reverse the bad food and agriculture policies that have come as a result of the Uruguay Round of trade negotiations.[38]

Beyond these campaigns and other organized efforts, each person can make a difference as a citizen and as a consumer by buying local and organic produce whenever possible and by looking for the Fair Trade label on coffee and other tropical food products.[39] People can also work to get their schools, workplaces, or places of worship to spend money in ways that help local family farmers as much as possible. All politicians are food consumers, and all drink water. They know they are somehow connected to this system, but most need help to see how their decisions as leaders can make a real difference. Talking to them can help them in this process.

Collective and individual actions are most powerful when they are set within a supportive policy framework. If the local government or drinking water agency provides technical and financial support for farmers making the transition to organic farming, the process will be sped up.

What if all food that was not organic had to be labeled instead of making organic growers shoulder this added cost? If the federal government required labeling on all foods that were treated with dangerous chemicals or genetically engineered, all of us would have the information we need to make healthier, more ecologically sound choices.

What if we had an international trade policy that kept out unsafe products and encouraged local food cultures to flourish? What if trade rules were designed to protect human rights, like the right to food and shelter, as strongly as they protect intellectual property rights?

We know how to grow food safely and sustainably. We know the health impact of our diets. We know the social and political justice issues that confront us every day in the food industry. What we need is political action to turn what we know into public policies and personal practices that return food production to its proper role in creation.

NOTES

1. See Mark Ritchie, *Loss of Family Farms: Inevitable Result or Conscious Policy* (Minneapolis: Institute for Agriculture and Trade Policy, 1979).

2. One of the most dramatic cases was the overturn by the WTO of Oregon state laws designed to help smaller brewers through an excise tax break; see "GATT Finds U.S. State Laws on Beer Discriminate against Foreign Brewers," *Wall Street Journal*, March 13, 1992.

3. For an overview of some of these cases, see Marlene Halverson, *The Price We Pay for Corporate Hogs* (Minneapolis: Institute for Agriculture and Trade Policy, 2000).

4. Television personality Oprah Winfrey got a taste of this power when she had to stand trial in Texas after being accused of criticizing the feeding of ground-up dead and diseased animals to beef cattle, a common practice that is seen as the likely cause of the deadly mad cow disease epidemic in the United Kingdom.

5. Dennis Avery, *Saving the Planet through Pesticides and Plastics*, 2d ed. (Indianapolis: Hudson Institute, 2000).

6. Centers for Disease Control and Prevention, "Preliminary FoodNet Data on the Incidence of Foodborne Illnesses, United States, 1999," March 2000, www.cdc.gov/epo/mmwr/preview/mmwrhtml/mm4910a1.htm. See also Centers for Disease Control and Prevention, "Food-Related Illness and Death in the United States," http://www.cdc.gov/ncidod/eid/vol5no5/mead.htm.

7. For more information, see *Congressional Record* submission by Congressman David Obey (D-WI), July 23, 1997, "How the Rural Crisis Fuels Antigovernment Movement," by Joel Dyer.

8. "Health and Safety," *Atlantic Monthly*, June 2000, 12.

9. For an excellent overview of the full range of issues, see K. J. Donham, "The Impact of Industrial Swine Production on Human Health," in *Pigs, Profits, and Human Communities*, ed. K. M. Thu and E. Paul Durrenberger (Albany: State University of New York Press, 1998, 73–83).

10. Food and Agriculture Organization, Technical Background Documents 1–5, *World Food Summit*, 1:4–5, Rome, November 13–17, 1996.

11. See Frances Lappé, Joseph Collins, Peter Rosset, and Luis Eparaza, *World Hunger, Twelve Myths*, 2d ed. (Oakland, CA: Grove Press, 1998).

12. C. D. Fulhage, *Gases and Odors from Swine Wastes*, publication G01880 (Columbia: University of Missouri, 1993).

13. Thu and Durenberger, *Pigs*, 80.

14. Halverson, *The Price We Pay for Corporate Hogs* (Minneapolis: Institute for Agriculture and Trade Policy, 2000).

15. Halverson, *Price*, 30.

16. Farm Safety Program, *Farm Injury and Fatality Data* (St. Paul: University of Minnesota, Biosystems and Agricultural Engineering Department, 1998).

17. K. J. Donham, "Respiratory Disease Hazards to Workers in Livestock and Poultry Confinement Structures," *Seminars in Respiratory Medicine* 14 (1) (1993): 49.

18. "Cultivating Resistance to Antibiotics," *Washington Post*, April 27, 2000.

19. D. Strauch, *Animal Production and Environmental Health* (New York: Elsevier, 1987).

20. Halverson, *Price*, 62–65.

21. S. Wing and S. Wold, *Intensive Livestock Operations, Health and Quality of Life among Eastern North Carolina Residents: A Report Prepared for the North Carolina Department of Health and Human Services, Division of Public Health* (Chapel Hill: University of North Carolina School of Public Health, Department of Epidemiology, 1999).

22. C. Ison, "State Health Department Acknowledges Health Risks of Feedlots," *Minneapolis Star Tribune*, February 20, 2000.

23. See "Board Smells Lower Land Values Near Hog Farm," *Peoria Journal*, May 6, 1998.

24. Another legal but deadly impact of the drive to huge factory hog farms is the destruction of biodiversity. Current practices have led to the loss of habitat that is now endangering many species, including salmon, elk, and eagles.

25. S. B. Levy, "Multidrug Resistance: A Sign of the Times," *New England Journal of Medicine* 338 (19) (1998): 1376–78.

26. Quoted in Halverson, *Price*, 32.

27. A. Salyers, *Antibiotic Resistance Transfer in the Mammalian Intestinal Tract: Implications for Human Health, Food Safety, and Biotechnology*. Austin, TX: Molecular Biology Intelligence Unit, R. G. Landes, 1995.

28. P. Huovinen, "Immediate Need for Antibiotics Policy in the Community." In *The Threat of Antibiotic Resistance: A Nordic Perspective* (Stockholm: Swedish Academy of Pharmaceutical Sciences, 1997).

29. U.S. General Accounting Office, *Report of the Comptroller General of the United States on the Need to Establish Safety and Effectiveness of Antibiotics Used in Animal Feeds* (Washington, DC: General Accounting Office, 1977).

30. For example, H.R. 3266, 106th Cong., 1st sess., introduced on November 9, 1999.

31. U.S. Department of Agriculture, National Agricultural Statistics Service, *Hogs and Pigs Report*, MT An 4(12–99) (Dec. 28, 1999)

32. Geoffrey Lean, "Hi-Tech Crops Are Bad for the Brain," *The Independent*, April 23, 2000.

33. The most important of these treaties is the Nuremberg Accords, developed after World War II in response to Nazi experimentation on concentration camp prisoners.

34. For additional information on this situation, see Centers for Disease Control and Prevention, *Request for Assistance in Preventing Deaths of Farm Workers in Manure Pits*, NIOSH Publication 90–103 (Washington, DC: National Institute of Occupational Safety and Health, 1990).

35. The most important studies on the impacts of genetically engineered corn on butterflies and other beneficial insects can be found at http://www.biotech-info.net/risks.html#beneficials.

36. For more information on the terminator gene, contact RAFI International, 110 Osborne Street, Suite 202, Winnipeg, MB, R3L 1Y5 Canada; http://

www.rafi.org. A simple but complete description, "How the Terminator Termi-nates," is found at www.bio.indiana.edu/people/terminator.html.

37. See John Lauck, "Toward an Agrarian Antitrust: New Direction for Agri-cultural Law," *North Dakota Law Review* 75 (3) (1999).

38. For more information on these campaigns, contact the Institute for Agri-culture and Trade Policy, 2105 First Avenue South, Minneapolis, MN 55404; www.iatp.org.

39. For more information on the Fair Trade system, contact Headwaters Inter-national, 2105 First Avenue South, Minneapolis, MN 55404; http://www.peacecoffee.com.

9

Accountability in the Pesticide Industry

Peter Riggs and Megan Waples

Introduction

Many people perceive the power of agrochemical interests as a major obstacle to the development of sustainable agricultural alternatives. Promoters of sustainable agriculture face a series of obstacles from agrochemical concerns. Pesticide use is expanding in spite of widespread awareness of its dangers. Agrochemical companies' influence on national development plans continues unabated. Pesticides that are banned or restricted in industrial countries are aggressively marketed in the global South. The industry-promoted notion of "safe use" of pesticides in the tropics has become a cruel joke perpetrated on farmers and agricultural laborers who lack the power to bargain for improved occupational health and safety standards. The science regarding the ecological and public health consequences of pesticide misuse is unequivocal. We know that these products cause serious and lasting harm. Nevertheless, the prevailing attitude of government officials, public health workers, and nongovernmental organizations can be summed up as follows: Despite the existence of viable agricultural alternatives, and despite a broad understanding of the problems and risks associated with these products, deceptive marketing and outright dumping of these chemicals in the farm sector continues. Establishing accountability for these companies has been a challenging task for public interest activists.

While additional controls are needed, a number of important regulatory and judicial handles already exist that should enable us to curb the worst pesticide abuses, at least in theory. However, the full range of what those handles are, and how they might be used to this end, have not yet been fully described or attempted. Similarly, although the public generally understands many of the problems associated with pesticides, we believe that specific information about the long-term downside risks of investments in pesticides is not being adequately communicated to market analysts. We further believe that efforts to help to provide this information in ways useful to financial service professionals represent a profoundly constructive contribution both to ensuring greater corporate accountability and to safeguarding public and environmental health.

Recent investor concerns about the inadequacy of U.S. corporate disclosure rules have fueled across-the-board declines in stock prices. As of July 2002, President George W. Bush's moves to tighten reporting requirements and punish corporate wrongdoers had not calmed the markets. On the contrary, the preceding few months saw one of the sharpest falloffs in major stock indexes in more than fifteen years. It is clear that this massive loss of confidence in the financial markets will permanently alter our perceptions of what constitutes adequate corporate responsibility (see also Klinger and Sklar, in this volume).

In this climate, the Rockefeller Brothers Fund in June 2002 brought a small group of concerned scientists, lawyers, socially responsible investment professionals, and advocates of sustainable agriculture to the fund's Pocantico Conference Center for a meeting on accountability in the pesticide industry. This chapter distills the participants' brainstorming and suggestions. We hope that creative deployment of the strategies discussed here can help to correct financial market perceptions of investment risks in the pesticide industry. More generally, we hope that our recommendations may serve as a blueprint for using financial disclosure and improved transparency to increase corporate accountability in any economic sector. Thus, this chapter will outline concrete policies and strategies that widen the range of options that can be envisaged with respect to other industries discussed in this volume.

The Harm Caused by Pesticides

Pesticides are chemical or biological agents designed to eliminate unwanted pests from agricultural systems or places of human habitation. The most prevalent class of pesticides is insecticides, but weed killers (herbicides), fungicides, and chemicals used for animal control (e.g., rodenti-cides) also fall into this category.

Pesticides work by interfering with the biological pathways of unwanted plants and animals—that is, by being toxic to the target species. Although there has been a trend away from "broad spectrum" pesticide use and toward more precise targeting of particular pests in chemical-control efforts, pesticide use inevitably leads to impact on nontarget species—other plants and animals, including humans. (*Broad-spectrum pesticides* are relatively nonselective chemical formulations that eliminate not just tar-geted pest species, but a range of other insects or life-forms that may help to maintain the overall ecological balance in the field environment. DDT is one example of a broad-spectrum pesticide. A great deal of pesticide research focuses on reducing toxicity to nontarget species.)

Farm workers are the most likely to be exposed to toxic pesticides, and numerous studies have pointed out the serious adverse health impacts of pesticide use on rural populations. Effects can be acute (based on onetime exposure) or chronic and cumulative. Exposure to pesticides can lead to reduced immune system function, impaired neuromuscular coordination, and reproductive abnormalities. In severe cases, pesticide exposure can lead to death. Impacts are not just limited to farm workers, however; every human being carries some "body burden" of chemical pesticides. These effects are still difficult to quantify, however, and the potentially synergis-tic impacts of two or more chemicals in the body are even less well under-stood.

At the ecosystem level, pesticides can cause tremendous harm to assem-blages of soil organisms, to native insect fauna, and to higher-order ani-mals (such as birds) that prey on these species. Pesticides frequently reduce biodiversity and cause shifts in plant communities. Absorbed into soil, pes-ticides can persist over several growing systems; these chemicals can also be carried by water and thus inflict damage on ecosystems far from the site of their use.

Reducing Chemical Reliance in Agriculture

As our knowledge of the true risks and costs of pesticides has grown, so too have attempts to reduce agriculture's reliance on agrochemicals. The cur-rent volume of pesticides used globally is unnecessary to maintain global food production. In fact, current overreliance on chemical shortcuts is degrading the productive agricultural resource base, making future increases in yields much more difficult. Substituting less toxic chemicals, accelerating production and deployment of safer botanical pesticides, and, most importantly, vigorously promoting farmer-centered, ecologically based approaches to pest management should be the primary goals for the future of agriculture.

These are hardly radical assertions. Over the past several decades, research in the fields of ecology and public health has shown the problems associated with pesticide use. Regulatory systems designed to control pesticide use at both national and international levels have evolved in response to this body of research. In addition, research and activism at the local level has convincingly demonstrated that viable alternatives to chemical-dependent agriculture are both possible and profitable.[1] The dramatic success of farmer-led integrated pest management (IPM) programs in curbing excessive pesticide use shows that ample room for reductions exists even within the commodity-focused "industrial agriculture" paradigm. While there is legitimate disagreement regarding the speed at which major changes to our food-production systems can be made and the degree of economic disruption that will occur as a result, there is a broad professional consensus on the importance of reducing chemical reliance in agriculture.

However, implementing the changes necessary for reducing pesticide reliance will inevitably challenge the vested interests of the existing industrial sector, including pesticide production, formulation, and marketing. An accelerated move away from pesticide dependency is likely to dramatically decrease the agrochemical sector's profitability and growth prospects—and therefore the sector's attractiveness to investors. Rational behavior of firms in this industry, however, inevitably includes attempts to expand their markets, prolong the patent-protected life and overall use of their products, and shape IPM programs to ensure a future role for their chemicals.

Another widely held view that informs this chapter is the likelihood that corporations will face larger liabilities than they do now as a result of harms imposed on people and nature around the world. This has already occurred with tobacco and with asbestos claims. Liabilities in the latter case have exceeded profitability for many companies, resulting in a slew of bankruptcies. As evidence of the damage caused by pesticides grows, agrochemical companies are likely to face rising legal costs and liabilities and declining revenues. Perception of rising risk levels in this sector will discourage new investment.

Our point of departure is thus a perceived disconnect among three observed facts:

- the broad consensus on the need for a move away from pesticide reliance;
- the increasing possibility that pesticide companies will incur major financial liabilities; and
- financial markets' continued unquestioning support of the agrochemical industry.

This cognitive dissonance persists because of misunderstanding and underestimation of the industry's risks, liabilities, and long-term viability. A major challenge, therefore, is to better document and communicate these risks and liabilities to investors, analysts, and consumers so that they will be able to better assess the market value of agrochemical firms.

Many issues of pesticide manufacture and use should concern investors, even if the immediate financial impacts are unclear. These issues need to be raised with investors even as our collective understanding changes regarding what fiduciary responsibility actually entails. We will begin by laying out what we perceive as the major risks faced by the pesticide industry and by those who invest in it. The next section will cover investors' concerns about quality of management and reputational risks. We will then look at the institutional changes necessary to inject the information laid out here into financial decision making, considering the variety of relevant decision makers. Finally, we will provide an overview of the most promising near-term opportunities for action. The number and variety of such opportunities already being pioneered provide grounds for optimism.

Pesticides Are Inherently Risky for Investors

The types of risks and liabilities that the pesticide industry faces can effectively be grouped into four categories: legal liabilities, market trends, regulatory trends, and long-term uncertainties. In this section we will divide the last of these topics into three headings: gaps in safety testing; disaster response, disposal, and cleanup costs; and unwelcome surprises. In addition, we explore potential problems related to quality of firm management and broader corporate reputation risks.

Accelerating Legal Liabilities: Trends in Product Liability Suits

Pesticides are inherently risky products. Pesticide producers are always at risk of product liability claims as a result of poisonings, deaths, and other damages. Product liability suits against the pesticide industry as a whole, although relatively limited in their size and scope to date, have the potential to become a major threat. To date, plaintiffs bringing claims against pesticide producers have faced serious hurdles in their pursuit of redress, hurdles that raise questions about access to justice in a globalized economy. Much of the harm caused by pesticides takes place in developing countries, among workers who may have little access to formalized systems of justice. Establishing jurisdiction for civil actions in these countries is fraught with difficulties. Developing-country plaintiffs may face procedural barriers and high filing fees, as well as justice systems that are weak, corrupt, or vulnerable to outside political pressures.

When sued in the United States, pesticide companies have generally found protection from product liability claims in one of three ways. The first is a doctrine of *forum non conveniens*, which allows a court to dismiss a case in the interests of the convenience of the parties when the majority of evidence is in another country. The second is known as "FIFRA preemption." Pesticides are regulated at the U.S. federal level under the Federal Insecticide, Fungicide, and Rodenticide Act (FIFRA), first passed in 1947. FIFRA sets requirements for the testing, registration, use classification, and labeling of pesticides. Finally, pesticide companies have successfully argued that damage was caused by misuse of their products, and liability thus falls to the user or agent responsible rather than to the producer.

Several recent cases have undermined these traditional defenses and opened new doors for plaintiffs. As more cases are pursued, pesticide companies may face increasing liability for their products. Legal activists have also been working to hold the pesticide industry, especially transnational corporations operating in a global economy, accountable in other ways, therefore increasing the trend of upholding the "polluter pays" doctrine.[2]

Market Trends toward Organics and IPM

Market trends are a key concern for potential investors. If a technology or a group of products is becoming obsolete or losing consumer favor, a company whose business strategy depends on that technology or product market leader will usually not fare well over the medium to long term. Trends in agricultural product markets are obviously relevant to pesticide markets in particular. Farmers are the immediate consumers of pesticides, but their production choices are driven by the preferences of those who purchase food and fibers. Several trends developing in these markets indicate a growing public unease with pesticides (and with genetically engineered crops) and a clear preference for foods grown in a less damaging, more sustainable way. These trends are visible at the level of the individual consumers' increasing preference for organic foods and at the supplier level among food processors and retailers, as the following examples show.

- In 2001, the Co-op Group—one of the United Kingdom's top five food retailers and Britain's largest grower—announced that it was "banning over 20 pesticides used for food production worldwide amid rising consumer concerns about the impact on human health and the environment of chemical residues." The ban applies not only to all fresh produce but also to canned, frozen and processed foods. Six products still permitted for use in the United Kingdom are among the pesticides for which the Co-op Group will show zero tolerance. The Co-op Group also seeks to impose "restrictions on the use of over 30 other chemicals where the Co-op will ask growers to use more benign alternatives." The group has also embarked on a stringent testing program for pesticide residues to ensure implementation by growers and suppliers around the world.[3]
- Food processors and retailers are coming under increasing pressure to incorporate IPM standards into their production protocols and standards. Large processors such as Campbell's and Unilever are implementing such measures.
- The market for organically grown produce is growing rapidly. Consumer polls in the United States, United Kingdom, Japan, and the European Union (EU) show increasing concern about pesticides and the embracing of organic produce as a safer alternative. Although currently representing just a small share of overall food sales, the relative growth rate of organic foods—largely as a result of consumer concerns about food safety and harmful pesticide residues—is impressive. According to the Food and Agriculture Organization (FAO), "sales values [of organic foods] have increased in most markets at an annual growth rate of 20 to 30 percent" since the early 1990s; this trend has accelerated since the FAO "World Markets for Organic Fruit and Vegetables" report was published in 2001.[4] "The

organic fruit and vegetable market offers significant potential for countries to increase their export earnings and diversify their agricultural base," states a November 2001 press release from FAO[5] that coincided with the publication of the report.

- The use and acceptance by consumers of both "ecolabels" and "fair trade" designations is expanding. Retailers can increasingly market the particular qualities associated with these specialty labels in the expectation that the claims can be verified and that consumers understand what the label represents. The Fairtrade Labelling Organizations International recently issued a guideline stating that no dangerous pesticides can be used in the production of an item seeking the Fair Trade label.[6]

Based on these examples, there is ample reason to believe that the market for pesticides will shrink with decreased public acceptance of the risks and costs of pesticide use.

Regulatory Trends away from Pesticide Use

Regulatory trends play a critical role in determining a company's future value. Since regulations can greatly alter the costs of doing business and the marketability of certain products, any uncertainty in the regulatory environment should be of concern to investors. With the trend toward increasingly stringent regulation of pesticide use in both the developed and developing world, the picture for those investing in agrochemicals is not encouraging. Europe, in particular, is leading the way. EU regulations are increasingly establishing liabilities for pollution caused by pesticides, thereby affecting pesticide sales and creating legal liability costs for the industry. In addition to the dramatic changes in Europe, the following trends should be borne in mind:

- In the developing world, government-mandated IPM programs designed to reduce pesticide use have become more widespread. National IPM programs also help to protect the health of farmers and farm workers as well as to reduce the financial costs incurred by farmers. Increasingly, such programs also assist farmers in gaining new access or maintaining existing links to export markets. Under these programs, farmers receive training in methods that significantly reduce the need for pesticide use. As these programs grow more widespread and their success and cost-effectiveness

become more obvious, the developing world's markets for pesticides
will shrink. This is particularly important because the developing
world is now the only major growth market for pesticides.

- Both the EU and the United States are reviewing lists of registered
pesticides with an eye toward reducing use of these products. In the
EU it is anticipated that this review will substantially reduce the
number of pesticides re-registered for use beyond 2003. As residue
tolerance levels are revised downward, markets for pesticides phased
out in the EU come under pressure in countries exporting to the EU,
including many developing countries.

- In the United States, the Food Quality Protection Act, passed in
1996, requires the Environmental Protection Agency (EPA) to
establish new safety standards that better protect children from pesticide exposure and then to reassess permitted pesticide uses and
food residues according to these standards within ten years. The law
mandates that the EPA focus on pesticides considered most hazardous to children, a sensible strategy widely endorsed by advocates.
The pesticide industry and other conventional agricultural interests
bitterly opposed the Food Quality Protection Act, and lawsuits and
settlements have been and continue to be required to ensure even
lackluster progress in its implementation. Still, the law has already
forced the EPA to ban completely, for all home and garden uses, two
widely used insecticides and to reduce, or bring to a zero-point,
almost two thousand pesticide-residue limits for a variety of foodstuffs. Based on consent-decree-driven deadlines and explosive new
information being generated about pesticide impacts, health and
environmental activists expect the Act's implementation to pick up
speed in coming years, leading to many more cancellations and
restrictions on pesticide use.

- National reviews of agriculture and crop protection policies over the
past decade have sought to ensure the safety of drinking water supplies, enhance the sustainability of agricultural production, and
respond to consumer concerns about pesticides in their food and
environment. The Netherlands provides a dramatic recent example:
its "Ten Year Policy on Plant Protection" aims for a 95 percent
reduction in the environmental burden caused by the use of chemical pesticides and asks farms to seek IPM certification by 2010.

- In addition to national policies, there are trends toward more stringent pesticide regulation at the subfederal level. For example, in
addition to having tougher state pesticide laws (as allowed under
FIFRA), California has passed a number of other laws affecting pesticides. A case in point is California's Proposition 65, a voter initia-

tive passed to address citizen concerns about exposure to toxic substances, including pesticides, that cause cancer or have reproductive
toxicity.

- More and more public spaces, or places frequented by "vulnerable
  populations" (e.g., children, pregnant women, the elderly), are being
  designated as free of pesticides. At least thirty-three states have
  adopted regulations addressing protection of children by focusing on
  pesticide use in, around, or near schools.

These regulatory trends demonstrate a consistent and increasing concern
about the costs and impacts of pesticides. Over time, these regulations will
both reduce the markets for pesticides and attach higher costs and liabilities to their use.

Long-Term Risks I: Gaps in Safety Testing

The approval and registration of pesticides in the United States is managed primarily under FIFRA. Relying on EPA oversight of FIFRA, many
investors and consumers believe that pesticides on the market are safe or
at least that their risks are well known and managed. But this is not necessarily true. Although in 1972 FIFRA was amended to require that all
pesticides used in the United States be assessed for long-term environmental and human health impacts, many pesticides in production have
not gone through that level of assessment. Pesticides that were registered
before 1972, when regulations were significantly less rigorous, were supposed to be re-registered under the new guidelines. However, that
process has been extremely slow, and many pesticides still on the market
consequently have not been adequately retested for long-term environmental and human-health risks. Pesticides produced only for export are
not required to go through the safety testing required for U.S. registration. However, these chemicals are still manufactured and transported
within the United States, creating the same risks of exposure and contamination.

The EPA does not itself test chemicals. In the interests of "commercial
security," companies perform those tests in-house and submit their results
to the EPA for review. This system creates a great deal of leeway for companies to choose which results and which data sets to submit. This means
that the EPA may be approving and registering pesticides on incomplete
or possibly even misleading information, sending to market pesticides that

may in fact pose significant health risks. These risks, in turn, create larger liabilities for the companies involved.

This system has already failed farmers, farm workers, and consumers many times. The list of products once judged beneficial and harmless enough to be registered under FIFRA and later discovered to have serious health and/or environmental consequences begins with DDT and continues to grow. Without a more stringent system of third-party review and testing, the risks posed by pesticides will not be well known and managed. It is worth noting that in-house testing of asbestos and tobacco failed to effectively prevent product-related injuries or to prevent lawsuits and liabilities resulting from these injuries.

Further, the statute requires an analysis comparing health and environment risks to the aggregate financial benefits from pesticide use. Not only is the former more difficult to quantify than the latter, but the resulting figures are not strictly comparable. Public interest activists suggest that this approach creates a strong bias toward product approval, even in the face of considerable scientific uncertainty, and propose the "precautionary principle" as a preferable conceptual framework for FIFRA.

Long-Term Risks II: Disaster Response, Disposal, and Cleanup Costs

By far the best-known case of widespread harm caused by pesticide manufacture is the case of the 1984 explosion and release of toxic gas from Union Carbide's plant in Bhopal, India. While Union Carbide settled with the Indian government, the case nonetheless has dragged on in various courts. The Bhopal incident did lead to changes in how agrochemical firms viewed their liability—most companies moved to isolate, to the maximum extent possible, the legal liability for particular manufacturing plants or subsidiaries from the parent corporation as a whole.

The body of law regarding this restricting of legal liability is quickly evolving. Disposal costs, procedures, and liabilities are also changing rapidly. It has become much more difficult for industrialized nations to export hazardous wastes to the developing world. Just as firms in other industries have had to shoulder major cleanup costs for oil spills and other disasters, pesticide companies should expect that they would also be liable for such costs in the event of a major spill.

Finally, it must be acknowledged that national security concerns now extend to the possibility of attacks on chemical industry production facilities. Unfortunate and unfair as this may be, companies that produce or store large quantities of pesticides are exposed to additional risks (and costs) associated with the potential for terrorist use of these materials. Lawmakers are flexing their muscles in this field: a bill pending in the Maryland State Legislature would require background checks on anyone seeking access to restricted-use pesticides. In 2002 HB 809, entitled "Agriculture Restricted Use Pesticide Use and Access," did not go to a vote in the House or Senate. It was reintroduced in 2003 as SB 540, but again did not go to a vote in either house.

Long-Term Risks III: Unwelcome Surprises

In addition to known data gaps, researchers continue to bring forward unexpected data about pesticides. These revelations serve as a reminder that important questions often go unasked before new chemicals are introduced into the environment and the food chain. In the past decade, such revelations have included the following:

- We have seen the emergence of a previously unexamined category of risk—hormone disruption—for which few pesticides have been tested. This emerging body of data has sent shock waves throughout the international environmental and policy communities, in large part because effects have been noted at exposure levels as low as parts per billion. In addition to pointing to the need for more research regarding such effects, these findings highlight the weakness of relying on cancer as the main end point in risk assessments.
- Research in recent years, including a groundbreaking study from the National Research Council, has demonstrated that childhood exposure to pesticides is associated with increased cancer risk. With these findings came the realization that safety thresholds for childhood exposures had never been evaluated as part of EPA's registration process. For decades, then, national and international markets were flooded with pesticide products whose effects on this particularly susceptible population were unknown.
- A report published by the World Resources Institute[7] raised the possibility that by reducing immune function in already weakened populations in developing countries, pesticide exposures might be contributing to excessively high death rates from infectious diseases in these regions.
- It has been discovered that pesticide overuse is contributing significantly to an international decline in the population of insects, birds, and other animals that perform pollination functions, frogs

and other amphibians, and other animals. The economic value of animal pollination to world agriculture has been estimated at $200 billion per year. One recent effort to assess the economic significance of this newly identified problem concluded that "serious problems for world food supply, security, and trade could be in the offing if current declines in pollinator abundance, diversity, and availability are not reversed."[8]

Many pesticide risks may remain incompletely described or still unrecognized. Experiences in other industries provide many examples of risks that were underestimated or initially not observed. Precautionary approaches are a more appropriate basis for pesticide regulation than the risk/benefit framework underpinning most national systems and trade agreements.

Quality of Management

Most serious investors and investment analysts devote significant effort to assessing the quality of a company's management, since that quality affects the company's ongoing financial welfare and competitiveness throughout its operations. Corporate irresponsibility may indicate a failure of management, giving rise to fiduciary concerns. A widespread loss of confidence in corporate management is likely to contribute to a precipitous decline in share value.

Certain patterns of corporate conduct on the part of agrochemical companies may serve as reliable indicators of a higher quality of overall corporate management. These potential indicators include: adhering to international codes and conventions and taking a leadership role in the implementation of voluntary codes; adopting uniform companywide performance standards rather than defaulting to lower environmental and occupational health standards permitted by local regulations; demonstrating life-cycle concern for products; and achieving an above-average level of transparency with respect to company operations.

Conversely, the kinds of pesticide abuses that concern public interest activists may indicate a divisionwide or even companywide management failure. Because institutional investors (such as pension funds, mutual funds, foundations, and endowments) must be guided by their fiduciary duty to prudently manage the assets under their control, these investors must seriously consider any demonstrable pattern of imprudent behavior by those who manage the companies in which these institutions invest.

Patterns of irresponsible conduct by agrochemical corporations represent precisely the kind of imprudent behaviors that give rise to fiduciary concerns, since these behavior patterns pose real risks of financial injury to investors as well as of harm to public health and the environment.

The following examples demonstrate how the behavior of particular firms with respect to pesticide use may be indicative of a more general failure of management.

Compliance with International Codes and Conventions

Because the pesticide industry deals in products that are, by design, harmful to life, sales and use of these products are governed by both national and international standards. The extent to which companies observe or neglect these standards is a powerful indicator of management quality. Although such standards vary in form, focus, and type of compliance required, many will include guidelines for reducing reliance on pesticides and minimizing the risks to users, public health, and the environment. Other standards deal more generally with rules governing public partnerships or are broad statements regarding corporate ethics, including issues such as transparency, conflict of interest, due diligence, and corruption. While most of these standards are voluntary, some are legally binding, including two recent conventions with provisions requiring implementation by ratifying governments.[9]

Nonbinding, normative standards can provide pesticide companies with a frame of reference for considering best practice, corporate responsibility, product stewardship, and good environmental management. These standards can also help investors evaluate the management strength and performance of individual companies and can provide a way of comparing a specific company's performance to that of other firms in the industry.

The pesticide industry has offered its own set of standards for best practices. The American Chemistry Council (ACC) developed the Responsible Care® program in 1988 in response to public concerns and the need to improve the environmental safety and health performance of the industry. According to ACC literature, "Responsible Care® is advancing in 47 countries, representing over 85 percent of the world's chemical production." The program is essentially an environmental management system for chemical manufacturers. In fact, the ACC has developed a certification system, called RC 14001, that will award both Responsible Care® and ISO14001 certificates in a single audit process. The program has developed from a simple statement of codes of management practice to one driven by a series of performance matrices.[10] The ACC has pointed to Responsible Care® as evidence that the industry is capable of policing itself and does not require further regulation.[11] Some companies' annual reports and Securities and Exchange Commission (SEC) filings refer to participation in the program as evidence of strong environmental management.

Another particularly relevant convention, with substantial normative force in the developing world, is the FAO's International Code of Conduct on the Distribution and Use of Pesticides. CropLife International, the trade association representing the pesticide industry, has "actively supported the FAO Code of Conduct, and has made compliance with the FAO Code by national associations and their members a condition of membership."[12] Given the broad level of support for the FAO Code of Conduct and the industry's professed desire to comply with it, the code is a good measuring stick by which to evaluate company practice and management.

Feedback from the field, especially from developing countries, suggests that these standards of behavior and self-regulation are frequently ignored in daily practice.

- Guidelines for partnerships between international organizations and the private sector emphasize transparency and avoidance of conflicts of interest. However, a review of partnerships with pesticide companies under World Bank projects revealed broad conflicts of interest and noncompliance with bank safeguard policies.[13] Similar concerns have been raised about partnerships with pesticide companies under the United Nations Global Compact.
- Companies have frequently failed to live up to their commitments to "cradle-to-grave product stewardship" as described in Responsible Care Program and other industry literature. As described later in this chapter, there are serious problems with obsolete pesticide stocks in most countries. To date, pesticide manufacturers and distributors have strongly opposed efforts by the FAO, World Wildlife Fund, Pesticide Action Network, and other groups to increase the industry's historically insignificant financial contributions to the disposal of obsolete pesticides in developing countries.
- In 1987 and 1993, the FAO conducted comprehensive reviews of the implementation of the FAO Code of Conduct.[14] These reports show significant shortcomings related to trading practices, advertise-

ment, collaboration to recall hazardous products, and labeling information, among other areas. Their findings are consistent with those documented by numerous nongovernmental and civil society organizations during the past two decades; ongoing advertising of unsubstantiated claims is among the persistent problems documented by such monitoring efforts.

Properly documented and publicized, such cases would demonstrate that many companies are out of step with internationally accepted standards and norms for good management and corporate responsibility. (This issue comes up again in the section on reputational risks later in the chapter.)

Product Use in Developing Nations and Consistency of Corporate Behavior

Many of these problems regarding violations of codes and conventions relate generally to the inconsistencies and double standards employed by the pesticide industry in dealings with developing countries. Perhaps the most famous example is that of the "circle of poison," where pesticides banned in industrialized countries are nevertheless produced there and then exported for use in developing countries, only to be reimported to the developed world as residues on foods. This tidy concept has captured the public's imagination, but double standards and inconsistencies are much broader and more damaging.

The idea of the circle of poison usually refers to pesticides that have been banned in the industrial North but that are still used in the global South. In fact, relatively few pesticides are actually banned; many more are restricted with respect to uses. Use can be restricted to particular crops, to trained applicators, or conditions of use (for example, requiring special protective equipment, or specific weather conditions, before spraying is allowed). Monitoring of actual field conditions in developing countries invariably reveals serious obstacles to complying with the restrictions intended to protect human health and the environment from significant pesticide damage. These damages can include the following:

- lack of protective clothing and face masks for pesticide applicators;
- lack of water for washing after spraying or for laundering work clothes;
- absence of a separate storage facility for pesticides or for clothes used in spraying pesticides;

- absence of disposal facilities for either large obsolete stocks or for used containers;
- reuse of pesticide containers for storage of food and water;
- lack of access to health care services;
- poor literacy levels, making complex labeling instructions meaningless;
- poor-quality (leaking) sprayer units; and
- lack of equipment maintenance.

Whenever a pesticide is restricted or banned for actual or potential health or environmental problems in a particular locality, data exist to demonstrate reasons for the ban. At the very least, it must be considered ethically questionable to continue marketing those chemicals in countries that lack the ability to effectively regulate or enforce restrictions on their use or that have not yet performed the local tests likely to result in a ban. Nonetheless, companies routinely and aggressively market chemicals that they know have serious human health consequences to people in the developing world. Additional concerns are generated by the fact that the agricultural workforce in the developing world includes a high proportion of women and children and by the fact that they often perform such tasks as spraying pesticides or picking crops soon after they have been sprayed.

In response to widespread public concern about these practices, many companies have embarked on "safe-use" programs designed to train growers in developing countries in how to handle and apply these pesticides. There is a substantial body of literature showing that safe-use training does not provide workers with adequate protection. One industry-funded report even stated that any pesticide manufacturer that cannot guarantee the safe handling and use of its toxicity Class I products should withdraw these products from the market.[15] However, many manufacturers continue to market their most toxic pesticides in developing countries with no such guarantees.

Disposal of Obsolete Stocks

Obsolete stocks of pesticides are a growing international environmental health problem. The FAO has documented more than forty-seven thousand tons of obsolete pesticide stocks in fifty-three countries, but this is far from a complete inventory; global estimates suggest that the actual amount of obsolete stocks may be closer to half a million tons. It is likely that nearly every developing country has obsolete stocks of pesticides, and cleanup costs range from twenty-five hundred dollars to five thousand dollars per ton, depending on volume and circumstances.[16]

Pesticides become obsolete if their use is banned while the product is kept in storage or if a product has deteriorated because of poor storage conditions. In some cases pesticides were imported (frequently under foreign aid programs) to combat a particular pest emergency that never came to pass. Some stockpiles have been accumulating for as long as forty years. These stocks frequently are not stored securely and may cause environmental contamination and human health problems.

Governments generally feel that companies should bear a significant share of the disposal responsibility—particularly if supplying companies irresponsibly pushed to have the chemicals imported. For example, company representatives or others that stand to gain financially may overestimate the amount of a pesticide needed for a particular project or pest outbreak; sometimes, poorly supervised company agents will suggest chemicals that are not technically appropriate for a given agricultural project. There are also cases where companies have explicitly used donor projects or loans to off-load stocks that are about to be banned in a developed country. Yet companies have adamantly refused to contribute significantly to the cleanup and disposal of their stocks. The pesticide industry has contributed less than 1 percent of the $30 million spent worldwide in the 1990s on the disposal of obsolete pesticide stocks.[17]

While there is currently no legal mechanism to require companies to take responsibility for their role in handling obsolete stocks, there is growing public pressure for companies to live up to their own claims of cradle-to-grave product stewardship by contributing to cleanup and disposal. A continuing refusal to accept responsibility and to play a meaningful role in reducing the problem creates a reputational risk and demonstrates a failure to meet the principles of corporate environmental management systems, provisions of the FAO Code of Conduct, Responsible Care Program guidelines, and other relevant standards.

Compliance with Export Labeling and Shipping

Arguing that it is unfair for competitors to have ready access to details regarding their production and trade, pesticide companies have sought to have export labeling and shipping notification requirements considered "confidential business information," not to be shared with the public. This practice prevails at the global level. Even in the case of international treaties intended to reduce or eliminate trade in specific chemicals, the industry has insisted that it will release only limited information regarding production and trade of the target chemicals.

Companies do not comply even with the minimal standards that do exist. Huge quantities of chemicals are shipped interstate and internationally without adequate labeling and/or with product documentation that is out of compliance with legal requirements. Between 1992 and 2000, approximately 3.8 billion pounds of pesticides—63 percent of total exports—were not clearly or specifically identified in shipping manifests. A significant percentage of the 1.5 billion pounds of pesticides exported during the 1996–2000 period were identified only as "weed killing compound" or "pesticide" rather than by specific names.[18] Many products are shipped unlabeled or are labeled incorrectly. A significant percentage of these shipments likely would run afoul of federal regulations requiring hazardous materials to be specifically named in shipping documents. In addition, the paucity of relevant information regarding shipments can greatly hinder the preparation of emergency preparedness plans, increase the costs of responding to an emergency response to a spill, and result in much more severe environmental and human-health damage than would otherwise occur.

Reputation Management

All of the concerns and behaviors described here would risk damaging name brands and corporate reputations. The idea of reputational risk is difficult to define but is becoming increasingly accepted as an important business issue. This risk has been more obvious for consumer product companies: campaigns against Nestle and other corporations have shown that concerted public education and media outreach efforts can have a lasting impact on a company's reputation. This, in turn, can affect a corporation's market share, damage investor relations, and hinder its ability to move into new business areas and attract quality employees. Of course, corporate image and reputation are important for all companies, not just those that have retail product brands. This can be seen from the fact that several of the major pesticide producers have recently attempted to reposition themselves as "life science" companies—a generic but appealing term behind which it is more difficult to perceive an explicit association with chemical pesticides or genetically engineered crops.

Reputational risk is an area where nongovernmental organizations and public interest activists have had substantial impact. Establishing reputational risks requires working to document and dramatize to the public the bad actions of particular companies as well as to document and communicate bad press and ongoing public concerns to company managers and investors. Nongovernmental organizations have used this strategy very effectively in other sectors. For example, a coalition of groups successfully lobbied Home Depot to halt sales of wood from endangered rainforests and to give preference to sustainably harvested wood products. Public interest activists have also persuaded treated-lumber manufacturers and retailers to stop stocking lumber treated with chromated copper arsenic and other arsenic compounds. These campaigns have involved a combination of street theater tactics at Home Depot stores, media, shareholder activism, and dialogue with senior management, as well as the provision and promotion of viable alternatives. The pesticide industry is vulnerable to reputational risks due to inconsistencies in their practices at home and abroad and their lack of compliance with accepted codes of conduct.

Reaching the Markets

There is urgent need for improved communication regarding the risks we outlined previously in this chapter. Continuing lack of awareness in the finance community with respect to these risks allows corporations to pursue business as usual, including routinely marketing extraordinarily toxic chemicals and taking advantage of underregulated developing-country environments. To protect investors (and public and environmental health) and to create market incentives for developing sustainable alternatives such as IPM and organic agriculture, it is essential that financial markets accurately account for pesticides' true costs and risks. Improved communication of such information will also fill an important gap in the materials available to the public regarding pesticides.

To more accurately account for these risks and costs, we recommend the following actions.

- Document the true extent of the global risks and liabilities associated with this industry, and seek legal and financial accountability.
- Increase the socially responsible investment (SRI) community's engagement with the pesticide industry and related issues.
- Use the power of private and institutional investment monies to move the agricultural sector away from a financially risky and environmentally destructive overuse or abuse of pesticides and toward

more socially responsible, beneficial, and accountable industries and
activities.

- End direct and indirect public subsidies to the pesticide industry and
  increase public support for sustainable alternatives.
- End public agencies' partnerships with pesticide companies wher-
  ever these partnerships create a clear conflict of interest or violate
  the codes of the public agency in question.
- Use the pesticide industry as an important test case to enhance current efforts to improve corporate disclosure, governance, accountability, and ethics.

Any attempt to use financial leverage in these ways must be multifaceted
and reach a wide variety of audiences. Different strategies are required to
reach these different aims and to bring the different constituencies into
stronger alignment.

The Socially Responsible Investment Community

The research and investment companies involved in the SRI movement
have helped lead the way in making financial markets account for the
environmental and social costs of different industries. Different SRI firms
use different strategies, including screening (choosing not to invest in
companies that create environmental and social risk or investing only in
those companies considered best in class), shareholder activism (seeking
to improve corporate behavior through dialogue and resolutions), and
community development (investing in opportunities that support communities and sustainable development). Although most SRI funds are not
invested in pesticide companies, these funds are well positioned to play a
lead role in strategies involving shareholder activism and in improving the
level of due diligence on pesticide companies. Other SRI investors, pursuing a best-in-class approach, can help strengthen support for international
codes of conduct and other mechanisms that distinguish proactive management from mere legal compliance.

Pension Funds and Other Institutional Investors

Pension funds and other institutional investors are a strong force in financial markets, commanding 30 percent of invested capital in the New York
Stock Exchange. Institutional investors represent concentrations of in-

vestor power and thus are an easier target for public interest activists than are individual investors. Many pension funds are quite sensitive to concerns not considered strictly financial. For example, public pension funds in some states have a mandate to invest in ways that benefit the state and might view support for companies producing products that degrade groundwater and surface water quality as inimical to state interests. Foundations—particularly those with programs in health, environment, or rural development—should be willing to vote their proxies or invest in ways that support their program goals. Students can pressure universities to use their endowments and consumer power in socially responsible ways (as has been demonstrated both in the fight against apartheid in South Africa and more recently in anti-sweatshop campaigns). Given these other interests, institutional investors may become allies for shareholder activism and potentially for pursuing divestment.

Shareholder Activists

In addition to SRI and institutional funds, other types of shareholder activists can affect investment patterns in the pesticide industry. A great deal of shareholder activism presently occurs on issues of good corporate governance, including improved reporting, that would overlap with efforts to more accurately reflect the disclosure concerns discussed here.

For example, the issue of obsolete pesticide stocks lends itself well to engagement by shareholders. Although most SRI funds are not likely to be invested in pesticide companies, there may be some opportunity to work with the SRI community on this issue. In addition, it may be possible to align with other institutional investors and shareholder activists to work with companies to request data disclosure or company action on the issue of obsolete pesticide stocks.

Analysts

Financial analysts play an essential role in the financial markets, researching and valuing companies according to various models and recommending that fund managers buy or sell particular stocks. How an analyst perceives and values a company can affect how its stock is treated on the market. While analysts work in an information-rich environment, they often rely primarily on company-based sources and may not be aware of broader contextual issues or of the views of other stakeholders. Analysts with interests in long-term market forecasting would be particularly interested in the kinds of materials and information presented here.

The Securities and Exchange Commission

The SEC oversees the U.S. stock markets and regulates company-reporting requirements. Recent events have pressured the SEC to play a stronger role in monitoring the corporate sector by adopting broader definitions and standards of disclosure. Working with the SEC could be important both in improving data disclosure and reporting across the industry and in pursuing omissions or misleading statements by particular companies. The impact of impending regulatory changes in Europe may be considered as material business issues, therefore subject to disclosure.

Public Agencies

Public funding from governments and international bodies such as the World Bank continues indirectly to support the pesticide industry around the world. This support can be in the form of tax breaks, subsidies, funding for safe-use programs, or procurement of products through foreign aid programs. International agencies such as the United Nations and the World Bank have begun to establish public-private partnerships with these companies, providing positive public relations benefits to the companies and sometimes helping to open new markets for them. However, governments and public agencies are accountable to the public and are required to act in the public interest. Multiple opportunities exist to work with governments and public agencies to redirect these monies to more sustainable alternatives. For example, improved implementation of World Bank Safeguard Policy 4.09, which requires the use of farmer-based IPM strategies in the pest-management component of any agriculture loan, is an important vehicle by which a public agency could assist in shifting this sector away from its current costly and damaging overreliance on pesticides.

Consumers

Consumers are important actors in corporate accountability efforts. Working with consumers is essential to raise social awareness of the health and environmental impacts of pesticide use. Consumers obtain investment advice and use financial service products, use foodstuffs and fibers that may be contaminated with pesticides, and may purchase other products sold by companies that make pesticides (e.g., Bayer Aspirin, DuPont cookware).

Insurers, Bond Analysts, and Banks

Insurers may prove to be an interesting audience for pesticide concerns in two ways: as major investors and as underwriters of disaster insurance to specific companies. Indeed, the underwriting industry estimates the cost of complying with environmental cleanup costs and legal fees to be in excess of $100 billion.[19] Insurance companies obviously have a strong interest in reducing such costs and fees. Bond analysts are at first glance an unlikely target audience, but analysis done for bond markets is relatively thorough and long term in its orientation, which may suggest a direct interest in improving data disclosure requirements for companies floating commercial paper. Companies planning major new initiatives are likely to have a close relationship with one or more investment banks, so it may be effective to channel accurate risk information to these banks.

Strategies and Opportunities

Given the risks and liabilities outlined in this chapter and the potential target audiences, the most promising immediate opportunities for action include the following.

Research and Analysis

A first and essential step is to improve understanding of the major pesticide manufacturers worldwide. The pesticide industry is highly concentrated, with seven manufacturers currently controlling upwards of 80 percent of the global pesticide trade. The "Big Seven" have made considerable investments of staff time and money in shaping the strategies of CropLife International, the pesticide and agricultural biotech industry association. CropLife International was formally launched in June 2001; previously, the agrochemical industry association was known as the Global Crop Protection Federation. Its U.S. affiliate, CropLife America, describes itself as representing the "developers, manufacturers, formulators, and distributors of plant science solutions for agriculture and pest management in the

United States." Its member companies "produce, sell and distribute virtually all the crop protection and biotechnology products used by American farmers."[20] CropLife International rolled out a new, aggressively positive public relations initiative, "Promoting Capacity Building for Sustainable Agriculture," at the Rio + 10 World Summit on Sustainable Development.

TABLE I.   Top Seven Agrochemical Companies: 2001 Sales

Company	Sales ($ billions)	Change since 2000
Syngenta (Switzerland)	5.385	–8.5%
Aventis CropScience (France)	3.842	+5.0%
Monsanto (United States)	3.755	–3.3%
BASF (Germany)	3.105	+39.4%
Dow AgroSciences (United States)	2.612	+11.3%
Bayer (Germany)	2.418	+7.4%
DuPont (United States)	1.917	–4.6%

Sources: Agrow, World Crop Protection News, March 1, 15, 29, June 28, 2002; Global Pesticide Campaigner 12 (2) (August 2002): 26.

Research approaches to understanding individual companies, industry associations, and the overall market structure of this industry are needed, including

- a thorough assessment of pesticide producers' finances and financial accounting procedures;
- a thorough assessment of the companies' product lines, past and current behaviors, and potential liabilities;
- information on corporate structure, including relationships to other companies, developing world subsidiaries, board members, conflict-of-interest policies, public relations profiles, and so on, as well as information on the internal corporate culture;
- the status of various mergers and divestitures, which has rapidly changed the face of the pesticide industry in recent years;
- case studies regarding other products at one time commonly used but later withdrawn as a result of health concerns, leading to massive industry liabilities (for example, asbestos cases);
- studies of legal trends related to liability; and
- sector-specific research on the financial implications of environmental performance (for example, the World Resources Institute report on the pulp and paper industry).[21]

Credible research is required for continued work on corporate accountability. Results must be prepared in formats most useful to target audiences; thus, different products may be needed to target the financial services community, the media, and so forth.

Advancing Social Reporting

The SEC requires companies to disclose information judged material to
business concerns so that potential and current investors have an accurate
picture of firms' health. Current regulations require disclosure of "information that a reasonable investor would be likely to consider important in
the context of all the information available." The SEC goes on to say that,
"facts can be considered material if they bear on the ethics of management, its integrity, or its law compliance record, irrespective of the sums
involved."[22] The requirement includes forward-looking statements, market uncertainties, and trends that may affect future financial performance.

However, many companies fall short of fulfilling these reporting
requirements. Even when adequacy of compliance is more precisely defined, company reporting is often found to be lacking. For example, the
SEC has stated that companies must report on any pending legal proceedings: specifically, "Environmentally related proceedings must be disclosed
if: they are material; they involve a claim for more than 10 percent of current assets; or they involved the government and potential monetary sanctions greater than $100,000."[23] Studies have found that companies often
fail to report on legal proceedings fitting this definition. Superfund liabilities must also be disclosed but frequently are not.

Improving data disclosure across the board is essential for improving the
performance of financial markets and creating appropriate incentives for
strong environmental management. Information disclosure has been shown
to improve environmental management, and companies practicing
improved disclosure are less vulnerable to adverse market impacts when
outside information becomes available. Event studies show that stock market prices do react to environmental news, confirming that investors consider environmental and social information relevant.

The pesticide industry in particular needs to improve its data disclosure,
particularly in two areas: operating data and discussion of risks and uncertainties. Pesticide companies frequently do not disclose accurate data
regarding their products, export practices, sales in developing countries,

location of obsolete stocks, and production-related pollution issues. Activists, investors, and other stakeholders cannot adequately assess a corporation's environmental management or risk exposure without these data. For example, information about exports of pesticides is extremely difficult to pin down: aside from the inadequate labeling issues described earlier, some pesticide companies even withhold their names from shipping manifests.

Many issues regarding pesticide industry practices as well as pesticide market and regulatory trends are not adequately or accurately described within company reports. For example, the pesticides molinate, atrazine, and paraquat have been the subject of a great deal of public controversy due to their high toxicity and environmental impacts. One of their manufacturers, Syngenta, acknowledged the risk of product liability lawsuits briefly in its 2001 annual report. Their conclusion glossed over the depths of the problem, stating only:

> We designed our environmental management program with the aim of ensuring that our products and their manufacture pose minimal risks to the environment and humans. The crop protection industry is subject to environmental risks in three main areas: manufacturing, distribution and use of product. We aim to minimize or eliminate our environmental risks by using appropriate equipment, adopting "best industry practice" and providing grower training and education. The entire chain of business activities, from research and development to end use, operates according to the principles of product stewardship. We are committed voluntarily to the responsible and ethical management of our products from invention through to ultimate use.[24]

This stance is reflected in the literature of most companies as well as that of CropLife International. Agronomists, health professionals, and public interest activists are demanding that such statements be evaluated against the patterns of behavior noted earlier in this chapter, such as promoting use of World Health Organization Class 1 products in developing countries; manipulating procedures and rules to speed access to markets; providing financial incentives to decision makers to override health and environmental concerns; and refusing to assist in the disposal of obsolete pesticide stocks. In sum, there is a major gap between stated corporate environmental management objectives and field practices. Although the SEC has been reluctant to enforce environmental-risk-reporting requirements, it is likely that a "reasonable investor" would be interested in information about the perceived gap between rhetoric and actual business practices.

Prodding the SEC

Several coalitions are working to improve SEC guidelines on social and environmental risk disclosure and to improve enforcement of regulations pertaining to these disclosure requirements. The Corporate Sunshine Working Group, a coalition of more than sixty organizations, is urging the SEC to hold corporations accountable for reporting significant environmental expenses. The Social Investment Forum (the trade association of socially concerned investors) is also asking for SEC action on these compliance issues.

Another important effort has been the Environmental Fiduciary project of the Rose Foundation for Communities and the Environment. This project makes the financial case for incorporating environmental factors into portfolio management policies. Socially responsible investor groups are also pushing the SEC on disclosure requirements. Domini Social Investments has asked the SEC to require that all mutual funds publish their proxy voting policies and votes.

World Resources Institute has also paid careful attention to the SEC's administrative proceedings, noting that "of the more than 5000 Administrative Proceedings initiated by the SEC over the last twenty-five years, only three are based on insufficient disclosure of environmental risks or liabilities."[25] Over that same period, the SEC brought only one civil action against a company on the grounds of inadequate environmental disclosure.[26]

In conjunction with such efforts, two approaches are particularly relevant for advancing social reporting.

- Filing challenges and complaints with the SEC regarding specific omissions or misleading statements in a particular company's filings. The SEC imposes specific requirements on the accuracy of communications associated with proxy fights, including information that a company may publish in response to a proxy. Increasing the number and specificity of challenges on these issues helps to build demand and momentum for change within the SEC. Such challenges can also be used in public information campaigns to bring attention to issues of corporate misrepresentation.
- Requesting improved guidelines for social and environmental

reporting. Reiterating such requests alongside specific challenges would build public pressure on the SEC to improve reporting requirements and compliance monitoring.

Investor Education on Data Disclosure

In addition to those at the SEC, there are ample other opportunities to directly work with and educate investors about data disclosure problems. For example, one strategy might be the preparation of addenda to the annual reports to be circulated to investors. These would detail particular areas where the company has provided incomplete or misleading information. Working with shareholders to file resolutions requesting that specific reports and data be disclosed can also create pressure on companies and lead to opportunities for dialogue with management on improving disclosure. Again, SRI firms are in the vanguard of this effort.

Supply Chain Management—Investor and Consumer Activism

Although pesticide companies may not be particularly vulnerable to consumer pressures, their downstream customers are. As described in the earlier section on market trends, major food and product retailers are moving toward tighter management of their supply chains to reduce pesticide contamination in their purchasing. This is part of a larger trend toward supply-chain management as a form of corporate responsibility. Kodak, Volvo, Ford, Procter and Gamble, Toyota, Texas Instruments, and many other firms have pursued better supply-chain management, working with suppliers to improve corporate safety and environmental performance and/or to support "design for environment" production goals.

Given the trend toward supply-chain management and precedents set by Campbell's, Unilever, the United Kingdom Co-op Group, the Fairtrade Labelling Organizations International, and others with respect to pesticides, a promising approach is to work with food retailers, food processors, and fiber and clothing companies to implement similar measures. This strategy could be particularly conducive to shareholder activism and appeals to SRI funds that hold shares of food and fiber companies but not of agrochemical companies. Concerns regarding supply chain issues should probably also address issues related to the introduction and marketing of genetically engineered crops. Most major pesticide companies make questionable claims to promote genetically engineered crops as a means of reducing pesticide use.

Increasing Funding to Alternatives

Working with food and fiber companies on supply-chain management nicely complements the goal of increasing funding to more sustainable alternatives, including farmer-centered IPM and organic agriculture. As consumers drive food and fiber companies to use and produce products according to these principles and standards, farmers will have an increased economic incentive to pursue such alternatives. There are numerous ways to increase public and private funding to promote farmer-centered IPM and organic agriculture, including the following.

- Pesticide companies actively solicit public capital (through bilateral aid programs, multilateral development banks, or Department of Agriculture programs) in support of their safe-use and IPM training programs. As mentioned earlier, these programs can actually increase pesticide use, introduce small farmers to pesticides they cannot afford to use properly, and reinforce a chemical-centered view of agriculture. Chemical-centered IPM considers pesticide use as the primary mode of crop protection, while ecologically based, farmer-centered IPM acknowledges the existence of pests and seeks not their elimination, but rather to prevent outbreaks that will cause high levels of economic harm to farmers' crops. To compare, a total IPM program administered by AgroEvo, a pesticide manufacturer in Brazil, only reduced the number of pesticide applications from forty to twenty-eight. By contrast, a program in Mexico supported by Campbell's Soup—a company with a clear interest in supply chain management—and using an ecologically based approach, managed to achieve a reduction in pesticide sprayings during the cropping season from forty to just two. In Brazil, farmers have remained heavily dependent on AgroEvo pesticides, and AgroEvo obviously has little incentive to promote the type of IPM used in the example from Mexico. Redirecting these funds to farmer-centered, ecologically based IPM training programs, such as those run by the Global IPM Facility and other financially disinterested IPM programs, would promote better farm economics and reduced pesticide use.
- The incentive structure for sustainable agriculture would be strengthened by removing existing subsidies and tax breaks that benefit pesticide companies and redirecting these monies instead to organic and other, less toxic, sustainable farmers and suppliers. Public information is needed to pressure governments and public agencies to reallocate their subsidies and funding for research. One ongoing effort, Pesticide Action Network North America's "World Bank

Accountability Project," attempts to push this largest of the multi-lateral development institutions to embrace organic and sustainable agriculture principles, better implement its own Safeguard Policy 4.09 on IPM, and clarify the nature of its partnerships with pesticide firms.

- As mentioned earlier, community development is one of the central tenets of socially responsible investing. Working with SRI funds to identify investment opportunities that support farmer-centered IPM and organic agriculture would be a natural fit for many funds, providing much-needed capital to those efforts. Efforts to broaden investor awareness generally can start with the SRI community.

Advancing Legal Precedent

Establishing greater legal and financial liability for the negative health effects of pesticides is clearly a very powerful way to change investors' perceptions of risk with respect to this industry. In recent years, the level of legal activism regarding pesticide misuse has intensified. Groups such as EarthJustice and the Environmental Working Group have ongoing efforts to bring suits against industry actors; in so doing, these groups advance precedents that establish or expand legal liability. One current focus is finding new legal avenues for foreign workers affected by pesticides. Efforts to find new legal strategies within the United States and Europe establishing the right to bring suit over occurrences in the developing world may broaden the liability applied to the pesticide industry. It is also necessary to increase public and investor awareness of such cases and their outcomes, thereby establishing the public perception that these companies are responsible for the impact of their products. This is difficult and long-term work, but it is not without precedent: such litigation was essential in helping to curb tobacco industry abuses. Decades of litigation were key to forcing the tobacco industry into legal settlements and acceptance of new regulations.

Decertification Campaigns

Like other companies concerned about reputational risks, pesticide firms crave recognition by international bodies. As described earlier, a number of conventions and codes apply to the pesticide industry, including the FAO Code of Conduct and the industry-led Responsible Care Program. Pesticide companies also have been actively pursuing partnerships with the World Bank and the United Nations. The participation of agrochemical companies in the UN's Global Compact has been something of a public relations disaster for this global institution. Finally, several pesticide companies have been included in indexes such as the FTSE4Good and the Dow Jones Sustainability Index that are intended to highlight best-in-class companies, or firms with superior environmental management records.

Public perceptions of such companies can be altered by research into corporate noncompliance with the FAO Code of Conduct, violation of guidelines of public/private partnerships, and other egregious behaviors. The screening criteria used in obtaining listings for such indexes can also be challenged; many public health activists think there is no place for pesticide companies on any index that implies corporate social responsibility. Performing rigorous "audits" that document violations and cases of insufficient or inaccurate reporting, and publicizing the results, can help investors understand the degree to which companies have made compliance with the code a routine part of corporate behavior; such audits can also shed light on management's decision-making procedures. Applying pressure to the UN to end pesticide companies' participation in the Global Compact and other partnerships would both remove any inappropriate public relations advantage that companies gain from participation and signal that there are well-founded concerns regarding those companies' performance. The FTSE4Good and Dow Jones Sustainability Index includes companies with best-in-class records but excludes companies that deal in what are clearly socially harmful products, such as weapons and tobacco. Some advocates believe there is no place for agrochemical companies in these indexes, and attempts to get them delisted would send a strong message regarding the social utility of pesticides in light of available alternatives.

Worker-Oriented Strategies

There are several different labor constituencies (waged agricultural workers, workers in pesticide production facilities, workers in the food/fiber processing and retail sectors) with specific occupational interests in pesticides. Various labor pension funds may be interested in working with issues of special importance to these constituencies. Unions have particular expertise and sophistication regarding these issues. Indeed, some of the strategies described above are already being used by the International Union of

Foodworkers, and public interest advocates involved with pesticide issues should improve their understanding of worker concerns and objectives.

Conclusion

The issue of corporate social responsibility has greater salience and attention today than at any point since the 1930s. The need is not to undertake a new campaign but rather to incorporate information such as that collected in the Pocantico Forum into existing work on sustainable agriculture, corporate responsibility and accountability, and multilateral institutional reform. Each of these different campaigns should understand and develop initiatives pertaining to the financial risks of continued pesticide use. Each of these different reform efforts will also benefit from awareness of the others.

Two final points should be made. The first is that the tactics discussed here are strategies of engagement. Sustainable agriculture activists have frequently sought direct engagement with pesticide producers and distributors but have, for the most part, been frustrated. As can be seen from the new "sustainable agriculture" program announced by CropLife International, the industry frequently appropriates approaches (e.g., IPM) and manipulates definitions ("sustainable agriculture") from those advancing a different, more ecologically based and social benefit oriented development agenda. The strategies outlined here will increase engagement with additional actors involved with the industry. This broadening of tactical approaches can be expected to create new opportunities and incentives for change within the industry and the multiple arenas that constitute its operating environment.

Finally, this chapter frequently uses the term *investors*. Who are these investors? One Pocantico meeting participant summed it up this way: "They are retired teachers, public employees, steelworkers, widows and orphans, colleges, hospitals, and foundations." In other words, they are all of us. Building a broader engagement to pursue social change necessitates that we all look to our investments. At the very least, we should not be complicit through our portfolios in funding activities that run counter to our beliefs and values. Nor should we ever be placed in the unfortunate position of being duped, watching our investments crash down around us, simply because a company that was not required to disclose certain information failed to do so. To ensure that our investments uphold our values, we must first seek to obtain the information necessary to make those critical judgments.

NOTES

Research for and writing of this chapter was undertaken while the authors were program officer and program associate, respectively, at the Rockefeller Brothers Fund. The authors gratefully acknowledge the assistance of RBF staff and board colleagues in preparation of this manuscript.

This chapter was based on discussions at a forum at the fund's Pocantico Conference Center, June 25–28, 2002. An earlier version was issued as Pocantico Paper 5. In addition to the authors of this chapter, the Pocantico Forum included the following participants: Andreas Bernstorff (Greenpeace, Germany), Barbara Dinham (Pesticide Action Network, United Kingdom), John Harrington (Harrington Investments), Adam Kanzer (Domini Social Investments), Sanford Lewis (Strategic Counsel), Steve Lydenberg (Domini Social Investments), Monica Moore (Pesticide Action Network North America), Jill Ratner (Rose Foundation for Communities and the Environment), Erika Rosenthall (EarthJustice Legal Defense Fund), and Carl Smith (Foundation for Advancements in Science and Education).

This chapter is in many ways the result of a collective effort, for which the authors sincerely thank the participants as well as several outside reviewers whose schedules prevented them from attending in person. However, the authors take final responsibility for any errors. The opinions represented here should not be assumed to represent the positions of the Rockefeller Brothers Fund or its staff members or board members.

1. Jules Pretty and Rachel Hine, *Reducing Food Poverty with Sustainable Agriculture: A Summary of New Evidence* (Colchester, UK: Centre for Environment and Society, University of Essex, February 2001); Greenpeace and Bread for the World—Germany, "Recipes against Hunger: Success Stories for the Future of Agriculture," http://www.farmingsolutions.org.

2. Michael R. Neilson, "Pesticides: FIFRA Preemption," *Chemical Regulation Reporter* 25 (1) (April 23, 2001): 728–37; "*Guzman v. Amvac* Ruling: Implications for the Agrichemical Industry," *Agrichemical and Environmental News,* November 2000, http://www.aenews.wsu.edu/Nov00AENews/Nov00AENews.htm#anchor 971146. See also Gurdial Singh Nijar, "Developing a Liability and Redress Regime under the Cartagena Protocol on Biosafety: For Damage Resulting from the Trans-Boundary Movements of Genetically Modified Organisms," *Third World Network* (2001), http://www.twnside. org.sg/title/blplpdf.

3. http://www.cooponline.coop/about_campaigns_consumer6.html.

4. International Trade Centre, Technical Centre for Agriculture and Rural Cooperation, Food and Agriculture Organization, "World Markets for Organic Fruit and Vegetables—Opportunities for Developing Countries in Production and Export of Organic Horticultural Products" (Rome: FAO, 2001). Available at http://www.fao.org/docrep/004/y1669e/y1669e00.htm.

5. "Bearing the Fruit: FAO Study Urges Countries to Develop Organic Food Market, Provides Caution Too," Press Release 01/90, Food and Agriculture Organization, Rome, November 13, 2001. Available at http://www.fao.org/organicag/doc/press_y1669e.htm.

6. Fairtrade Labelling Organizations International, "Generic Fairtrade Standards for Small Farmers' Organizations," Bonn, Germany, January 2003, p. 5, available at http://www.fairtrade.net/sites/standard/sp.html. Rule 3.1.1.2 prohibits use of pesticides in WHO Class 1a and 1b, pesticides in the Pesticide Action Network's "Dirty Dozen" list, and those in the FAO/UNEP Prior Informed Consent Procedure list. The rule is repeated in the Fairtrade Labelling Organizations International guidelines for farmers using hired labor: "Generic Fairtrade Standards for Hired Labour," Bonn, Germany, January 2003, p. 7.

7. Robert Repetto, *Pesticides and the Immune System: The Public Health Risks* (Washington, DC: World Resources Institute, 1996).

8. P. G. Kevan and T. P. Phillips. "The Economic Impacts of Pollinator Declines: An Approach to Assessing the Consequences," *Conservation Ecology* 5 (1) (2001): 8 (http://www.consecol.org/vol5/iss1/art8).

9. Treaties on Prior Informed Consent (PIC) and Persistent Organic Pollutants (POPs) will enter into force when ratified by 50 signatories. As of July 2002, 73 states and regional economic organizations had signed the PIC agreement (the Rotterdam Convention), and 23 had ratified it. The POPs treaty (the Stockholm Convention) had 151 signatories and 16 ratifications as of August 2002. Both treaties are intended to be international legally binding instruments.

10. Information in this section comes from the American Chemistry Council Web site (www.americanchemistry.org). For information concerning international efforts of the council, access Responsible Care® from the home page. For information on RC 14001, click on Responsible Care® then any of the links under the RC 14001 heading. For information on the use of codes of management practices and performance metrics, access Responsible Care®, then General Information, then Responsible Care Management System and Performance Measures.

11. For example, in a recent press release criticizing the European Union's regulatory approach as misguided, and urging that it not be adopted worldwide, the ACC pointed to Responsible Care as an example of the industry's commitment to environmental protection and self-regulation. "Chemical Leader Calls for Aggressive Global Advocacy—ACC President and CEO Greg Lebedev Criticizes EU Regulatory 'Fog'," Press Release, American Chemistry Council, Arlington, VA, April 2, 2003, http://www.accnewsroom.com/docs/1200/1140?DocTypeID=4& TrackID=.

12. Croplife International, "Integrated Pest Management: Our Contribution to Sustainable Agriculture," http://www.gcpf.org/library/documents/Stewardship.

13. Marcia Ishii-Eiteman and Jessica Hamburger, "Pesticide and Biotech Companies: The Wrong Partners for the World Bank," http://panna.igc.org/resources/ documents/badPartners.dv.html. See also D. Forno, H. van der Wulp, and G. Fleischer. "Pest Management in World Bank Projects: Report to the Second Governing Group Meeting of the Global IPM Facility," Kakamega,Kenya, October 2000.

14. See http://www.fao.org/ag/AGP/AGPP/Pesticid/Default.htm.

15. *Safe and Efficient Use of Crop Protection Products in Developing Countries*, ed. J. Atkin (Novartis Crop Protection Sector) and K. M. Leisinger (Novartis Foundation for Sustainable Development) (Oxfordshire, UK: CABI Publishing, 2000).

16. "Baseline Study on the Problems of Obsolete Pesticide Stocks," www.fao.org/DOCREP/003/X8639E/x8639e02.htm; see also P. Costner, M. Simpson and D. Luscombe, *Technical Criteria for the Destruction of Stockpiled Persistent Organic Pollutants* (Amsterdam: Greenpeace, 1998).

17. The authors have compiled a mass of data on obsolete pesticide stocks, much of it contradictory. Among the issues confounding the data are finding proper definitions for "obsolete" and judging whether enhanced storage security can be counted as "disposal." The authors acknowledge the problems in the data regarding Disposal of Obsolete Pesticide Stocks; we quote a figure used by Pesticides Trust at http://www.pan-uk.org/pestnews/Pn34/pn34p8.htm.

18. "Exporting Risk: Pesticide Exports from U.S. Ports, 1992–1994," FASE Research Report, spring 1996, http://www.fasenet.org/pesticide_report92–94.pdf.

19. U.S. Office of Technology Assessment estimate. See, for example, "US Environmental Protection Agency's Budget Slashed," Sierra Club Fact Sheet on Economic Harms of EPA Budget Bill, July 28, 1995.

20. http://www.croplifeamerica.org (access About link).

21. See, for a comparative example, Robert Repetto and Duncan Austin, *Pure Profit: Financial Implications of Environmental Performance* (Washington, DC: World Resources Institute, 2000).

22. "SEC Staff Accounting Bulletin no. 99: Materiality," http://www.sec.gov/interps/account/sab99.htm.

23. Ibid.

24. Syngenta Corporation, annual report, 2001.

25. Robert Repetto and Duncan Austin, *Coming Clean: Corporate Disclosure of Financially Significant Environmental Risks* (Washington, DC: World Resources Institute, 2000), 11.

26. Ibid.

10

Titans of the Enron Economy

The Ten Habits of Highly
Defective Corporations

Scott Klinger and Holly Sklar

Introduction

The pivotal lessons from the Enron debacle do not stem from any criminal wrongdoing. Most of the maneuvers leading to Enron's meltdown not only are legal but are widely practiced. Many of the problems dramatically revealed by the Enron scandal are woven tightly into the fabric of American business. This part of the story is widely understood: the cold betrayal of employees by rapacious executives amassing personal fortunes as the company's fortunes unraveled. The images of loyal employees suddenly losing their jobs, homes, and life savings are etched into our minds.

The negative externalities associated with the Enron scandal are clear. Reaching far beyond its employees, the long list of Enron casualties includes a wide array of individual and institutional investors and the broader taxpaying public. Shareholders have lost tens of billions of dollars in share value. State and municipal pension funds lost more than $1.5 billion on Enron stock. The state of Florida alone lost $335 million; Georgia lost $127 million, Ohio $115 million, and New York City $109 million on Enron investments.[1] This money ultimately will have to be made up by increased taxpayer contributions to state pension coffers. Diverting tax money to make up for Enron losses means that less funding is available for other vital public services.

Before Enron imploded, it was embroiled in another scandal—profiteering from the deregulation of energy markets at great consumer expense and hardship. During the 2000 California electricity crisis, consumers faced blackouts and were overcharged an estimated $40 to $70 billion.[2] As the Consumer Federation of America reported, the California Independent System Operator, manager of the state's power grid, documented energy supplier "price gouging (economic withholding) or hoarding (physical withholding) in virtually every hour of every day for almost a year." California was not alone. New York, Massachusetts, Montana, and other states have also suffered huge price increases and service problems.[3] Enron engaged in legalized piracy in many parts of the world. In India, the company made millions of dollars in "educational payments" to government officials in exchange for a power contract that Enron expected would generate more than $30 billion over the next twenty years. The Indian public, which engaged in massive protests against the plant, ended up paying twice the rate charged by the next-most-expensive power producer and more than seven times the cheapest power rate in the region before the plant was shut down by the Indian government. Enron turned to Vice President Dick Cheney and other U.S. government officials to try to bully the Indian government into making payments to the company.[4]

The Stock Option Scam

American taxpayers subsidized Enron's profiteering at home and abroad. When Enron executives received multimillion-dollar stock option payoffs, taxpayers were unwitting contributors. This is because corporations maintain two sets of accounting books, one for shareholders and the other for the government. In the income statement shown to shareholders, stock options are invisible. Unlike cash salaries and bonuses, stock options are not counted as an expense. But when executives cash in their stock options, reaping fortunes, the set of corporate books shown to governmental regulatory agencies reflects a full deduction of the engorged value of the option, not its much smaller worth at the time it was granted. Thus, stock options represent a powerful tool for keeping corporate earnings artificially high and taxes legally (but artificially) low.

Although excluded from the profit calculations, corporations are required to report the latest three years' stock option activities in a footnote to their financial statement. Using the option data contained in

the footnotes to financial reports, a [March 18, 2002] Tax Notes article
. . . estimated the impact of options on the corporate tax base. According to those estimates, exercised stock options may have reduced corporate taxes [for all U.S. corporations] by as much as $28 billion in 1998,
$42 billion in 1999, and $56 billion in 2000.[5]

According to a study by the Institute on Taxation and Economic Policy of
the 1996–98 taxes paid by 250 of the nation's largest and most profitable
companies, the top 10 firms avoided $10.4 billion on taxes as a result of
stock option deductions. The 250 firms in the study avoided paying a combined $25.8 billion in taxes.[6]

Enron's exorbitant option-related pay scheme was a principal factor in
the company's ability to not only avoid all federal corporate income taxes
but also to get the Treasury to rebate $395 million during the three-year
period ending in 2000 in spite of the fact that Enron reported net profits of
more than $1.1 billion.[7]

Not coincidentally, Enron's twenty-nine top executives reportedly net-
ted $1.1 billion from stock options in the three years before the company
declared bankruptcy.[8] Many companies treat stock options as a license to
print money for executives and, increasingly, for directors. As *Business
Week* reported, chief executive officers (CEOs) receive about 60 percent of
their total pay from stock options, and the two hundred biggest companies
(by revenue) allocate more than 16 percent of their outstanding shares of
stock for options. Not counting options for Time Warner, which AOL
acquired in January 2001, AOL Time Warner's earnings would have been
reduced by 75 percent during 1996–2000 if options had been expensed. In
2000, AOL Time Warner got a $711 million tax break thanks to exercised
options. Cisco earnings would have been reduced by 26 percent; Cisco got
an option-related tax break of $1.4 billion.[9]

The Federal Reserve believes that by not expensing options, "corporations were able to add three percentage points to their average annual
earnings from 1995 to 2000. Operating earnings would have grown an
average of 5% during this period, not the reported 8.3%."[10] That means
more than a third of the miraculous earnings growth of the late 1990s may
have stemmed not from wise corporate strategy or increased productivity
but from a common, misleading stock option accounting maneuver that
legally left tens of billions of dollars of expenses off official income statements.

While a few companies such as Global Crossing, a telecommunications company that shared Enron's penchant for tax dodging and insider trading, have followed Enron into bankruptcy court, scores of other companies have seen their stock prices shattered as they rush to restate earnings in the face of greater regulatory scrutiny. Credit has become more expensive for companies because of tougher scrutiny and ratings downgrades.[11] Many analysts worry that the lingering accounting controversy is creating a drag on the whole economy. "The accounting problem does seem to have legs and it is spreading," said Craig Thomas, a senior economist with the consulting firm Economy.com.[12] Still, outside the spotlight on Enron's rise and fall, government policies and accounting practices continue to reward and shelter many firms with harmful practices.

Negative Externalities of Enron and Other Defective Corporations

This chapter examines ten Enron habits that resulted in negative externalities—costs, of one kind or another, borne by people who had nothing to do with generating those costs. All of these habits ultimately contributed to the company's demise, yet all of them are common in corporate America. It explains the negative consequences of each habit and examines other companies with similar behavior. The chapter concludes with a ten-step program to break corporate addictions to Enronesque habits and prevent future Enronlike debacles.

We have found that at least ten practices or "habits" of legitimate companies generate substantial risks and harm to their employees, investors, clients, and society at large (see table 1). They are all well illustrated by the Enron case but at the same time highlight how common and widespread these practices are throughout the corporate world.

The first three habits of defective corporations create risk for workers while rewarding executives: tying up employee retirement funds in company stocks, providing compensation and incentives for management to engage in fraudulent accounting, and laying off workers to distract attention from management problems.

Habit 1. Tie Employee Retirement Funds Heavily to Company Stock and Let Misled Employees Take the Fall When the Stock Tanks—While Executives Diversify Their Holdings and Cash Out before the Bad News Goes Public. In the days following Enron's meltdown, the news media were filled with grim stories of employees with wiped out retirement accounts. Over the past two decades, defined contribution plans such as 401(k)s, in which employees reap the rewards—and bear the risk—of stock market performance, have supplanted traditional defined-benefit pensions, in which employers are responsible for guaranteed monthly pension payments.

A key problem is that whereas defined-benefit plans by law must be diversified, 401(k)s are heavily weighted with company stock. According to a study by the Profit Sharing/401(k) Council of America, stock of the sponsoring company accounted for 39.2 percent of 401(k) plan assets in 2000. This was even truer in large companies: In firms with more than five thousand 401(k) participants, more than 43 percent of assets were in company stock.[13]

TABLE I.   The Ten Habits of Highly Defective Corporations

Risk for Workers, Rewards for Executives
1. Tie employee retirement funds heavily to company stock and let misled employees take the fall when the stock tanks—while executives diversify their holdings and cash out before the bad news goes public.
2. Excessively compensate executives and set incentives that encourage them to cook the books and overstate profits for personal gain.
3. Lay off employees to reduce costs and distract from management mistakes; increase executive pay for implementing this cost-cutting strategy.

Corrupt the Watchdogs
4. Stack the board with insiders and friends who will support lavish compensation and not ask difficult questions about the business.
5. Pay board members excessively for their part-time service; pay them heavily in stock so they have a disincentive to blow the whistle on business practices that may cause the stock price to decline.
6. Give your independent auditors generous nonaudit consultant work, creating conflicts of interest for those charged with assuring that the company follows the rules and protects shareholder interests.

Buy-Partisanship: Profiting from Political Influence
7. Give campaign contributions to gain access to decision makers; diversify your political investments in a portfolio of candidates from both major parties.
8. Lobby lawmakers and regulators to eliminate pesky oversight, safety, environmental, and other rules and to pass favorable regulations, subsidies, tax breaks, and other items on the company wish list.
9. Get the government to finance and insure dubious overseas investments, especially those opposed by the local citizenry.
10. Avoid taxes; use tax deductions, credits, and clever accounting to pay little or no tax and hopefully even to get tax rebates.

Though Enron's 401(k) plan was 58 percent invested in company stock, it was far from the worst among large companies. Ninety-four percent of Procter and Gamble's 401(k) is invested in company stock, and twenty-seven large companies have greater shares of company stock in their employees' 401(k) plans than did Enron.[14] Moreover, 85 percent of all plans impose some restrictions on the sale of company stock held in their 401(k)s.[15] Common restrictions include preventing employees from trading until they reach age fifty, requiring employees to hold company stock for a set period of time, and blackout periods during which trades are not permitted while account administrators are changed. It is noteworthy that Enron's last blackout period coincided with the stock's final free-fall. Companies often entice employees into failing to diversify their retirement assets by offering a higher-percentage matching contribution if the employees invest their portion of the 401(k) in company stock.

Habit 2: Excessively Compensate Executives and Set Incentives That Encourage Them to Cook the Books and Overstate Profits for Personal Gain. (See table 2.)   Between 1998 and 2000, Enron CEO Kenneth Lay received more than $211 million in total compensation, including salary, bonuses, exercised stock options, life insurance, and a host of executive perks, including more than $300,000 worth of personal travel in the company jet in a recent year. During the same period, Enron president Jeffrey Skilling made more than $130 million. Despite Lay's lavish compensation, he was only tenth among CEOs at large companies ranked by *Business Week* during the period. Lay had an incentive to inflate earnings. Corporate executives' compensation packages often include performance benchmarks that in theory are designed to align the interests of corporate managers with those of shareholders. Lay's compensation package included restricted stock (direct grants of stock, the ownership of which cedes to the executive over time). In Lay's case, the stock was scheduled to become his over four years, but the plan also had an accelerated vesting procedure under which control of the stock would be granted earlier if the company's stock price outperformed the Standard and Poor's 500 by more than 20 percent.[16] This offered Lay and others a powerful incentive to inflate Enron's stock price. With the stock price up, Lay was granted the stock; he could then sell it for personal gain without waiting the full four years. In 2000, Lay received 347,830 stock options.[17] He cashed in millions of dollars worth of Enron stock while pumping the stock to employees and outside shareholders.

Habit 3: Lay off Employees to Reduce Costs and Distract from Management Mistakes; Increase Executive Pay for Implementing This Cost-Cutting Strategy. Enron laid off 4,250 workers in late December 2001. While laid-off workers received severance pay of $4,500, several executives drew six- and seven-figure bonuses as an incentive to stay.[18] The penchant for rewarding Enron's executives continued: in late March 2002, the company petitioned the bankruptcy court to allow it to pay $130 million in retention bonuses to seventeen hundred employees, an average of $76,000 per employee, or almost seventeen times the severance pay provided each sacked worker who paid for the debacle with his or her job.[19] "Payoffs for layoffs" was a routine business practice before Enron's collapse, with devastating consequences for workers and sometimes for companies. In fact, Al Dunlap had a reputation for coming into businesses and ruthlessly slashing payrolls in the name of boosting shareholder value. Dunlap destroyed more than fourteen thousand jobs and decimated the century-old Scott Paper in the mid-1990s while pocketing $100 million for his efforts. Next he turned his attention to household appliance maker Sunbeam. As Dunlap was working his magic, laying off workers and reporting a rebound in profitability, Sunbeam was discovered to be cooking its books. Arthur Andersen, which played a central role in the Enron scandal, was Sunbeam's auditor. For Dunlap, crime paid, even though he had to cough up $15 million to settle a shareholder suit over the fraudulent accounting; Arthur Andersen paid $115 million.[20]

Layoffs to trim costs have been a common practice among other large corporations as well. In addition, a survey of corporate executives indicates

TABLE 2.   Top Ten Companies by CEO Pay, 1998–2001

Company	CEO(s)	Total Compensation (1998–2001)
Oracle	L. J. Ellison	$ 796,624,000
Computer Associates	C. B. Wang / S. Kumar	$ 704,708,000
Disney	M. D. Eisner	$ 700,093,000
Citigroup	S. I. Weill	$ 524,799,000
Tyco International	L. D. Kozlowski	$ 396,944,000
AOL Time Warner	S. M. Case / G. M. Levin	$ 350,960,000
IBM	L. V. Gerstner Jr.	$ 349,558,000
General Electric	J. F. Welch Jr.	$ 315,630,000
Cisco Systems	J. T. Chambers	$ 280,162,000
JDS Uniphase	K. N. Kalkhoven / J. Straus	$ 262,523,000

Source: "Executive Pay," *Business Week,* April 15, 2002; "Executive Pay," *Business Week,* April 16, 2001.

that layoffs will remain a permanent strategy for reducing corporate costs. To encourage this approach, executives who slash jobs receive the highest pay. A 2001 report by United for a Fair Economy found that "CEOs of firms that announced layoffs of 1,000 or more employees earned about 80 percent more, on average, than executives at 365 top firms surveyed by *Business Week*. The layoff leaders earned an average of $23.7 million in total compensation in 2000, compared with a $13.1 million average for executives as a whole."[21]

The next three habits generating negative externalities fall under the general theme of corrupting the individuals and institutions that should be providing regulatory oversight. Companies accomplish this by stacking the board with insiders and friends, creating disincentives for board members to blow the whistle on the company, and by providing the company's auditors with consulting work independent of auditing, creating a conflict of interest.

Habit 4: Stack the Board with Insiders and Friends Who Will Support Lavish Compensation and Not Ask Difficult Questions about the Business. The same people who were supposed to be watching over Enron's business practices granted Lay his lavish compensation package: the company's board of directors. Sound corporate governance policy holds that corporate boards should be made up of a majority of independent individuals, without direct or indirect ties to the company. Some institutional investors seek an even higher standard. The Council of Institutional Investors, a coalition of corporate, public, and labor pension funds with combined assets of more than $2 trillion, believes that corporate boards should be composed of at least two-thirds independent directors.[22]

Because there are no national standards, methods of determining independence vary. While all definitions exclude direct employees and people earning fees from companies (outside legal counsel, consultants, and so on), other definitions of independence are murky. The Investor Responsibility Research Center (IRRC) reported that of the directors elected at Enron's 2001 annual meeting, 64 percent met traditional standards of independence.[23] Yet the nine directors categorized as independent include some with close informal ties: for example, director John Mendelson is president of the University of Texas's M. A. Anderson Cancer Center, to which Enron and the Lay family contributed more than $1.9 million, and director Charles Lemaistre is past president.[24] Wendy Gramm, wife of U.S.

Senator Phil Gramm (R-TX), was another supposedly independent director. Though Enron's political investments flowed freely in Washington, no member of Congress benefited more than Senator Gramm, who received $72,000 from Enron between 1995 and 2000.[25]

Habit 5: Pay Board Members Excessively for Their Part-Time Service; Pay Them Heavily in Stock So They Have a Disincentive to Blow the Whistle on Business Practices That May Cause the Stock Price to Decline. Board members not only set their own salaries but select one another as well, since the board's slate of nominees faces opposition only in rare cases of corporate takeovers. At typical large companies, boards meet once a month. Even factoring in a few days of preparation time, being a corporate director is a part-time job with pay most full-time workers can only dream of, plus plenty of perks. According to the IRRC, Enron's nonemployee directors received $353,140 in compensation in 2000, ranking Enron fourth among companies with more than $5 billion in annual revenues.[26]

Like most firms with director megacompensation, a large share of the Enron directors' pay—about 80 percent—came from stock awards. Compensating corporate directors with stock is a growing trend. The theory is that directors should share the interests of shareholders and be well compensated only if the company performs well. While that holds true to a point, excessively large awards have the potential to compromise the board's willingness to responsibly hold management accountable for taking excessive risks. In the case of Enron, directors had personal fortunes largely tied to the company's soaring stock price. What incentive did any of them have to blow the whistle on increasingly troubling business practices, which masked $1 billion in phantom profits? The board wrote a scathing report about Enron's now-famous duplicitous partnerships—but only after the scandal had brought down the company.[27]

In maintaining a cozy relationship with beholden directors, Enron was only behaving like most other large corporations. The Raytheon board, for example, refused to adopt an annual election of directors despite majority shareholder support for such a policy at the company's 2000 and 2001 annual shareholder meetings.[28] When an exasperated former employee and shareholder rose at the company's 2001 annual meeting to ask why the company has shareholders vote if their will is not implemented, CEO Daniel Burnham replied, "Because the SEC [Securities and Exchange Commission] says we have to."[29] So much for corporate democracy!

Habit 6: Give Your Independent Auditor Generous Nonaudit Consultant Work, Creating Conflicts of Interest for Those Charged with Assuring That the Company Follows the Rules and Protects Shareholder Interests. The interests of the auditor should be independent from the interests of its client. However, the image of Arthur Andersen employees shredding Enron documents belies this practice. The independent auditor is supposed to objectively review management's presentation of accounting data to shareholders. In the course of conducting financial audits, accounting firms gain a great understanding of their clients' businesses. About two decades ago, the major auditing firms discovered there was significant money to be made by adding consulting businesses to their auditing work. This consulting work covers such things as tax strategy development, advice on mergers and acquisitions, and suggestions for restructuring and improving management information systems. Not only does nonaudit consulting work carry higher profit margins, but most clients have been enticed to spend more on their consulting contracts than on their audits. The objectivity of auditors is compromised when challenging a problematic accounting method may result in the loss of valuable consulting business.

In Enron's case, Arthur Andersen was not willing to jeopardize $27 million in consulting contracts by blowing the whistle on the accounting excesses discovered during the audit process, for which it was paid a $25 million fee in 2000.[30] Complicating matters further at Enron, CEO Ken Lay, Enron board member Herbert Winokur, and David Duncan, Arthur Andersen's lead auditor on the Enron account, all served together as board members of the American Council for Capital Formation, a Washington, DC–based group that advocates for corporate tax reductions.[31]

As reported in *Business Week*, a new study of more than three thousand proxy statements from 2001 by accounting professors Richard Frankel, Marilyn Johnson, and Karen Nelson found that "the more consulting services a company bought from one of the Big Five auditors, the more likely its earnings met or beat Wall Street expectations. . . . Companies using their auditors as consultants tend to 'manage earnings'— maneuvers such as moving debt off the books into partnerships and booking gains in pension funds as income." Frankel says, "Investors should be wary of the quality of a company's earnings if it hires its auditor as a consultant." Unfortunately, 95 percent of companies studied paid their auditors for some consulting work.[32] In February 2002, Walt Disney Company, under pressure from union shareholders, became the first Fortune 500 company to

adopt a policy forbidding its independent auditor from engaging in nonaudit consulting work. Consulting work undertaken by independent auditors
was significantly limited under the provisions of the federal Sarbanes-
Oxley corporate reform bill, which President George W. Bush signed into
law on July 30, 2002.

The final four habits associated with negative externalities fall under the
general theme of the use of political influence by companies to encourage
laws and policies that benefit the companies. Companies use political
influence by making generous campaign contributions to key decision
makers, by lobbying lawmakers, by convincing the government to back up
overseas investments, and by avoiding taxes.

*Habit 7: Give Campaign Contributions to Gain Access to Decision Makers;
Diversify Your Political Investments in a Portfolio of Candidates from Both
Major Parties.*   No asset was more valuable at Enron than the company's
political capital. Enron was the biggest corporate supporter of George W.
Bush's 1994 and 1998 Texas gubernatorial campaigns and a leading backer
in Bush's run for the presidency.[33] Lay's close ties with both Presidents
Bush are well known. But Enron had a diverse portfolio of political investments, distributing $1.1 million in campaign gifts to 257 different mem-
bers of Congress from 1989 through 2001.[34] Ninety-eight of these legislators were Democrats, demonstrating the company's buy-partisan spirit.
Moreover, since 1992, Enron contributed at least $1 million to Republican
Party conventions and an undisclosed amount to hold parties in conjunction with Democratic conventions.[35] Enron acquired its political capital
with campaign gifts, and reinforced it with jobs. Wendy Gramm presided
over the Commodity Futures Trading Commission when it made the land-
mark decision to exempt over-the-counter energy contracts (those not
made through a regulated commodity exchange) from certain antifraud
provisions, perhaps the single greatest boost that changed Enron from a
pipeline operator to a Wall Street star. Five weeks later, Gramm was
offered a new role as one of Enron's directors.[36] Gramm had plenty of company in the revolving door. Enron hired former Secretary of State James
Baker and former Secretary of Commerce Robert Mosbacher as consultants.
    Before becoming secretary of the army, with its $91 billion budget,
Thomas White was vice chair of Enron Energy Services. At Enron "he'd
been the guy charged with making sure the company got its piece of the

pie as the Pentagon privatized its own utilities. Once ensconced as army secretary, White sent a memo down the chain of command [in November 2001] calling for a bigger, better privatization program." White made millions while at Enron and millions more selling Enron stock before it plummeted, raising allegations of insider trading. The supposedly profitable Enron Energy Services "was a fraud, hemorrhaging money while covering up its losses with accounting maneuvers."[37] As Al Hunt wrote in the *Wall Street Journal*, Enron "played with funny money. But their political investment helped prolong the Ponzi scheme."[38] Most importantly for the future, Enron's influence resulted in a host of regulatory appointees it favored and a long trail of harmful policies, such as the consumer-harming energy deregulation policies.

Again, Enron was not alone or even unusual in its use of campaign contributions as an investment in company profitability. For example, after heavy lobbying and campaign contributions from the banking and credit card industry, both the House and the Senate passed the 2001 Bankruptcy Reform Act by wide margins, and President Bush said he would sign it. (The bill, however, died in conference committee after an impasse was reached over the issue of whether antiabortion activists could declare bankruptcy to avoid fines relating to their political activities.) "In congressional circles, a bill like this one is known as a 'money vote,'" observed journalist William Greider, "because it's an opportunity for good fundraising from moneyed interests (or, if you vote wrong, you face the risk of those interests financing your next opponent)."[39] Credit card giants Citigroup and MBNA were among the ten largest campaign contributors during the 2000–2002 period. On the same day that the House voted on the bankruptcy reform bill, MBNA contributed $200,000 to the National Republican Senatorial Committee, according to an exposé written by investigative journalists Donald Barlett and James Steele for *Time* magazine.[40]

Under current law, consumers overwhelmed by debt have the option of filing for chapter 7 bankruptcy protection, under which the family's assets are sold off to settle debts. Primary homes, retirement assets, and a few personal possessions cannot be touched. The bankruptcy reform bill, championed by the credit card industry and opposed by consumer groups, not only would make filing for bankruptcy considerably more difficult but also would put credit card companies in a more favorable position, allowing them, for example, an equal standing to claims for child support.

Other measures of the bill are also troubling. According to Barlett and

Steele, "if a mother tapped an ATM to buy necessities such as food or pre-scription drugs six weeks before filing for bankruptcy, the withdrawal could be considered a fraudulent transaction." Like Enron, which claimed that energy deregulation would save consumers money, the credit card industry has promised customers that bankruptcy reform will save the average household more than $400 a year. Barlett and Steele observed, "Some people unquestionably use bankruptcy court to escape bills they could afford to pay, but their numbers are insignificant. The vast majority of bankruptcy filers have neither income nor the assets to pay creditors. Most turn to bankruptcy as a last resort."[41] Ironically, while companies like Enron Corporation easily avail themselves of bankruptcy protection to cover the lies and misdeeds of corporate executives, the innocent Enron employees who suddenly lost their jobs may not be so easily able to protect themselves or their families if the Bankruptcy Reform Act becomes law.

Habit 8: Lobby Lawmakers and Regulators to Eliminate Oversight, Safety, Environmental, and Other Rules and to Pass Favorable Regulations, Subsidies, Tax Breaks, and Other Items on the Company Wish List.   Corporate lobby-ing has received a lot of attention with the scandal over Vice President Cheney's energy task force. A House Committee on Government Reform report prepared for Representative Henry A. Waxman (D-CA) has detailed "How the White House Energy Plan Benefited Enron."[42] The problem, of course, is much larger than Enron's undue influence. The Bush administration's making of energy policy is a case study in undemocratic corporate influence. According to the *New York Times*, while Energy Sec-retary Spencer Abraham "helped the Bush administration write its national energy report [in 2001, Abraham] heard from more than 100 energy industry executives, trade association leaders and lobbyists, accord-ing to documents released by the Energy Department." Despite their efforts to meet with him, "Mr. Abraham did not meet with any represen-tative of environmental organizations or consumer groups." Among those who met with Abraham were eighteen energy industry contributors, including Enron, ChevronTexaco, El Paso, and ExxonMobil, which have donated a combined $16.6 million to Republican candidates since 1999.[43]

It is difficult to know exactly what kind of resources Enron spent lobby-ing. The company's postbankruptcy disclosures included the information that it underreported its lobbying for the first six months of 2000 by a fac-tor of three—instead of $825,000, it was really $2.5 million.[44] As reported by the Center for Responsive Politics, Enron lobbied on a wide range of issues from energy, broadband, and international trade bills and regulations to energy taxes and repeal of the corporate alternative minimum tax.[45]

Habit 9: Get the Government to Finance and Insure Dubious Overseas Investments, Especially Those Opposed by the Local Citizenry. Enron's most significant business partner was the government. "Since 1992, at least 21 agencies, representing the U.S. government, multinational development banks and other national governments, helped leverage Enron's global reach by approving $7.2 billion in public financing toward 38 projects in 29 countries," says *Enron's Pawns*, a revealing report published by the Institute for Policy Studies.[46] Such U.S. government agencies as the Overseas Private Investment Corporation (OPIC), Export-Import Bank, and several others paid more than half that amount—$3.68 billion for twenty-five projects. The World Bank and Inter-American Development Bank, both heavily influenced by the U.S. government, kicked in another $1.5 billion to support Enron's ventures.[47] This was another way Enron shifted costs and risks to taxpayers.

Enron's targets of overseas investment are almost all poor nations, most with a lot of internal dissent about the moves made by government leaders. This dissent often centers on disputes over environment and development issues, such as the building of Enron power plants or the sale of public water supplies to Enron. Enron's extremely controversial Dabhol power plant project in India is a case in point. The $30 billion contract to build this plant—the most expensive contract in the country's history—sparked protests by the Indian people. After Enron provided $30 million in "educational payments" to the Indian government as political power changed hands in India, the plant was short-circuited. U.S. Secretary of State Colin Powell and Vice President Dick Cheney both twisted the arms of Indian officials on behalf of Enron. Powell warned Indian Foreign Minister Jaswant Singh in an April 2001 meeting that "failure to resolve this [Dabhol] matter could have a serious deterrent effect on other investors."[48]

The Bush administration even went so far as to form a Dabhol working group within the National Security Council to help Enron collect on its debts.[49] The combination of Enron's bankruptcy and the Indian government's continued unwillingness to pay bloated power costs may have dealt the plant its final blow. The controversial project filed for bankruptcy, and the plant was placed in the hands of a court-appointed receiver.[50]

Cheney was the right man for the role of Enron bagman seeking to collect on the Indian debts that left OPIC and the Export-Import Bank on the hook for hundreds of millions of dollars thanks to Enron rip-offs. These same agencies were very good to Cheney while he served as CEO of Halliburton, a leading global energy services and engineering/construction company, prior to joining President Bush in his bid for the White House. When it comes to receiving corporate welfare, Cheney has blinders. During the 2000 vice presidential debate in Danville, Kentucky, Democratic candidate Senator Joseph Lieberman from Connecticut invoked the memory of Ronald Reagan when he asked the audience, "Are you better off than you were eight years ago?" Without pause, Lieberman turned to Cheney and said, "And I'm pleased to see, Dick, from the newspapers, that you're better off than you were eight years ago too." Cheney retorted with a straight face: "And I can tell you, Joe, that the government had absolutely nothing to do with it."[51]

On the contrary, under the direction of Cheney—a former congressman, White House chief of staff, and secretary of defense—Halliburton received $1.5 billion in government financing and loan guarantees, a fifteenfold increase from the pre-Cheney days. The company also garnered $2.3 billion in direct government contracts, more than double the amount received in the five years preceding Cheney's half decade tenure.[52] Over the 1992–2000 period, during which Enron received $7.2 billion in government financing and loan guarantees, Halliburton was close behind at $6 billion.[53] Halliburton doubled both its campaign finance and lobbying expenditures, to $1.2 million and $600,000, respectively, during Cheney's tenure.

The bills Halliburton lobbied to pass included a measure for OPIC's reauthorization and the Foreign Operation Appropriations Bill, which would fund OPIC, the Export-Import Bank, and the Trade and Development Agency.[54] These lobbying and campaign finance expenditures offered huge returns on investment. Like Enron, Halliburton wanted protection from overseas risks. Halliburton legally circumvented U.S. sanctions against Iraq (while Saddam Hussein was still in power), Burma, and Libya by using foreign affiliates. The company also conducted business with Iran; Azerbaijan, which was subject to U.S. sanctions for ethnic cleansing (Cheney lobbied for removal of these sanctions while CEO of Halliburton); and Indonesia, where one of the company's contracts was voided in a post-Suharto cleanup of corruptly awarded contracts.[55]

Habit 10: Avoid Taxes; Use Tax Deductions, Credits, and Clever Accounting to Pay Little or No Tax and Hopefully Even to Get Tax Rebates.   Tax advice is a key element of those lucrative accountant consulting contracts. Enron was one of Arthur Andersen's star pupils. In the five years ending in 2000, Enron reported $1.8 billion in profits. Instead of paying $625 million in corporate income taxes under the federal corporate tax rate of 35 percent, Enron received $381 million in rebate checks from the U.S. Treasury. Enron's eight hundred partnerships in such tax havens as the Cayman Islands offer a partial answer to the question of how Enron cut its corporate taxes. In addition, deducting billions of dollars of stock option gains reduced Enron's tax burden by nearly $600 million over five years. The Institute on Taxation and Economic Policy studied the 1996–98 taxes paid by 250 of the nation's largest and most profitable companies and found that instead of a 35 percent tax rate, the average company paid just 20.1 percent of its income in federal income taxes in 1998. This was sharply lower than the 26.5 percent rate paid a decade earlier, after the 1986 Tax Reform Act closed many corporate loopholes. The study also found that 41 of these companies paid no federal taxes in at least one of the three years of the study despite earning a collective $25 billion in pretax profits during those no-tax years.[56]

From 1995 to 2000, according to *Business Week*, "Corporate earnings jumped by more than a third, but taxes rose by only about 17%. As a result, the spread between book income and taxable income is widening. Harvard University economist Mihir A. Desai estimates that just among companies with assets in excess of $250 million, book earnings in 1998 exceeded taxable income by a staggering $287 billion."[57] Corporations just cannot get enough tax breaks, though. As Enron was crumbling in the fall of 2001, the Bush administration proposed an "economic stimulus" bill that included the retroactive repeal (back to 1986) of the corporate alternative minimum tax, which was enacted to ensure that highly profitable companies paid at least some federal taxes. According to Citizens for Tax Justice, sixteen large companies—including IBM, Ford Motor, and ChevronTexaco—would have shared $7.4 billion in refunds if the alternative minimum tax were repealed retroactively. Enron's share of the loot would have been $254 million.[58]

Conclusion/Policy Implications

If American corporations are to recover from their Enronlike habits, the United States must reregulate corporate practices for the protection of workers, consumers, and shareholders. It will not be easy to change destructive corporate habits that have been nurtured by a set of rules and regulations that—by intent or inadvertently—have fostered a culture of short-term selfishness. Recognizing the dysfunctionality of these cultural norms, it is not enough simply to decide that they should change. It is necessary to change the institutional environment that legitimated this culture. Our policymakers can begin by taking the following steps.

1. Improve corporate disclosures so that they are clear and easy for the average citizen to understand. The SEC, under the leadership of former Chair Arthur Leavitt, moved companies toward a "plain English" disclosure standard for corporate reporting. The SEC should mandate stricter disclosure in the following areas:

- conflicts of interest for management, board members, and auditors, including charitable relationships (e.g., gifts from CEOs and companies to directors' charities);
- taxes—including how much corporate cash actually went to governments in the reporting year, what were the most significant tax credits received by the company, and how much was received from state and local tax expenditure financing;
- amount of financing from governmental agencies and multinational agencies; and
- recipients of corporate campaign contributions and amount of lobbying expenses;

2. Require stock options to be expensed on an annual income statement, with the amount of tax deduction limited to the value of the stock option at the time of the grant. Stock options do have value before they are exercised. Thousands of stock option contracts trade publicly every day. Corporations should be obliged to value stock options at the time of the option grant and count them as expenses on income statements. For tax purposes, corporations should deduct the value of options at the time they are granted, as companies would do with compensation paid in cash. This would eliminate the huge tax-cut windfall that presently stems from stock option grants.

In an important change in policy, the Council of Institutional Investors reversed its previous policy on stock option accounting. In March 2002, noting that times have changed, the council came out strongly in support of expensing of stock options.[59] After years of lobby-fueled resistance, congressional efforts to require the expensing of stock options are finally bipartisan. The chief sponsor of S. 1940, the Ending the Double Standard for Stock Options Act, is Senator Carl Levin (D-MI), along with Senators John McCain (R-AZ), Peter Fitzgerald (R-IL), Dick Durbin (D-IL), and Mark Dayton (D-MN).

The Levin-McCain-Fitzgerald-Durbin-Dayton bill would not legislate accounting standards for stock options or directly require companies to expense stock option pay but would require companies to treat stock options on their tax returns the exact same way they treat them on their financial statements. In other words, a company's stock option tax deduction would have to mirror the stock option expense shown on the company's books. If there is no stock option expense on the company books, there can be no expense on the company tax return. If a company declares a stock option expense on its books, then the company can deduct exactly the same amount in the same year on its tax return.[60]

Expensing stock options is an important step in the right direction. At the same time, there should also be a limit to tax deductibility of executive compensation, as in step 5.

3. Apply ERISA diversification rules covering traditional pensions to defined-contribution plans—including 401(k) plans—as well. A strict law, known as the Employee Retirement Income Security Act (ERISA), presently protects the nation's defined-benefit pension plans. This law has many safeguards, including limits on the concentration of stock to no more than 5 percent in any single security. ERISA rules also subject pension plans to periodic oversight by government regulators, something not required of 401(k) plans.

4. Prohibit inclusion of pension fund gains in the presentation of corporate earnings. The pension fund accounting fiction allows earnings from company operations to be overstated. Because executive compensation is frequently tied to reported earnings, this accounting trick leads to padded executive pay packages. Doing away with this accounting rule would restore some incentive to pass along more market gains to retirees in the form of cost-of-living adjustments.

5. End taxpayer subsidies for excessive compensation, whether in cash or stock. Current law permits tax deductions of "reasonable business expenses." However, the tax code is conspicuously silent on reasonable

levels of executive pay. Representative Martin Sabo (D-MN) has attempted to close this gaping loophole through his Income Equity Act, which would permit corporations to deduct as a "reasonable business expense" all compensation for a given individual up to twenty-five times the pay of the lowest-paid employee in the firm.

6. Amend corporate laws that mandate shareholder primacy. Current laws maximizing shareholder returns would give way to rules balancing the needs and interests of all stakeholders—shareholders, customers, employees, and communities. Modern corporations serve a range of constituencies and depend on these different stakeholders for long-term viability and success. More than three dozen states presently have laws that allow directors to evaluate the effects of corporate mergers on stakeholders other than shareholders, but the scope of these laws is limited. Enron's fanatical focus on inflating earnings to boost stock prices pitted shareholders' short-term interests against the long-term well-being of employees, customers, and the broader society and finally hurt the long-term best interests of most shareholders.

7. Adopt a regulatory standard of board independence. The SEC should issue a universal ruling defining what constitutes an independent director. Scandals offer opportunities for useful reforms, on which we should capitalize. For example, after the collapse of DaeWoo, a South Korean corporation, that country mandated that corporate boards of large companies have at least half their seats filled by outsiders.[61] The New York Stock Exchange (NYSE) and NASDAQ stock exchange have each proposed new listing requirements that would mandate a majority of independent directors for companies whose shares trade on the NYSE or NASDAQ. However, these requirements require the approval of the SEC, which has been slow to act.

8. Require auditors to be changed every five years. In response to Enron, Singapore is requiring all banks to switch auditors every five years and is considering extending the rule to all firms.[62] This would prevent overly cozy relationships and create checks and balances among firms. Corporations should also consider obtaining their auditors through a bidding process. With Pricewaterhouse Coopers being sued for lax accounting, one of its clients, the Russian corporation Gazprom, is holding a competitive bid to determine its next auditor.[63]

9. Change the focus of U.S. and international trade and finance agencies to include sustainable-development criteria and democratic input from affected peoples. Require companies to disclose when and why these agencies turn down financing requests. One of the primary functions of international trade and finance agencies is to provide insurance against political risk. Rather than issuing bailouts after controversial projects collapse, political risks could be minimized at the outset by making certain that the voices of affected people are heard and incorporated in any decisions to provide funding.

10. Adopt a progressive corporate income tax. While Big Business can afford to spend millions on accountants to mine the tax codes and millions more on lobbyists to press for specific tax breaks, small businesses are at a disadvantage. Higher tax rates only add to the competitive disadvantage small businesses already face in their purchases of raw material, their cost of employee benefits such as health care, and their cost of capital. Congress should do away with most corporate tax loopholes, reduce the overall corporate tax rate, and make corporate taxes progressive—that is, the bigger the business, the higher the tax rate. This would create greater competition in the marketplace and a healthier, more sustainable climate for small businesses, which remain the true engine of job creation in the United States. This change would also provide a disincentive for corporations to grow unchecked in ways that lead to concentrations of vast political and economic power and increase the risks for both our economy and our democracy.

This ten-step rehabilitation program would make it easier for people to understand what is going on inside corporations and to see how individuals (including shareholders), society, and the environment may be affected by corporate actions (steps 1–3). It would protect shareholders, workers, and other stakeholders while exerting some reasonable degree of restraint on executive rewards (steps 4–6). It would empower and motivate those who are supposed to be the watchdogs, especially directors and auditors (steps 7–8), and reduce the political and economic dominance of large corporations (steps 9–10). These are some of the institutional and regulatory changes that are needed to alter the corporate culture that has produced the disaster of Enron along with a large number of other equally defective corporations.

NOTES

This chapter is adapted from a report published by United for a Fair Economy, April 2002 (www.faireconomy.org). Research assistance was provided by Chris Hartman and Ben Boothby.

1. Christine Dugas, "Enron Won't Hurt Public Pension Fund Receipts," *USA Today*, January 24, 2002, p. 3B.

2. Kathleen Sharp, "Price Gouging Inquiries Target Enron," *Boston Sunday Globe*, March 3, 2002, p. A12.

3. Mark N. Cooper, *Electricity Deregulation and Consumers: Lessons from a Hot Spring and a Cool Summer* (Washington, DC: Consumer Federation of America, August 2001).

4. Arundhati Roy, *Power Politics* (Cambridge, MA: South End Press, 2001), 53ff; Richard Oppel Jr. and David Sanger, "Loan Agency Wants Inquiry into Enron," *New York Times*, April 2, 2002, p. C1; John Nichols, "Enron: What Dick Cheney Knew," *The Nation*, April 15, 2002, p. 14; U.S. House of Representatives, Minority Staff, Committee on Government Reform, *How the White House Energy Plan Benefited Enron* [report prepared for Representative Henry A. Waxman] (Washington, DC: U.S. House of Representatives, January 16, 2002), 18.

5. Martin A. Sullivan, "Economic Analysis—Corporate Tax Revenue: Up, Down, and All Around," http://www.tax.org/federal/federal.htm.

6. Robert S. McIntyre and T. D. Coo Nguyen, *Corporate Income Taxes in the 1990s* (Washington, DC: Institute on Taxation and Economic Policy, October 2000), 2 (http://www.ctj.org/itep/corpoopr.htm).

7. Citizens for Tax Justice, "Less Than Zero: Enron's Income Tax Payments, 1996–2000," http://www.CTJ.org/html/enron.htm.

8. Leslie Wayne, "Enron's Collapse: Before Debacle Enron Insiders Cashed in $1.1 Billion in Shares," *New York Times*, January 13, 2002, sect. 1, p. 1.

9. "Too Much of a Good Incentive?" *Business Week*, March 4, 2002, p. 38.

10. "Don't Blame the Stock Options," *Business Week*, April 15, 2002, p. 26.

11. "A New Credit Crunch," *Business Week*, February 18, 2002, p. 32.

12. Eric Palmer, "Will 'Enronitis' Torpedo Recovery?" *Kansas City Star*, March 6, 2002, p. C1.

13. "Enron Debacle Will Force Clean Up of Company Stock Use in DC Plans," *DC Plan Investing*, December 11, 2001.

14. Ibid.

15. Matthew S. Scott, "What Investors Can Learn from the Enron Mess," *Black Enterprise*, April 2002, 73.

16. Enron 2001 proxy statement.

17. Ibid.

18. Jim Yardley, "Enron's Collapse: The Hometown," *New York Times*, January 14, 2002, p. A1.

19. Bloomberg News Service, "Enron's Many Strands: The Workers," *New York Times*, March 30, 2002, p. C5.

20. "Sunbeam, Debtor Units Extend Deadline to Vote on Reorganization," Associated Press, April 1, 2002.

21. Sarah Anderson, John Cavanaugh, Chris Hartman, and Betsy Leondar-Wright, *Executive Excess 2001* (Boston: Institute for Policy Studies and United for a Fair Economy, August 28, 2001), 1.

22. Council of Institutional Investors, "Corporate Governance Policies," http://www.cii.org/corp_governance.htm.

23. Alesandra Monaco and Stacey Burke, *Board Practices/Board Pay 2001* (Washington, DC: Investor Responsibility Research Center, 2001), 162.

24. Christopher Schmitt, Julian E. Barnes, and Megan Barnett, "As Enron Fell, Even Its Outsiders Became Insiders," *U.S. News and World Report*, February 11, 2002, 28.

25. Center for Responsive Politics, "Top Senate Recipients of Enron Contribution's, 1989–2001," http://www.opensecrets.org/news/enron/enron_senate_top.asp.

26. Monaco and Burke, *Board Practices*, 196.

27. Report of Investigation by the Special Investigative Committee of the Board of Directors of Enron Corporation, February 1, 2002.

28. Steven Syre and Charles Stein, "Shareholder Democracy Issues Gain," *Boston Globe*, May 2, 2001, p. C1.

29. Daniel Burnham, Raytheon annual shareholder meeting, April 25, 2001, Lexington, Massachusetts.

30. Alesandra Monaco, *The Audit/Non-Audit Fee Landscape Analysis and Benchmarks* (Washington, DC: Investor Responsibility Research Center, 2001), 63.

31. Mark Babineck, "Lay, Auditor, Director Sat Together on Board," *Boston Globe*, February 19, 2002.

32. Charles Haddad, "When Auditors Also Consult," *Business Week*, March 4, 2002, p. 12.

33. Center for Responsive Politics, "Enron: Other Money in Politics Stats," updated January 29, 2001, www.opensecrets.org/news/enron/enron_other.asp.

34. Center for Responsive Politics, "Top Congressional Recipients of Enron Contributions, 1989–2001," http://www.opensecrets.org/news/enron/enron_cong.asp.

35. Center for Responsive Politics, "Enron: Other Money in Politics Stats."

36. "Did Enron Write Its Own Rules?" *Futures*, March 2002, 78–82.

37. Robert L. Borosage, "White Must Go," *The Nation*, March 11, 2002, p. 7; Robert L. Borosage, "White—It Gets Worse," *The Nation*, April 22, 2002, p. 6. See also Jonathan S. Landay and Chris Mondics, "Army Secretary Denied Wednesday That He Had Insider Information When He Sold Enron Stock," Knight Ridder/Tribune News Service, March 28, 2002.

38. Al Hunt, "Enron's One Good Return: Political Investments," *Wall Street Journal*, January 31, 2002.

39. William Greider, "Not Wanted: Enron Democrats," *The Nation*, April 8, 2002, p. 11.

40. Donald Bartlett and James Steele, "Soaked by Congress," *Time*, May 15, 2000, 64.

41. Ibid.

42. U.S. House of Representatives, Minority Staff, *How the White House Energy Plan Benefited Enron.*

43. Don Van Natta Jr. and Neela Banerjee, "Bush Energy Paper Followed Industry Push," *New York Times,* March 27, 2002, p. A20.

44. Pete Yost, "Enron Lobbying Correction: $2.5 Million for Six Months of Pressing Its Agenda on Bush Administration," Associated Press, March 7, 2002.

45. Vikki Kratz, "Enron: A Look at the Company's Lobbying in 2001," *Money in Politics Alert* (Center for Responsive Politics), January 14, 2002.

46. Jim Vallette and Daphne Wysham, *Enron's Pawns* (Washington, DC: Institute for Policy Studies, 2002), 3.

47. Ibid.

48. Ibid., 8.

49. Ibid., 9.

50. Khozem Merchant, "Assets of DPC in Hands of Receivers," *Financial Times,* April 4, 2002, p. 20.

51. Kevin Sack, "Campaign 2000: The Debate: In Civil Clash, Cheney and Lieberman Reinforce Tickets' Sharp Differences," *New York Times,* October 6, 2000, p. A1.

52. Michael Douglas, "Dick Cheney, Government Man," *Akron Beacon Journal,* October 8, 2000, p. B2.

53. Jim Vallette and Kenny Bruno, "Cheney and Halliburton: Go Where the Oil Is," *Multinational Monitor,* May 1, 2001, 22.

54. Douglas, "Dick Cheney."

55. Vallette and Bruno, "Cheney and Halliburton."

56. McIntyre and Nguyen, *Corporate Taxes.*

57. Howard Glickman, "Tax Dodging: Enron Isn't Alone," *Business Week,* March 4, 2002, p. 40.

58. Citizens for Tax Justice, "House GOP Stimulus Bill Offers 16 Large, Low-Tax Corporations $7.4 Billion in Instant Tax Rebates," October 26, 2001, http://www.ctj.org/html/amtdozen.htm.

59. Council of Institutional Investors, "Council of Institutional Investors Backs Expensing of Stock Options," March 25, 2002, http://www.cii.org/press/expensing.htm.

60. Sen. Carl Levin, "Stock Options" Web site, http://levin.senate.gov/issues/stockoptions.htm.

61. John Rossant, Jack Ewing, and Brian Bremner, "The Corporate Cleanup Goes Global but Not All Reforms Will Follow the U.S. Model," *Business Week,* May 6, 2002, p. 80.

62. Phillip Day, "In Singapore, a Glimpse of the World Post-Enron," *Wall Street Journal,* March 14, 2002.

63. Rossant, Ewing, and Bremner, "Corporate Cleanup."

Profiting through Influence

The Pharmaceuticals and Lobbying Industries

Ken Silverstein and Jess Taylor

If they can offer an 80 percent discount, there was something wrong
with the price they started off with.
—JAVID A. CHOWDHURY, INDIA'S MINISTER OF HEALTH, COMMENT-
ING ON WESTERN PHARMACEUTICAL MAKERS' REVISED PRICING FOR
HIV/AIDS DRUGS IN AFRICA, *NEW YORK TIMES*,
DECEMBER 1, 2000

Introduction

Disputes surrounding the pharmaceuticals industry have become so
numerous in recent years that it is hard to keep track of them:

- Taxpayers, via grants to research institutions and the National Institutes of Health's awarding of patents, underwrite the development
  of most new prescription drugs launched by U.S. pharmaceuticals
  firms.
- Pharmaceuticals giants bribe upstart competitors to keep generic
  substitutes off the market, thereby getting around patent termina-
  tions and guarding monopolies for flagship brands via brazen violations of antitrust statutes.
- Very high U.S. drug prices have consumers pushing—with U.S.
  drug makers' enthusiastic support—for a prescription benefit under
  Medicare.
- U.S. agencies and officials strong-arm numerous governments to
  protect drug manufacturers' monopolies virtually worldwide.
- Foreign drug manufacturers who seek—entirely legally under both

their own countries' laws and international trade agreements—to
undercut those monopolies are branded as pirates.
- Throughout the developing and industrialized world, questions of
profitability overrule medicine, leaving patients stranded because
drugs are unaffordable, unavailable, or unprofitable either to make
or devise.
- Each year, tens of thousands of Africans die (to take the example of
just one continent and one disease) because the AIDS drugs they
need, though readily available, are priced beyond the means of
almost all the world's HIV- and AIDS-affected population; thousands more die of diseases like malaria and sleeping sickness because
it is not cost-effective to manufacture or invent the drugs to cure
them.

The issues and policy concerns related to the highly profitable and influential pharmaceutical industry are complex and interconnected. Even those
who attend to it every day, like India's health minister, may not perceive
the full network of laws, research priorities, diplomacy, public relations,
and cash flow that holds together the worldwide business of pharmaceuticals. At the same time, this industry remains quite adept at not being seen.
As the New York Times noted in its series on "Medicine Merchants" published in late 2000, this is "one of the world's most lucrative, and secretive,
industries."[1] Naturally, high degrees of lucrativeness and secretiveness
figure in the tangle of controversies sampled here. Both are greatly aided
by an activity that almost all press coverage overlooks: ardent courting of
the U.S. government.

The pharmaceutical sector racks up the largest legal profits of any industry. As of 1999, pharmaceuticals' projected growth over the next four years
was triple the average for the Fortune 500.[2] This high-profit, high-growth
business also reinvests a healthy chunk of its income in lobbying and campaign contributions: America's drug makers lay out bigger expenditures
than any other industry to secure influence in Washington.

This combination of record-setting positions that pharmaceuticals
enjoy speaks bluntly of cause and effect: largesse toward Washington
boosts revenues. But this is just part of the picture. The benefits blow both
ways; legislators and government functionaries also profit hugely. The
questionable synergies between them and Big Pharma's political action
committees (PACs) and lobbyists are myriad. Such a sophisticated,
multiflanked alliance calls for an accounting of the effect of supplement-

ing commercial power with governmental power and of the corrupting effect that corporate handouts have on our government.

Even a limited survey of the drug companies' methods of establishing, maintaining, and expanding their dominance and of the uses they make of its benefits reveals multiple connections between the industry and public officeholders; such a survey also exposes how the industry's highly beneficial and essential work shields its well-funded, well-rewarded, and socially deleterious activities.

A linchpin among these activities, integral to the machinery of most of the practices listed previously, is the industry's mastery of the give-and-take of influence peddling. The influence industry—lobbying plus its vassal trades of campaign finance, fund-raising, PAC-making, political consulting, and artificial "grassroots" organizing—holds favored slots in Washington's power structures analogous to the positions pharmaceuticals hold in real-world commerce. Big money and shadowy operations are essential components. But unlike the drug companies' actions, the influence industry's capitalization and annual dollar turnover are next to impossible to tabulate. The long-established image of the revolving door—through which cabinet members, members of Congress, and staffers move on to lobbying shops, where they essentially rent out their privileged access to former colleagues—has a less visible counterpart: the revolving door through which favors (perks, contributions, virtual bribes, sweetheart legislation, weakening of regulatory bodies) circulate between our elected representatives and government appointees, on one side of the portal, and the representatives of corporate America on the other.

Whatever its contribution to the gross domestic product, the influence industry's real significance can be measured only in an unquantifiable commodity: power. Influence peddling generates substantial negative externalities, most of them hard to observe fully and measure. That requires considerable patience and a global reach. Chowdhury and his staff at the Indian Ministry of Health could readily give us a partial estimate by diagramming the way "free trade" and its champions, prominent among them U.S. drug lobbyists, have repeatedly choked off the flow of affordable AIDS drugs to developing nations.[3] Unlike many other industries, lobbying's positive externalities and by-products are few.

The symbiotic relationship between the two industries in question—pharmaceuticals and lobbying—reveals a great deal about both. Representative examples of their cooperation shed light on the more egregious of the pharmaceuticals firms' practices and their effects. Examining the two industries in combination enables us better to address problems of both. A look at lobbying reveals some of what enables the pharmaceuticals giants to get away with so much, and a look at drug issues reveals how far out into the world the lobbyists' tinkering can reach.

A detailed catalog of abuses by these industries is beyond the scope of this chapter (and has already been published by numerous journalists, activists, and researchers, myself included).[4] A look first at the drug makers and at their efforts via lobbyists provides a background against which to view the lobbyists' practices. An advantage of looking at this real-world context in which lives are at stake is that it shows the effects of influence peddling outside Washington. One reason lobbyists' impact on government provokes little public outcry is that much of the public regards Washington as intrinsically corrupt and its goings-on as irrelevant. A look at the intersection of these two industries and the success of their collaboration demonstrates that efforts to reform the control and distribution of pharmaceuticals—increasingly recognized as an urgent national priority—require a corresponding effort to reform lobbying.

The Pharmaceuticals

A panorama of the pharmaceuticals industry's antisocial impacts can be pieced together through examples of five of its practices, all relating to the earlier list and all well established and widespread. Two prevail in the industry's domestic workings, two in its foreign operations, and one bridges both.

- The use of tax money to develop drugs with no reciprocal financial benefit to taxpayers/pharmaceuticals buyers.
- Exorbitant, uncontrolled U.S. prices for drugs on which firms hold effective monopolies.
- The neglect of major diseases, leading to unavailability of drugs where needed.
- The use of federal agencies to champion drug makers' interests abroad.
- Efforts of drug manufacturers in foreign markets that mix strong-arm tactics on some issues with negligence toward others.

Both domestic examples reflect a mutually cultivated rapport with the federal government or at least with many of its officers. Much of the cost of drug research is borne by the government, which provides generous patent laws (and, since 1984, patent extensions) that help firms create single-product monopolies; the artificially high prices ensured by such monopolies support the funding of the drug makers' friends in Washington.

The price-profit relationship that this sustains is clear. Catalyzing factors in the equation are monopoly and subsidy, both enjoyed by U.S. drug manufacturers to a degree unequaled elsewhere in the developed world. The United States, alone among First World nations, does not control drug prices. As a result, prices here are about twice as high as they are in the European Union and nearly four times higher than in Japan.

The drug companies defend their extraordinary profit margins (and their disregard of various diseases, most of them tropical, that chiefly afflict the poor) by pointing to the risks and costs of research and development (R&D). According to the Pharmaceutical Research and Manufacturers of America (PhRMA), the industry's trade group, the costs average about $500 million per new drug. However, public health activists believe the number is wildly inflated. PhRMA gets the $500 million figure by extrapolating from a controversial 1987 Tufts University study that factored in such variables as "opportunity costs"—that is, the amount of money companies forgo by not investing their R&D funds in, for example, the stock market—pegged to an outrageous 9 percent rate of inflation.[5] Particularly compelling evidence against PhRMA's $500 million figure is its members' consistent refusal to disclose the R&D budgets for any of their products. Whatever the average lab bill for a pharmaceutical wonder, the lion's share of new drug development costs stems from preclinical research. Much—even most—of that is performed by universities and government-funded research facilities, not by industry.

This distribution of costs is illustrated by the second domestic example. Taxol, an important cancer drug, was discovered, tested, and manufactured by the National Cancer Institute and then turned over to Bristol-Myers Squibb for marketing. The company had an inside track on its bid to win marketing rights because it had hired Dr. Robert Wittes, an institute official familiar with the Taxol program, to help prepare the company's application. In return, Bristol-Myers was required only to supply the government with Taxol for clinical trials. The company purchased four hundred kilos of the drug from the institute's supplier, Hauser Chemical, paying twenty-five cents per milligram. When the Food and Drug Administration approved Taxol for sale in late 1992, the company announced a wholesale price of $4.87 per milligram. By 1999, Taxol was bringing in more than $1 billion annually for Bristol-Myers.[6] The government does not merely allow such profiteering but subsidizes it at the R&D level. While the government itself derives little benefit from this arrangement, numerous government officials do benefit: they support the arrangement as quid pro quo for kickbacks in the form of campaign money and lobbyists' largesse (discussed later in this chapter).

While all this hits the U.S. consumer with a double cost—high drug prices and use of tax money—a life-threatening product of the industry's practices is the scarcity or lack of drugs that are needed for illnesses but are unlikely to become profit centers. Two examples feature opposite approaches that produce the same unsatisfactory result. Ironically, the first case involves the drug companies' neglect of one illness, while the second involves their zealous pursuit of treatments for another. The sporadic, long-running campaign against malaria and the last two decades' concerted effort against AIDS have left Third World targets undefended.

Just fifty years ago, the discovery of new drugs and pesticides led the World Health Organization to predict that malaria would soon be eradicated.[7] By 1959, Laurie Garrett writes in *The Coming Plague*, the Harvard School of Public Health was so certain that the disease was passé that its curriculum did not include a course on the subject.[8]

Resistance to existing medicines, along with cutbacks in health care budgets, civil war, and the breakdown of the state has led to a revival of malaria in Africa, Latin America, Southeast Asia, Armenia, and Tajikistan.[9] The World Health Organization describes the disease as a leading cause of global suffering and says that by "undermining the health and capacity to work of hundreds of millions of people, it is closely linked to poverty and contributes significantly to stunting social and economic development."[10]

Total global expenditures for malaria research in 1993, including government programs, came to $84 million. That is a paltry sum when one considers that one B-2 bomber costs $2 billion—the equivalent of what, at current levels, will be spent on all malaria research over twenty years. In that twenty-year period, some 40 million Africans alone will die from the disease. In the United States, the Pentagon budgets $9 million per year for malaria programs, about one-fifth the amount it set aside in 2000 to supply troops with Viagra. For the drug companies, the meager purchasing power of malaria victims leaves the disease off the radar screen. As Neil Sweig, an industry analyst at Southeast Research Partners, puts it wearily, "It's not worth the effort or the while of the large pharmaceutical companies to get involved in enormously expensive research to conquer the Anopheles mosquito."[11]

AIDS is the one disease ravaging Third World countries that is the object of substantial drug company research because, unlike malaria, AIDS also plagues the First World. In many African countries, AIDS has wiped out a half century of gains in child survival rates. In Botswana, a country that is not at war and has a relatively stable society, life expectancy rates fell by twenty years over a period of just five. South Africa's health ministry issued a report in the late 1990s saying that 1,500 of the country's people are infected with HIV every day and predicting that the annual death rate would climb to 500,000 within the next decade. The legions of orphans that AIDS has created in southern Africa are stretching the social fabric now, and it is likely that by 2015 between 20 and 25 percent of all children in the region will be orphaned.[12]

Yet the few effective treatments and active research initiatives offer little hope for poor regions and poor people. A year's supply of one of the highly recommended multidrug cocktails in anti-HIV combination therapies (which joining antivirals and a protease inhibitor), costs about $15,000. That's exorbitant in any part of the world but is prohibitive in countries such as Uganda, where per capita annual income stands at $330. Further, research toward a vaccine focuses on the strains of HIV that prevail in the rich countries, although Genentech's AIDSVax, the major vaccine currently in phase 3 trials, does address the E strain prevalent in Africa and Southeast Asia, with trials running in Thailand as well as in the United States and Europe. Still, the overwhelming majority of research is concentrated on regions that are home to the affluent minority of those with HIV. "Without research dedicated to the specific viral strains that are prevalent in developing countries, vaccines for those countries will be very slow in coming," says Dr. Amir Attaran, an international expert who directs the Washington-based Malaria Project.[13]

From the drug companies' quarterly-earnings-driven perspective, this is all the natural working of the market. It will no doubt be some time before corporations take sufficiently long-range views to perceive that tackling such problems can indeed serve their interests and especially the wider interests of the industrial economies in which they operate. But is this the drug companies' responsibility? Why are they more obligated to combat malaria than Kraft is obligated to combat hunger or Boeing is obligated to provide aircraft to evacuate refugees from war-torn regions? To an extent, the pharmaceutical makers' social charge inheres in their enjoyment of such rich public subsidy (though Boeing has also signed on permanently to the federal dole). Uniquely, however, the drug industry has a particular obligation because it holds a particular monopoly on its products. In many cases, only one drug exists to treat a given illness; in others, the regimen of treatment obviates meaningful competition: people with HIV who can afford one of several available protease inhibitors cannot switch to another when the price of the first drug goes up. Such monopolies (utilities in particular) have historically been recognized as different and are subject to more stringent requirements.

All the blame for the neglect of tropical diseases cannot be laid at the industry's feet. Many Third World governments invest little in health care while investing heavily in arms, and First World countries have slashed both foreign aid and domestic research programs. Whatever its rank among the culprits, the industry owes a mounting debt to its chief accomplice, the U.S. government, which aggressively champions pharmaceuticals firms' interests abroad. Zealous in the role of the drug makers' enforcer, our government consistently squashes health care initiatives in developing countries.

For example, the best-proven treatment for HIV infection, the combination of protease inhibitors and antivirals, was beyond the financial reach of most of the world's patients. Yet in 1999 Vice President Al Gore pressured South Africa into barring the manufacture of cheap generic substitutes for those drugs.[14] The staunchly defended patents of the pharmaceuticals giants hold a much higher priority in our foreign policy than tens of millions of African lives.

Gore's efforts are just a sliver of the story when it comes to U.S. harassment of Third World nations over their drug policies. In the past few years, the Office of the U.S. Trade Representative (USTR), which is charged with promoting American commercial interests abroad, has become a virtual appendage of the drug industry. One of the OSTR's chief aims has been to discourage the use of generic drugs abroad. Such policies are especially cruel because the cost of drugs accounts for up to 60 percent of the health care budget in poor countries. "In the old days, the government made the world safe for Standard Oil," says Jamie Love of the Center for the Study of Responsive Law. "Now it's making the world safe for the drug companies."[15]

Among the products for which the world is deemed unsafe is Bristol's Taxol. The USTR has threatened at least seven countries with trade sanctions if they allow generic substitutes for the tax-financed cancer drug into their domestic markets. Bristol-Myers Squibb, one of the corporate world's most generous political donors, with soft-money contributions of $559,975 in the 2000 election cycle, also enlisted the services of Gore, who personally pressured South African officials to ban Taxol substitutes. The South Africans held firm.[16]

Thailand, too, felt the whip of USTR sanction threats when that country's government considered a bill requiring that generic substitutes be listed on the packaging of brand-name drugs. Argentina was punished because its drug companies opposed U.S. positions in international forums on patent protection and the intellectual property rights of multinational drug makers. Argentine firms "continue to work aggressively to frustrate our efforts," Trade Representative Charlene Barshefsky said in explaining a 1997 decision increasing tariffs on exports from Buenos Aires.[17]

The United States is also trying to outlaw the practice of "parallel imports," by which countries shop the world for the best prices instead of buying only from local distributors for U.S. pharmaceutical companies. Parallel imports can dramatically lower a country's drug bill because pharmaceutical firms charge different prices from nation to nation. As of 1995 identical amounts of SmithKline Beecham's antibiotic Amoxil cost eight dollars in Pakistan, fourteen in Canada, thirty-six in the United States, forty in Indonesia, and sixty in Germany. The USTR has for years been at war with New Zealand over the issue of parallel imports. In 1996 the U.S. ambassador to Auckland, Josiah Beeman, warned of "severe consequences" after that country's government removed restrictions on parallel imports. That prompted Prime Minister Jenny Shipley to blast back, "We will not be told how to run our country."[18] Such interference must be particularly galling when attempted by a U.S. administration pretending to be a great patron of free trade.

Free trade itself is a U.S. weapon for enforcing drug monopolies. The *New York Times* series devoted one article to India's generic drug companies, which operate completely legally and up to international standards under Indian patent law, intellectual property treaties, and the provisions of the Uruguay Round of trade talks. Wielding the threat to withhold or revoke WTO membership, the United States and the pharmaceuticals have put such producers of inexpensive medicines on the defensive.[19] Observed Frederick M. Scherer, emeritus professor of public policy at the Kennedy School of Government at Harvard University, "It's a marvelous piece of [public relations] to get these companies called pirates. What they're doing is perfectly legitimate, until 2005, under the Paris Convention and the Uruguay Round."[20] Pressure from Glaxo SmithKline recently forced one of the largest Indian firms, Cipla, to pull its generics for two AIDS drugs, AZT and 3TC, from Ghana's pharmacies.[21]

In 1983, Guatemala sought to counter the aggressive marketing tactics of multinationals with an "infant health law" that made it illegal to use pictures of babies on packaging for infant formula. Gerber, now a subsidiary of Novartis, claimed that the law constituted an unfair trade restriction and insisted that it be permitted to market its formula with a label sporting the Gerber baby. "A fat, chubby blue-eyed westernized baby is an absolutely winning marketing strategy for Gerber," United Nations Children's Fund legal adviser Leah Margulies told *Corporate Crime Reporter*. "It seduces the mother into using [formula] early." At issue is not merely an illustration but a point of truth in labeling. To an illiterate Guatemalan consumer, a picture is a text that makes claims for the product. Backed by the USTR, Gerber flagrantly violated the law. In 1996 the Guatemalan Supreme Court ruled that the infant health law could not be applied to imported products. The Gerber baby still smiles gaily from Guatemalan supermarket shelves.[22]

The rap sheet could go on with numerous, equally troubling examples.[23] They all illustrate how the industry's practices yield numerous and pervasive negative externalities. Each of these practices can be addressed individually, but it is clear that most of them share a short list of root causes. A common enabler is the industry's warm relationship with public servants. While many of them are officials of foreign governments—John Braithwaite compiled crushing evidence on the prevalence of bribes—there is plenty to be accomplished right here at home.[24]

The Power of the Purse

Again, the source of the drug lobby's vaunted power in Washington is no mystery. During the 1995–96 election period, pharmaceutical companies ponied up $6.1 million in soft money (contributions made to political parties or causes instead of candidates). Drug industry PACs tossed in another $3.2 million in campaign money. That buys a lot of calling cards in the capital, and the industry magnifies its Beltway might with squadrons of high-powered lobbyists. In 1996, industry reps shelled out $37 million to lobby the federal government. Among the big-name shops retained by

PhRMA are Barbour, Griffith, and Rogers, whose partners include former Republican National Committee chief Haley Barbour; and Akin, Gump, Strauss, Hauer, and Feld, home to Vernon Jordan, Bill Clinton's golfing pal.

Like many corporate employers of lobbyists, drug companies exploit the revolving door between Capitol Hill and K Street. One of the revolving door's great success stories is Dennis DeConcini. A member of the savings-and-loan scandal's Keating Five gang, a Democrat from Arizona, DeConcini chaired a Senate committee that oversaw drug patents until his retirement from Congress. He swiftly moved to Parry and Romani Associates, a firm run by his former chief of staff, Romano Romani, where DeConcini has represented such pharmaceutical makers as Pfizer, Genentech, Upjohn, and Glaxo-Wellcome, the world's largest drug company. Glaxo-Wellcome hired Parry and Romani to maintain a loophole in the General Agreement on Tariffs and Trade that extends patents on drugs such as Glaxo's Zantac.[25] The loophole is worth millions to DeConcini's client because it prevents consumers from buying generic alternatives to Zantac for another two years.

DeConcini told the *Washington Post* that he could not understand why anyone would criticize his efforts. "People who serve in government often go ahead and work for somebody later," said DeConcini, who was equally baffled by public reaction to his cozy relationship with Charles Keating of Lincoln Savings. "I think that's pretty natural."[26] Hand-in-glove arrangements between business and government constitute the established order in Washington.

Just as the drug industry leads in profitability and growth, it outpaces all others in spending to court politicians. In 1997, U.S. drug companies spent $74.8 million to lobby the federal government, more than any other industry; in the following elections these firms spent nearly $12 million on campaign contributions.[27] The figures suggest that highest profit correlates with greatest generosity to Washington insiders. Journalists and activists who decry lobbying focus on the influence industry's effect on government but tend to overlook its effect on the wider world.

Back in 1993, the hottest political issue in Washington was health care. President Clinton called the American system the "costliest and most wasteful" in the world.[28] The public would have enthusiastically supported a frontal assault on the health care industry, with polls showing Canada's socialized system as the most popular model for reform. The public, though, was largely excluded from the debate in Washington, which was dominated by the "health care profiteers" that Clinton had pledged to attack.[29] A report from the Center for Public Integrity found that some 660 groups shelled out more than $100 million to thwart reform between 1993 and 1994. About one-quarter of that amount took the form of political donations to members of Congress. A good chunk of the rest went to the hundreds of lobbying and public relations firms hired to influence the health care debate. At least eighty lobbyists working the issue were former members of Congress or the executive branch.[30] William Gradison was a member of Congress on Sunday and head of the Health Insurers Association of America, a trade group of 270 insurance companies and creator of the infamous "Harry and Louise" television ads, on Monday. The beltway firm Powell Tate was hired by Bristol-Myers Squibb, RJR Nabisco, T2 Medical, Pharmacia and Upjohn, and Searle. For $2 million, according to an internal memorandum, Powell Tate would "sow doubt" about Clinton's assaults on drug makers and his early calls for price controls on the industry. Since average citizens, including nearly 40 million Americans without health care coverage, were not heard from, talk of comprehensive health care reform soon faded. The public's minuscule influence on political affairs was seen in the fact that a Canadian-style system was swiftly discarded by Clinton and Congress because, said the pundits, it suffered from a lack of political support.[31]

Dollar for dollar, lobbying is a better investment than campaign contributions, one reason why business spends far more on the former than on the latter. In 1996, Philip Morris coughed up $19.6 million for lobbying programs versus $4.2 million for campaign donations, making it the leader in both categories. For 1996, Georgia Pacific spent $8.9 million for lobbying and handed out $527,000 in political money. Corresponding figures for AT&T are $8.4 million versus $1.8 million; for Pfizer, $8.3 million versus $775,000; for Boeing, $5.2 million versus $770,000; for ARCO, $4.3 million versus $1.4 million; for Lockheed, $3.5 million versus $1.26 million; for FedEx, $3.1 million versus $1.9 million; for Dow Chemical $1.5 million versus $578,000.[32]

In addition to in-house efforts, most big corporations spend lavishly for outside lobbying firms. Lockheed, for example, retains at least two dozen Beltway lobby shops to supplement its efforts, while FedEx has ten firms on retainer. In 1996, Boeing hired seven outside lobby shops for the sole purpose of pushing renewed most favored nation trade status for China, spending a combined total of at least $160,000.[33]

While corporate lobbying has long been a major force in American politics, it has also been greatly transformed during the past few decades. Today, many efforts involve stealth lobbying (e.g., mobilizing fake "grass-roots" campaigns) or with indirect methods, such as buying research from friendly think tanks to influence Congress and public opinion. All of this makes calculating corporate lobbying expenditures nearly impossible, though it is safe to say that lobbying has now become a multibillion-dollar-per-year industry. When the enormous benefits that the White House and Congress bestow on corporate America are considered, the sums companies spend to win favors are chump change. Lockheed's expenditure on lobbying and campaign contributions was about $5 million in 1996. That year, Lockheed's lobbyists, with help from other arms makers, won approval for the creation of a new $15 billion government fund underwriting foreign weapons sales. In 1996, Microsoft spent less than $2 million for lobbying and campaign contributions (the former accounted for more than two-thirds of that amount). The following year, Congress awarded the company tax credits worth hundreds of millions of dollars for the sale of licenses to manufacture its software programs overseas.[34]

Corporate lobbyists do not win every battle, but when they lose, it is often because a competing corporate faction bought up even more lobbying firepower. It is indisputable, though, that corporate citizens who retain lobbyists have an enormous advantage over the regular ones who merely vote. Tommy Boggs, perhaps Washington's best-known influence peddler, charged $550 per hour for his services in 1998. That's a drop in the bucket to Philip Morris, but Boggs's rate would eat up the average salary earner's entire annual income after a mere forty-three hours of lobbying activity.[35]

That lobbying has corrupted the political system is no secret. During his 1992 presidential campaign, Bill Clinton promised to "break the stranglehold the special interests have on our elections and the lobbyists on our government." Such promises were forgotten as soon as the election votes were counted. Republicans criticized Clinton for his coziness with special interests, but the GOP maintains the same intimate relationships. After winning control of Congress in 1994, the Republican House leadership met weekly with the Thursday Group, a pack of lobbyists and activists that helped plot legislative and media strategy on the Contract with America. Included in this elite troupe were hired guns representing the U.S. Chamber of Commerce, the National Federation of Independent Business, and Americans for Tax Reform.[36]

Lobbying is a practice almost as old as the republic. In the nineteenth century, future president James Buchanan was already complaining in a

letter to another future president, Franklin Pierce, about the "host of contractors, speculators, stock jobbers and lobby members which haunt the
halls of Congress."[37] During the past quarter century, however, the lobbying industry has exploded. By the late 1990s, the H to K Street corridor in
downtown Washington is infested with law offices, consulting firms, public relations companies, polling agencies, and lobby shops that effectively
form the fourth branch of government. There are estimated to be between
forty and eighty thousand lobbyists at work in Washington—a minimum
of seventy-five for every member of Congress.[38]

This huge army of influence peddlers, the great majority whom work for
business interests, has greatly enhanced corporate America's force in the
capital. The numbers speak volumes: in 1995, Congress showered businesses with $167 billion in "fiscal incentives," "export-promotion sup-
port," and other subsidies—in plain English, corporate welfare—a figure
that dwarfs the $75 billion that was allocated during the same year to pay
for all social welfare programs.[39]

The rapid growth of the lobbying industry has occurred because business—spurred by the populist upsurges of the 1960s and 1970s, especially
anticorporate campaigns led by Ralph Nader and the more general
upheavals surrounding the Vietnam War and the Watergate scandal—has
become far more aggressive in seeking to influence government policy. In
the early 1970s, most big companies did not even maintain Washington
offices. By the late 1990s, some six hundred corporations were operating in
the capital, as were an estimated five thousand national trade and business
membership groups. Most of these companies and organizations run in-
house lobby shops while depending on hired guns from outside firms to
provide supplemental firepower.

During this same period, the world of lobbying also has been transformed at the strategic level of tactics. Until as recently as the early 1990s,
lobbyists unbuckled vast sums of money to directly subsidize the day-to-
day life of elected officials. Sponsoring junkets, especially to exotic overseas locations, was another way for lobbyists to curry favor with lawmakers. Other lobbyists relied on less orthodox if more direct means to win
congressional support for their clients. Longtime senate staffer Roy Elson
recalled that for many years, lobbyists routinely supplied women to elected
officials. The straightforward cash bribe was long an accepted practice as
well.[40] This truly was a golden age of lobbying. As *Campaign and Elections*
magazine once wrote of the period, "There was a time when lobbying was

strictly a backroom affair. Affable men in suits would hang around swarming, sweaty legislative chambers, buttonholing lawmakers as they swaggered through lustrous bronzed doors, whispering in ears, slapping backs, winking knowingly. These were the same men who were always good for a free lunch, a round of cocktails, and at election time, a check from their fainthearted clients."[41]

Though this backroom world is far from extinct, lobbyists have been forced to develop new tactics as legal restrictions and tighter disclosure rules have dampened the effectiveness of time-honored techniques. Cash bribes passed under the table were replaced by campaign checks passed across the table. In a similar transition, junkets have given way to "fact-finding missions," where lawmakers give speeches or appear on panels in exchange for room and board at cushy resorts.

Producing a more profound change in strategies has been a growing public cynicism about business power, which has led corporations to disguise their direct involvement in lobbying campaigns. The most direct consequence has been an explosion of fake grassroots mobilizations. Back in 1993, the oil industry hired Burson-Marsteller to help build opposition to an energy tax that Clinton had proposed. A company executive, Jim McAvoy, was charged with coordinating rallies in small towns across the country. Just a decade earlier, the energy industry could have killed the tax with a handful of Beltway lobbyists, McAvoy lamented to the press at the time. "Now you have to hire 45 people and send them to 23 states because all the noise is supposed to have more credibility."[42]

In addition to "grassroots" activities, corporations now complement traditional lobbying with a multitude of other tricks: paying think tanks and "third party" experts to do the intellectual dirty work and testify on the corporations' behalf at public hearings and academic conferences; forming "independent" front groups to lead business-backed campaigns; hiring public relations firms to spin the industry's message and manipulate the media. "In the modern world, few major issues are merely lobbied anymore. Most of them are now managed, using a triad of public relations, grassroots mobilization, and lobbyists."[43]

Indeed, lobbyists' two great twentieth-century innovations were the PAC and the bogus grassroots organization. The first, devised to get around limits on campaign contributions by and to individuals, gave rise to the second. As the public became increasingly savvy about single-purpose PACs and suspicious of their (often few) supporters, corporate thinkers and their Washington agents began investing in organizations crafted to resemble the spontaneous banding-together of diverse citizens around a common cause.

In 1995, lobbyist Bob Beckel, campaign manager for Walter Mondale's 1984 presidential run and later founder of the Beckel Cowan lobby shop, was hired by the Competitive Long Distance Coalition, a group led by AT&T, MCI, and Sprint. The coalition paid Beckel at least $2 million to drum up opposition to a bill that would allow the Baby Bells to compete with the big long distance carriers.

With the help of NTS, a telemarketing firm based in Lynchburg, Virginia, Beckel's campaign generated 500,000 telegrams to members of Congress. There was just one problem: up to half the telegrams were fake. Many were signed by people who had never heard of the bill. Other telegram senders turned out to be dead. Indeed, the whole campaign was a fraud. NTS phoned people and asked if they were in favor of "competition" in telecommunications. If the response was affirmative, NTS asked if the person would like to send a telegram, at no cost, to his or her member of Congress. To heighten the drive's impact, NTS sent out four telegrams per person. Twenty-seven House members wrote to the Competitive Long Distance Coalition, saying, "Our constituents have been manipulated, lied to and misrepresented. . . . In our collective years of service none of us has ever before witnessed such reprehensible conduct."[44]

Welcome to the brave new world of corporate grassroots lobbying, which has become the Fortune 500's favorite way to influence government policy. Between mid-1993 and mid-1995, some $790 million was spent on grassroots lobbying during the two previous years, a jump of 70 percent.[45] Congress passed a lobbying reform bill in 1996, but conservatives succeeded in exempting disclosure requirements for "grassroots" lobbyists who push legislation but do not personally meet with lawmakers on the grounds that such restrictions would be a violation of free speech.[46]

From the mid-1980s onward, the strategic philosophy of corporate lobbying has shifted. Impressed by the organizing strength of unions, public interest groups, and civil rights organizations, businesses began to emulate those groups' techniques, giving rise to the new field of corporate "grassroots lobbying." To a large extent the model was corporate America's hated foe, Ralph Nader. Formerly a term that conjured up wholesome images of citizens spontaneously mustering to protect their interests, so-called grassroots lobbying is now an industry directed by enormously expensive Beltway consulting firms seeking to mime populist revolt. The phony grassrooters set up phone banks, manufacture letter-writing campaigns, arrange meetings between legislators and "white hat" community figures—preferably religious leaders or Little League coaches—and rent "third party experts" to draft op-ed articles or testify before elected officials.

At a 1994 conference (titled "Shaping Public Opinion: If You Don't Do It, Somebody Else Will") attended by dozens of corporate grassroots specialists, a public relations executive named Pamela Whitney claimed that her outfit could parachute into a community and within two weeks "have an organization set up and ready to go." According to an account in the newsletter *PR Watch*, Whitney said that the key to success was looking local. To further that end, she hired local "ambassadors," suggesting former PTA leaders as ideal candidates. "It's important not to look like a Washington lobbyist. When I go to a zoning board meeting I wear absolutely no make-up, I comb my hair straight back in a ponytail, and I wear my kids' old clothes." A special added touch was donning a baseball cap.[47]

And without being so blatantly fraudulent, such artificial grassroots groups (Astroturf organizations, as insiders call them) can be insidiously effective. For example, a convincing show was made by Citizens for the Right to Know, a PhRMA-funded group that peddles thoroughly cooked data blaming drugstores rather than drug companies, for high prescription prices. Experts do not buy the data, but Congress is eager to do so.[48]

The reach and effectiveness of these Astroturf organizations are demonstrated nicely by the success of Citizens for a Sound Economy (CSE).[49] If any informed citizen were asked to name Washington's top lobby-lawyer shops, the list would probably not include CSE, even though the Beltway newspaper *Roll Call* rated it the as the city's fourth-most-influential organization in 1995 (trailing the National Federation of Independent Business, the Christian Coalition, and the National Association of Wholesaler-Distributors). Since its formation in the late 1980s and in particular more recently, the CSE think tank has played a significant role in virtually every major issue of national importance. It has also been perhaps the leading proponent of the conservative economic agenda, especially in regard to welfare cutbacks, regulatory reform, and the call for lower taxes on the rich. A full-scale lobbying campaign by CSE is one of the primary reasons that President Clinton's 1993 budget did not contain a tax on energy producers or any significant new spending for social programs. The same can be said in explaining the defeat of health care reform in 1994.

One of CSE's triumphs in the 1990s was its assault on health care reform, which offers a good idea of what the group means by "grassroots" organizing. Out of a "truth squad" budget set at $321,000, CSE allocated $42,000 to shuttle its staffers around the country to distribute baseball caps, frisbees, and buttons. Another $8,000 was budgeted for counterrallies in towns to be visited by the Clintonites' Health Security Express bus tour, with CSE staffers on hand to greet the administration's troops with a towed bus called the Phony Express. The vast majority of the money— $266,000—was slotted to pay for a media campaign that painted Clinton's plan as the first step on the path toward "government-run health care," a Soviet-style nightmare in which everyone would "pay more for less care." The humiliating public relations debacle suffered by Clinton's forces foreshadowed the defeat of the administration's health care bill in Congress and the amputation of the topic from public debate for two years.[50]

CSE's central concern is money, not ideology. And since it does not directly lobby members of Congress or the White House but organizes "grassroots" campaigns, companies are not required to divulge their contributions to CSE, and CSE is not required to reveal who pays its bills.

What Could Be Done

In enumerating the excesses of lobbyists, as with those of the pharmaceuticals companies that number among the lobbyists' leading patrons, there is no shortage of examples. Of the two, the pharmaceuticals industry's troubling practices suggest remedies that are more readily apparent and more finite.

Certain remedies can and should originate by the companies' own initiative—although such remedies seldom do. Given the industry's profitability, it is clear that the companies could do more to increase drugs' availability in many countries and affordability everywhere. It is equally clear that companies will not do so unless forced. ACT UP's success in pushing drug companies to respond to the AIDS crisis in the United States is emblematic of how crucial but also how difficult it is to get the industry to budge.

While the industry's political clout currently insures against any radical government action, even minor reforms could go a long way. A retired drug company executive points to public hospitals, which historically were guaranteed relatively high profit margins but were obligated to provide free care to the poor in return. There is also the example of phone companies, which charge businesses higher rates to subsidize universal service. "Society has tolerated high profit levels up until now, but society has the right to expect something back," he says. "Right now, it's not getting it."[51]

The U.S. government already lavishly subsidizes industry research and allows companies to market discoveries made by the National Institutes of Health and other federal agencies. "All the government needs to do is start attaching some strings," says the Malaria Project's Attaran. "If a company wants to market another billion-dollar blockbuster, fine, but in exchange it will have to push through a new malaria drug. It will cost them some money, but it's not going to bankrupt them."[52]

Another type of string would be a "reasonable pricing" provision for drugs developed at federal laboratories. By way of explanation, Attaran recounts that the vaccine for hepatitis A was largely developed by researchers at the Walter Reed Army Institute. At the end of the day, the government gave the marketing rights to SmithKline Beecham and Merck. The current market for the vaccine, which sells for about $60 per person, is $300 million a year. The only thing Walter Reed's researchers got in exchange for their efforts was a plaque that hangs in their offices. "I'll say one thing for the companies," says Attaran. "They didn't skimp on the plaque; it's a nice one. But either the companies should have paid for part of the government's research, or they should have been required to sell the vaccine at a much lower price."[53]

Another proposal with a free-market appeal is to shorten the duration of drug patents and eliminate patent extensions. Open the market earlier to price competition, and give the drug manufacturers stronger encouragement to develop new drugs on which they can enjoy new, profitable patents. The knee-jerk argument that the shorter patent will dampen the profit motive has little force in light of the enormous profit margins new drugs enjoy.[54]

Most efficacious, however, would be to curb the drug makers' power in Washington. That requires reform of our system of lobbying (tied closely to our system of campaign finance), for which remedies are apparent but far-reaching and difficult to implement. Plenty of legislators no doubt hold stock in the big drug firms—but they will correctly view cutbacks in lobbying expenditure as lifted right out of their pockets.

While individual cases of effective lobbying present specific negative externalities, the consistently destructive outcome of lobbying is the erosion both of our democracy and of our faith in it. None of these remedies will produce more than temporary or cosmetic results without the substantial and sustained will of the people in our roles both as voters and as consumers. How, then, can the crooked world of lobbying be cleaned up? There are, obviously, no magic solutions. Indeed, given the flagrant political corruption that currently pervades the political system, it is hard to be optimistic.

Still, there are some hopeful signs, even if they come from around the country rather than from Washington itself. The American people know how Washington works and how lobbyists do the job for their clients. Citizens want the government to cut back on corporate welfare programs, and many Americans favor steep reductions in military spending. They are angry about the current state of affairs, as seen in polls that show widespread support for campaign finance reform and for efforts to curtail lobbyists' power. Public anger is also reflected in the fact that corporations so diligently seek to wrap their lobbying campaigns in grassroots packaging.

It is also encouraging that despite massive business spending for lobbying and public relations campaigns, the public remains hostile to many of corporate America's questionable goals. The American people don't want the government to cozy up to dictatorial regimes and generally favor putting human rights ahead of commerce in establishing foreign policy. Business groups have spent tens of millions of dollars to convince the public of the virtues of untrammeled free trade, but big pacts such as the North American Free Trade Agreement remain deeply unpopular. Corporate America believed that the GOP's 1994 takeover of Congress would open the way to a rollback of environmental laws, but the Republicans had to retreat on many fronts to avoid electoral disaster. By 1996, even Newt Gingrich was suggesting that conservatives hold photo sessions at zoos and national parks to demonstrate their devotion to protecting the nation's fauna and flora.

Finally, attempts to reduce lobbyists' influence should be seen as just one part of a broader battle to curtail corporate power. Winning better disclosure laws for lobbyists might not sound like a huge triumph, but even small steps like that can help reinvigorate democracy, especially if they are combined with victories on other fronts, from antisweatshop campaigns to campaign finance reform to efforts to protect the environment.

No reform is possible in isolation. There is no way to reduce lobbyists' power without first revamping the American system of financing elections. The cost of running for office is so high—about $500,000 on average to make a run for the U.S. House and more than $5 million to run for the U.S. Senate—that candidates spend much of their time raising funds.

Since lobbyists are among the few people in Washington who can afford to attend three to four fund-raisers a week at $500 a head, they receive much of the candidates' attention. Howard Marlowe, a past president of the American League for Lobbyists, says politicians and lobbyists have a "mutual addiction": "They need us for money and we need them to help our clients. We don't get access due to our ability or our knowledge of the issues, we get it with money. As a result, we spend way too much time trying to figure out how to buy access."[55]

Marlowe, one of just a few lobbyists who publicly call for cleaning up the profession, recalled meeting with a congressional staffer on behalf of a client. Two days later, the same staffer called to invite Marlowe to a fund-raiser and not so subtly reminded him of their earlier meeting. "We need to take the dollar sign out of the legislative process," Marlowe says. "That's the only way that the public will begin again to have faith in the political process."[56]

Second, lobbying disclosure laws need to be far tougher. While the 1996 reform bill forced greater numbers of lobbyists to register with Congress, the lobbying process is still riddled with loopholes. As a result, only a fraction of the capital's influence peddlers are required to disclose their activities. Henry Kissinger opens doors for businesses in China (and other countries) and frequently speaks out in favor of improving U.S.-Sino relations. But since he does not directly lobby members of Congress, he is not required to register as a paid agent of Beijing. (It is said that Kissinger's standard contract contains a clause that states that he will do nothing that would require him to register as a lobbyist.)[57] Disclosure laws must also be brought to bear on so-called grassroots lobbyists, who are currently exempted from all reporting requirements. Grassroots lobbying has nothing to do with the First Amendment, as its practitioners shamelessly claim, and everything to do with corporate power.

Bill Hogan of the Center for Public Integrity says that tougher disclosure rules would render lobbyists less powerful. He believes that members of Congress, like the executive branch, should be required to keep daily logs of visitors to their offices. "It would be useful if the public knew that lobbyist X had seen Congressman Y twenty times during debate on a bill," Hogan says. "That would be a source of embarrassment to Congressman Y and would reduce such contacts."[58]

Sunshine would help reduce the influence of special interests when it comes to congressional testimony as well. Mark Bloomfield, a top tax lobbyist, frequently testifies before Congress, where he identifies himself as the head of the benignly named American Council for Capital Formation. A "truth in advertising" law for congressional witnesses, as has been proposed by some watchdog groups, would require Bloomfield to also disclose the names of his corporate clients. Such a rule would allow the public to know who is paying for testimony and what interests are behind a given piece of legislation.

Front groups should also be required to be more up front about their membership and sources of funding. The public has a right to know if the "Citizens" involved with Citizens for the Sensible Control of Acid Rain are electric utilities and coal companies. The Internal Revenue Service does not force organizations to report such information on tax forms, but Congress could make full disclosure a requirement for any organization that sends representatives to testify on Capitol Hill.

Perhaps most importantly, something must be done to control the revolving door between the government and K Street. President Clinton promised that he would take action on this front, but nothing of consequence was forthcoming. Howard Paster, Clinton's first chief congressional lobbyist, resigned from the powerhouse firm of Hill and Knowlton to work for the president. But Paster spent less than a year at this post before announcing that he would return to his old firm to serve as chief executive officer.

Public officials cannot be permanently barred from lobbying, but they should be prevented from working as influence peddlers for a significant period of time—say, five years. That would force these officials to at least briefly make a respectable living and limit their effectiveness as lobbyists when allowed to again take up the trade. It might also serve as a disincentive to "clock punchers"—those people who come to Washington to learn the ropes and then exploit their knowledge for private gain. One simple step would be to revoke floor access to former members of Congress, a privilege that greatly increases their influence when they become lobbyists.

Perhaps the biggest barrier to reform is that the public's disgust with business as usual in Washington has generated far more apathy than revolt, thereby allowing our elected leaders to talk passionately about the urgent need for change but to take only the most innocuous steps to implement it. Until the public forces the establishment to take action, Washington will remain a place where corporations and lobbyists get their way and ordinary Americans have only the most minimal influence on political decisions.[59]

NOTES

1. Jeffrey Gerth, Gay Sheryl Stolberg, and Donald G. McNeil, "Medicine Merchants: Beyond Patents [article series]," *New York Times*, April 23, May 21, July 9, October 5, and December 1, 2000.

2. See Ken Silverstein, "Millions for Viagra, Pennies for Diseases of the Poor: Research Goes to Profitable Lifestyle Drugs," *The Nation*, July 19, 1999, pp. 13–19.

3. Bay Windows, "Ghana Battles Glaxo SmithKline," *International Briefs*, December 21, 2000. Available at http://www.baywindows.com/main .cfm?include =detail&storyid=35905.

4. This chapter draws extensively on Ken Silverstein, "Millions for Viagra"; and Silverstein, *Washington on $10 Million a Day: How Lobbyists Plunder the Nation* (Monroe, ME: Common Courage Press, 1998).

5. Silverstein, "Millions for Viagra," 15.

6. Ibid.

7. World Health Organization, available at http://www.who.int/health_ topics/malaria/en.

8. Laurie Garrett, *The Coming Plague: Newly Emerging Diseases in a World out of Balance* (New York: Penguin, 1995).

9. Ibid.

10. Cited in Silverstein, "Millions for Viagra," 14.

11. Ibid.

12. Ibid., 16; Medical Research Council, *The Impact of HIV/AIDS on Adult Mortality in South Africa*, Tygerberg, South Africa, 2001. Available at http:// www.mrc.ac.za/bod/.

13. Silverstein, "Millions for Viagra," 16.

14. Ibid.

15. Ibid.

16. Ibid.

17. Ibid.

18. Ibid.

19. Donald G. McNeil, "Selling Cheap 'Generic' Drugs: India's Copycats Irk Industry," *New York Times*, December 1, 2000, p. A1.

20. Ibid.

21. Bay Windows, "Ghana."

22. Silverstein, "Millions for Viagra," 16.

23. For more, see John Braithwaite, *Corporate Crime in the Pharmaceutical Industry* (London: Routledge and Kegan Paul, 1984); Braithwaite, "Transnational Regulation of the Pharmaceutical Industry," *Annals of the AAPSS* 525 (1993): 12–30.

24. Braithwaite, *Corporate Crime*.

25. See "GATT Rx: Profit Overdose," *Multinational Monitor* 16 (May 1995). Available at http://multinationalmonitor.org/hyper/issues/1995/05/mm0595_04 .html.

26. Quoted in Ken Silverstein, "Revolving Doors," *Multinational Monitor* 17

(May 1996). Available at http://multinationalmonitor.org/hyper/mm0596.08 .html.

27. Silverstein, "Millions for Viagra," 14.

28. Silverstein, *Washington on $10 Million a Day*.

29. Ibid.

30. Center for Public Integrity, *Well-Healed: Inside Lobbying Health Care Reform* (Washington, DC: CPI, 1994).

31. Silverstein, *Washington on $10 Million a Day*, 6, 7.

32. Ibid., 3.

33. Ibid.

34. Ibid.

35. Ibid., 4.

36. Ibid.

37. Jeffrey Birnbaum, *The Lobbyists: How Influence Peddlers Get Their Way in Washington* (New York: Times Books, 1992).

38. Silverstein, *Washington on $10 Million a Day*.

39. Ibid.

40. Ronald Kessler, *Inside Congress: The Shocking Scandals, Corruption, and Abuse of Power* (New York: Pocket, 1997).

41. *Campaign and Elections*.

42. Silverstein, *Washington on $10 Million a Day*.

43. Ibid., 17–21.

44. Ibid.

45. Ibid., 89.

46. *Campaign and Elections*.

47. Silverstein, *Washington on $10 Million a Day*, 88–91.

48. Gerth, Stolberg, and McNeil, "Medicine Merchants."

49. Silverstein, *Washington on $10 Million a Day*.

50. Ibid.

51. Silverstein, "Millions for Viagra," 18.

52. Ibid.

53. Ibid.

54. James Surowiecki, "The Talk of the Town: No Profit, No Cure," *New Yorker*, November 1, 2001, p. 46.

55. Silverstein, *Washington on $10 Million a Day*.

56. Ibid.

57. Ibid., 226.

58. Ibid.

59. Silverstein, *Washington on $10 Million a Day*, 224–27.

Contributors

Loretta Bondi directs the Cooperative Security Program at the SAIS Center for Transatlantic Relations. She focuses on international security, international organizations and coalitions, human rights, UN and regional sanctions, and the arms trade.

Richard A. Daynard is professor of law at Northeastern University and has worked with a number of organizations devoted to the study of tobacco and public health policy. His experience and expertise on tobacco law, policy, and litigation place him in the middle of the public debate over smoking, leading to appearances on *Nightline*, *Today*, *This Week with David Brinkley*, *Frontline*, and *Crossfire*, as well as a number of television and radio news programs.

Tom Diaz is senior policy analyst at the Violence Policy Center in Washington, DC. He is the author of *Making a Killing: The Business of Guns in America* (1999) and a number of monographs on specific aspects of firearms marketing, most recently *Bullet Hoses: Semiautomatic Assault Weapons? What Are They? What's So Bad about Them?* From August 1993 to January 1997, Diaz was lead Democratic counsel on firearms law and terrorism to the U.S. House Judiciary Subcommittee on Crime and Criminal Justice.

Patty Gerstenblith has been a professor at the DePaul University College of Law since 1984, specializing in law and the arts and cultural heritage law. She has served as editor of the *International Journal of Cultural Property* (1995–2002) and as a member of the President's Cultural Property Advisory Committee (2000–2003). She received a J.D. from Northwestern University School of Law and a Ph.D. in art history and anthropology from Harvard University.

Neva Goodwin is co-director of the Global Development and Environment Institute at Tufts University and editor of the Evolving Values for a Capitalist World series for the University of Michigan Press. She is involved in efforts to motivate businesses to recognize social and ecological health as significant, long-term corporate goals.

Herbert Howe is assistant professor of African studies at Georgetown University's School of Foreign Service. A specialist in African security studies, he is the author of *Ambiguous Order: Military Forces in African States*. He served in the Peace Corps in Nigeria from 1966 to 1967 and earned his M.A. from the Fletcher School of Law and Diplomacy and his Ph.D. from Harvard University.

John Warren Kindt is a professor in the College of Business and an associate in the Program in Arms Control, Disarmament, and International Security at the University of Illinois, Urbana-Champaign. He has several graduate degrees in law and business and served as a senior fellow at the London School of Economics. Professor Kindt's research has resulted in over thirty articles; he has also been cited for outstanding teaching.

Scott Klinger is co-director of the Responsible Wealth project of United for a Fair Economy. Responsible Wealth organizes affluent Americans to advocate for progressive taxes, living wages, and more equitable executive compensation. Prior to joining Responsible Wealth in 1999, Scott worked as a corporate social responsibility researcher, security analyst, and portfolio manager in the social investment industry.

Nikos Passas is professor of criminal justice at Northeastern University. He specializes in the study of terrorism, white-collar crime, corruption, organized crime, and international and transnational crimes and has published more than sixty articles, book chapters, reports, and books on financial crimes and other serious misconduct. He has acted as a consultant to law firms; private security companies; and various bodies, including the Financial Crimes Enforcement Network of the U.S. Department of Treasury (FinCEN), the United Nations Centre for International Crime Prevention, the World Bank, the Commission of the European Union, the U.S. National Academy of Sciences, and a number of government agencies in several countries. He has also served as an expert in international cases involving money laundering and other misconduct. He received a law degree from the University of Athens and a Ph.D. from the University of Edinburgh Faculty of Law. He is a member of the Athens Bar (Greece).

Peter Riggs is director of the Forum on Democracy and Trade and previously served as program officer at the Rockefeller Brothers Fund, specializing in East Asian environmental affairs. He has worked at universities, with nonprofit groups, and with UN agencies in Indonesia, China, Cambodia, and the former Soviet Union.

Mark Ritchie serves as president of the Institute for Agriculture and Trade Policy, focusing on the links between global and local natural resource, health, and community development policy in the food and agriculture sector. He holds degrees from Iowa State University and the University of Amsterdam.

Ken Silverstein is a Washington, DC–based investigative reporter who has written extensively on beltway lobbying and campaign finance. He is the author of several books, including *Private Warriors*, a look at the arms trade, and *Washington on $10 Million a Day*, which examines the world of lobbying.

Holly Sklar is a writer whose op-eds for the Knight Ridder/Tribune News Service have appeared in hundreds of newspapers. She is the coauthor of *Raise the Floor: Wages and Policies That Work for All of Us*, which argues, "A job should keep you out of poverty, not keep you in it." Sklar's other books include *Chaos or Community? Seeking Solutions, Not Scapegoats for Bad Economics* and *Streets of Hope: The Fall and Rise of an Urban Neighborhood*, the widely taught story of how the Dudley Street Neighborhood Initiative is rebuilding a long impoverished Boston community as a dynamic urban village.

Jess Taylor is an editor and translator. He works sporadically in international economic development and lives in Sao Paulo, Brazil.

Megan Waples, formerly program associate in the Sustainable Resource Use and Southeast Asia programs at the Rockefeller Brothers Fund, is currently attending the University of Connecticut School of Law. She is a graduate of Brown University and has also worked as a train conductor and as an environmental management consultant.